Literary Lives
General Editor: Richard Dutton, Professor of English
Lancaster University

This series offers stimulating accounts of the literary careers of the most admired and influential English-language authors. Volumes follow the outline of writers' working lives, not in the spirit of traditional biography, but aiming to trace the professional, publishing and social contexts which shaped their writing. The role and status of 'the author' as the creator of literary texts is a vexed issue in current critical theory, where a variety of social, linguistic and psychological approaches have challenged the old concentration on writers as specially gifted individuals. Yet reports of 'the death of the author' in literary studies are (as Mark Twain said of a premature obituary) an exaggeration. This series aims to demonstrate how an understanding of writers' careers can promote, for students and general readers alike, a more informed historical reading of their works.

Henry James

A Literary Life

Kenneth Graham
Professor of English
University of Neuchâtel, Switzerland

First published in Great Britain 1995 by
MACMILLAN PRESS LTD
Houndmills, Basingstoke, Hampshire RG21 6XS
and London
Companies and representatives
throughout the world

A catalogue record for this book is available from the British Library.

ISBN 0–333–43354–8 hardcover
ISBN 0–333–43355–6 paperback

 First published in the United States of America 1996 by
ST. MARTIN'S PRESS, INC.,
Scholarly and Reference Division,
175 Fifth Avenue, New York, N.Y. 10010

ISBN 0–312–12504–6

This book is printed on paper suitable for recycling and made from fully managed and
sustained forest sources.

10 9   8   7   6   5   4   3   2
04 03 02 01 00 99 98 97 96

Printed in Great Britain by Antony Rowe Ltd, Chippenham, Wiltshire

Contents

Acknowledgements   vi

1   Beginnings   1

2   American and Romantic   28

3   Victorian and Realist   52

4   Crisis and Experiment   99

5   Master and Modernist   140

Notes   189

Suggestions for Further Reading   196

Index   200

Acknowledgements

Like anyone writing today on Henry James, whether biographically or critically or, as in the present instance, a combination of the two, I am deeply indebted to Leon Edel's magisterial *Life of Henry James* (1953–72), which has become the definitive source of our factual knowledge of James's biography.

I would also like to thank Richard Dutton, as General Editor, for his great patience and his friendly encouragement at various stages.

KENNETH GRAHAM

The author and publishers are grateful to the following for permission to reproduce copyright material:

Harvard University Press for extracts from *The Letters of Henry James*, 4 vols, edited by Leon Edel, 1974– . Reprinted by permission.

Oxford University Press (New York) for extracts from *The Complete Notebooks of Henry James*, edited by Leon Edel and Lyall H. Powers, 1987. Reprinted by permission.

1

Beginnings

Henry James's literary career began in a time of war and national upheaval: an internecine struggle fittingly called, by some, the War between the States. When he published his first short story, 'A Tragedy of Error', in February 1864, and his first piece of criticism, a review of Nassau Senior's *Essays on Fiction* in the autumn of the same year – the year in which he became twenty-one – Sherman was marching and burning through Georgia, and bringing towards its conclusion what had been the bloodiest war in modern history. Lee finally surrendered in April 1865, a month after James published 'The Story of a Year', his second story and the first to bear his name as author, and itself set in the Civil War. And when James's career ended with his death more than half a century later, in 1916, it was again in a context of war and catastrophe. He died, a new British citizen, in February 1916, some months before the first battle of the Somme, his last year dominated by what he himself called the 'abyss' of the First World War, and his last piece of writing (he was too ill to correct the proofs) a passionate elegy for Rupert Brooke, and for Brooke's generation.

The Civil War marked dramatically the end of one phase of American history and the beginning of another. The old America in which James was brought up, an America of solemn New England idealism, leisured (though conscientious) contemplation, and Anglo-Saxon liberal thought, was gone, overwhelmed by a frenetic expansion of the nation's frontiers, its rapid (even rabid) industrialisation and commercialisation, and by a massive tide of immigration from Ireland, Germany, Russia, Poland, and Italy (460 000 in the single year of 1873). Socially and geographically, the centres of power had radically shifted; and the nation's values – how it saw itself – had shifted too. And no less dramatically, the subsequent abyss of the 1914–18 war was one that swallowed up not just Rupert Brooke and his contemporaries but a whole European tradition of social and political structures and of post-Christian and post-Romantic ideology.

Exactly between these two abysses – one American, the other

1

primarily European – lay the span of James's life as a writer. And his whole literary output can be seen as a dramatised investigation of personal and communal structures – moral, psychological, behavioural, even economic – under certain conditions of strain, of transition, of incipient breakdown. The basis of Jamesian comedy and Jamesian tragedy – and it would be difficult ever to agree on which of these two is predominant in his writing – is one of certain codes of values and behaviour being put to the test: either in laughter or in suffering. And one key to the tenor of his mind and of his technique as a novelist might be found, for example, in the way in which *The Bostonians*, published at the very mid-point of his career in 1885–6,[1] makes subtle and pervasive allusion to the Civil War as a metaphor for the other wars that activate the scene of that novel. There is the battle between the sexes, the struggle within the individual between principle and instinct, the stress between an older Boston and a brasher New York, the battle of publicity against privacy, of abstraction against felt experience, of age against youth, of words against action – and a dozen other oppositions, all richly qualified and non-schematic, even contradictorily handled, but amounting in the end to a masterful fable, both comic and tragic, of a whole culture and of certain fictional characters within that culture, in a state of crisis.

Because James's writing life begins in one period of vivid historic transition, and ends in another, it is more than usually necessary to look at all that led up to the twenty-year-old James's first appearance in print in 1864: the year after Gettysburg, when Dickens and Mrs Gaskell were still alive and writing, and three years before Marx's *Kapital* and the invention of the typewriter.

James was formed not by formal education but by family – including the family's principled opposition to a fixed education. The strains – in both senses of the word – that ran through the James family are almost a paradigm of certain formative aspects of American society between the Revolution and the Civil War. William James, the novelist's grandfather, was an Ulsterman and a Presbyterian who emigrated from Ireland in 1789, began by selling tobacco in a store, became a successful entrepreneur and banker, and died in 1832, leaving an estate (enormous at that time) of three million dollars. The puritanic, hard-working businessman, whose achievement of wealth so fitted into the ethic of his Protestantism, is a type, or a principle, that played an important role in the novelist's future examination of the stresses between action and contemplation, money-making and the imagination, in America, and above all in individual life – ranging from Barnaby Striker in *Roderick Hudson*, and Dr Sloper in *Washington Square*, to Caspar Goodwood in *Portrait of a Lady*, and down to the highly subtilised and qualified extrapolations from the type in figures like Chad Newsome in *The Ambassadors* and Adam Verver in *The Golden Bowl*. And the inherited dialectic in the James family was enriched by the fact that William James's son, Henry, the novelists's father, epitomised something dramatically contrary to the type of the self-made, practical man of affairs. Henry James Senior along with the other heirs of William James went to court to break the father's restrictive will, which placed moral conditions upon the inheriting of his wealth, and thereby not only signalised his difference from the puritanic type but by the same action gained the financial means that made the full difference possible. Money permitted leisure, permitted thought, permitted travel and experiment, permitted, perhaps above all, the creative self-indulgence of words: written and spoken. William James's money – like the 'wind' that Mr Touchett's legacy was designed to put in Isabel Archer's 'sails' in *Portrait of a Lady* – allowed Henry James Senior to become a philosopher, something of an intellectual dilettante, and a free-ranging, uncommitted critic of the human scene. And the same money, distinctly reduced in sum by now and passed on by him during his lifetime and after his death to his son, helped make possible the novelist's lifelong activities as a 'restless analyst' of the human predicament of action as against contemplation, commitment as against renunciation, and worldliness as against the spirit. James was in this way created by an American phenomenon – commercial wealth – and by the contradictions contained within that phenomenon; and in turn he took as the subject-matter of his fiction the very drama – the drama of those contradictions – that had made him.

The strains in Henry James Senior were very precise and personal, as well as being representative. A free-thinking but instinctively religious man, a believer in spirituality and divinity but a disbeliever in churches and all institutionalised religion, he underwent a crisis on a family visit to England when he was thirty-three and his son Henry was one year old (it was May 1844, and Dickens was still completing *Martin Chuzzlewit*). The crisis, remembered in the family as father's 'vastation', was one that anticipated certain later tensions in the younger James and certain crises – moments of anxiety when the world falls away – that appear in his fiction, like pressure-points in any system of strains and stresses. Out of the blue, without any premonitory anxiety or trouble, after dinner one evening James Senior was overwhelmed in his room, in a house rented with his family near Windsor, by what he described as 'a perfectly insane and abject terror, without ostensible cause, and only to be accounted for, to my perplexed imagination, by some damnèd shape squatting invisible to me within the precincts of the room, and raying out from his fetid personality influences fatal to life,'[2] The description is like a foretaste of his son's late tale of an encounter with a terrible, negative *doppelgänger*, 'The Jolly Corner' (1908); and also of the novelist's much-commented-on nightmare (probably dating from around 1910) of an 'awful agent, creature or presence' trying to break through the door of a room at him, while he fought to keep the door closed against the creature, filled with 'irresistible but shameful dread'.[3]

Both father and son overcame the moment of dread – more quickly in the case of the son, who turned the tables on his enemy within the very same dream, and set the beast to flight; the father only after much searching and advice, and only on discovering by chance that in the philosophic teachings of Swedenborg his oppressive shadow could at once be lifted from him. That neither man fell into despair is significant, and again suggests connections: not only as regards their essential temperamental toughness and survival qualities (the novelist, however sensitive and self-doubting, remained undespairing and confident in his vocation to the end), but even as to the manner in which each put his personal devil to flight. The son did so in his dream by tapping a resistant energy and aggression connected with his discovery that the room in which the appalling encounter was being played out was 'the tremendous, glorious hall', vivid to him from childhood visits, of the Galerie d'Apollon in the Louvre: a place that for him embodied 'glory' – 'not only beauty and art and supreme design, but history and fame and power, the world in fine raised to the richest and noblest expression.' The father won his victory not through such an image of art and power, but through a vision – his own vision of Swedenborg's vision – of human regeneration: the certainty that human nature could itself be a redemptive force, bringing the individual into unity with God and with all men, forming a truly transformed community on a new earth and in a new heaven. What the two men shared was a belief in transformation: transformation, no doubt, to somewhat different ends, and far more worldly in the case of the sceptical writer-son, but following the same basic principle of spiritual energy and creative change. The novelist wrote of his father's 'remarkable and constant belief, proof against all confusion, in the imminence of a transformation-scene in human affairs.' And in the previous volume of autobiography, he wrote of himself and his brother William: 'it is quite for me as if the authors of our being and guardians of our youth had virtually said to us but one thing, directed our course but by one word, though constantly repeated: Convert, convert, convert!'[4] James Senior achieved his mental equipoise by a belief in life as an unstoppable process of self-conversion in the direction of redemption. James Junior based his aesthetic – which in his case meant virtually the same as his mental equipoise – on the idea of the mind, the artist's and observer's mind, converting what the world so multifariously gave it into those organised forms of art (and consciousness) by which alone the world, and the individual within it, might be redeemed into the fullest meaning.

Just as significant as this duplicated pattern of crisis and recovery between father and son (between father and sons, rather, since William, the elder son, who was to become the most eminent of all American psychologists and thinkers, had his own profound crises of black depression and conscious self-remaking) was the effect on the son of James Senior's eccentrically liberal ideas concerning his children's education. Briefly, these seem to have been that a systematic and traditional schooling was a form of tyranny to be avoided for a child, whose mind ought to be kept free from doctrine and subjugation, and by perpetual novelty and challenge kept in a state of openness to experience, of well-balanced and critical alertness *vis-à-vis* the world, always communicative, articulate, and spontaneous. The idea of a perpetually intelligent spontaneity is an attractive one, and a profoundly American version of personal freedom. It is one of the most pervasive ideas in Henry James's fiction, and can be seen embodied in such early prototypes as Bessie Alden, in 'An International Episode' (1879), and Isabel Archer, in *The Portrait of a Lady* (1880–1). Even more integrally, the values of fluidity and free enquiry are celebrated by the whole development of James's narrative technique and linguistic style, which conscientiously resist the fixed, the stereotyped, and embody the many-faceted and the endlessly dynamic.

Subject to his father's strict doctrine that doctrine and authority must be resisted – a paradox that shadowed but did not invalidate the whole experiment – Henry Junior, with his three brothers and one sister, was moved from tutor to tutor, school to school, first in New York City (their official home from Henry's birth in 1843 until a move to Newport in 1858 and eventually to Cambridge, outside Boston, in 1864), and then in numerous short or prolonged excursions in the 1840s and 1850s to Europe: to Geneva, Paris, London, Boulogne, Bonn, in all of which the father's so-Jamesian restlessness resulted in an ever-changing series of schools and private teachers for his children. There must clearly be more than a merely analogical relation between such a wilfully unfixed mode of upbringing and the mature novelists's strong temperamental dislike, and indeed incapacity, for systematic, deductive thought, for general principles and conclusions, for any pattern of belief or a priori value. James was brought up in a vociferous, self-expressing household – in a perpetual babble of voices, according to various witnesses – and was moved from place to place, attitude to attitude, in order to retain freedom of thought. He became the novelist of freedom, quick to excoriate in his pages characters who were locked in egotism, or parochialism, or authoritarianism, or in the dehumanising grasp of stereotyped thinking, the habit of judging human behaviour not within the fluidity of experience but by the deadening application of some unscrutinised first principle. And in his own mental and emotional life, as well as in the lives of his fictional beings, he also demonstrated the other consequences of such freedom and such absence of system: the anxiety, the sense of alienation, and the proliferation of qualifications and nuances and hesitations and differing points of view which can be the terrible cost of such a systematically unsystematic mind and upbringing.

In those years just before the Civil War the intellectual tradition that sustained the James family's well-meaning and spiritually alert liberalism – and out of which grew James's own far more cosmopolitan and individualistic version of the play of free consciousness – was probably already past its peak, but certainly remained an active and influential presence in American culture for decades to come, perhaps never entirely to disappear. The idea of personal liberty, of course, has always been intrinsic to American history, its institutions, its codes of values. But the so-called American Renaissance of the 1830s, 1840s and 1850s – that outburst of speculative moral and social discourse that comprised the Transcendentalist movement, in such figures as Emerson, Thoreau, Margaret Fuller, Bronson Alcott, and Ellery Channing, and the very different writings of Hawthorne, Melville, and Whitman – represented one of the most energetic applications and reappraisals of the tradition of personal liberty. The James family household was much involved in the activities of the Transcendentalists, Henry James Senior being a born disputant, a man profoundly open to but also sharply critical of the intellectual currents of his day. By voluminous correspondence, articles, public meetings, and personal visits the Jameses were sewn into the fabric of that quintessentially New England movement – though James Senior's open-minded scepticism and nonconformity always kept him far from commitment to it. Emerson was a frequent visitor to the family home in New York, as Henry Junior clearly recalled (he also himself spent time with Emerson in later life). Thoreau, more of a recluse, visited at least once. And the others were household names, often discussed (unreverentially) in the family debates.

No budding writer in America, even as late as 1864, could have failed to respond to the excitements and to some of the absurdities and contradictions of Transcendentalist thought. The Jamesian principles of conversion, movement, and energy – both in the father's philosophy and the son's fiction – are equally fundamental to Transcendentalist ideas. The combination in the father's intellectual life of a Unitarian religious background touched (and warmed) by some subsequent mysticism echoes that of Emerson himself, who adopted from Hinduism and other sources what James Senior took, with a similar imprecision, from Swedenborg. And although James Junior was far from either rationalist Unitarianism or anything remotely mystic and oriental, the emphasis on individual consciousness and on a dynamic of transformation, personal and social, perceptual and moral, is common to all three. And if we extend the intellectual revolution represented by Transcendentalism – which began essentially with Emerson's essay, 'Nature', in 1836 – to include, dialectically, the far darker and tragic counter-arguments of Hawthorne and Melville, and also of Poe, then the case for James Junior's attachment to that revolution becomes even clearer.

The beginning author in 1864 embodied many of the contrary impulses of his culture at that time, a time of war in more ways than one, and his fiction set in action many of the essentially opposed strains of American thought – meaning New England thought – in the period between Emerson's 'Nature' and the collapse after 1860 into Civil War and subsequent industrialism. Throughout his fiction we find an Emersonian emphasis on the value of individual

consciousness in conflict with a Hawthornean and Melvillean insight into the destructive and self-destructive depths of individuality. Early heroes like Roderick Hudson, Christopher Newman, and
Isabel Archer, mid-period figures like Basil Ransom and Nick Dormer, and later examples like Fleda Vetch, Lambert Strether, and
Maggie Verver, all demonstrate something of the Transcendentalist
faith in self-help: self-transformation through the exercise of the
will, or the intelligence, or the moral imagination. The aim of their
self-transformation is never crudely materialistic but spiritual: personally spiritual, aesthetic, and refining, though not in as ethereal
or quasi-religious a direction as Emerson's ultimate 'Over-Soul'.
Non-material values can be validated or even created by such restless, morally or aesthetically ambitious, individuals as these characters of James's novels. The world is difficult, resistant to imagination
and spirit, but it is not fatally inert, and it is not impermeable to
consciousness. To that degree, right to the end of his career, James
is an optimist about human action and moral possibility, in the very
American tradition of Emerson, Thoreau, and Whitman (the poet of
Transcendentalist optimism). But against this tendency in James –
thereby constituting the tension of his outlook, and the tragic or
comic complexity of his fictional world – there also ran the unresolved, contrary fear that self-improvement and transformation come
too late, that the cost of it to the pragmatic self and to one's neigh-
bours is often too high, and that the tendency of experience is against
people of understanding and sensitivity and in favour of the unscrupulous and the worldly-wise: the Madame Merles, the Mona
Brigstocks, the Kate Croys. In this darker side of James's thinking
we can easily detect the sardonic tones of Hawthorne and Melville
– and even, just occasionally, the nightmare fears of Poe – and their
examinations of the human spirit baffled by the pressures of the
past and of the present, or in Melville's case (and Poe's) released
only through the self-destructively demonic power of the will.

The benignity, optimism, and even naivety of the Transcendentalist view of a self-redeeming human nature – to which even the
more sceptical Henry James Senior basically subscribed – always
ran counter to the much older tradition in America, which had
gone underground since the advent of eighteenth-century Deism
and the subsequent blandness of Unitarianism: that tradition of
Calvinist pessimism concerning the latent evil of human nature.
Transcendentalism dismissed evil, faintly, as a non-problem, and
saw no bounds to the human will to perfection. Whereas two of the

greatest American writers of the mid-century, Hawthorne and Melville, both of them heirs in their differing ways to the seventeenth century, expended all the powers of their minds on examining the tragedy of human evil and the imprisoning constrictiveness of circumstance, society, and history. And throughout James's writing career one might trace the perfect, because creative, interplay between these two currents, each affording a radical critique of the other.

Fundamental, too, to the Transcendentalists, and also to James Senior's version of Swedenborg (touched by the very influential social-reformist writings of Charles Fourier), was the concept of the brotherhood of man. The individual in search of the Oversoul discovers that the same soul flows through all people (and things), and therefore that personal and social conflict is an aberration and not of the essence of reality. Hawthorne and Melville, on the contrary, seem to expose the social, the communal, as a fatal trap and pressure – with only here and there in their writings the image of an ideal brotherhood, a dream of belonging and togetherness, just sufficiently present in the human imagination to highlight the disastrous fragmentation and isolation of actual human life. The James household, as a household of its times, was filled with the perpetual rumble of an idealised, socio-spiritual reformation towards a redeemed society of men – the kind of utopian vision that Hawthorne satirised in *The Blithedale Romance* in 1852 (and James too, more indirectly, in the satire of *The Bostonians* and *The Princess Casamassima* in 1885–6) – and what can be detected in James's fiction is again an interplay, though not an equal interplay, of these opposites. What James presents is a drama of individuals more or less at variance with their brothers, their society. The sensitive tend not to succeed in the courts of the world, and those who are most at ease with social life are mostly suspect in moral terms. Society either oppresses like a Wall of China – the image used for the Bellegarde duplicity that defeats Newman, in *The American* (1876–7) – or it is a dangerous game, a theatrical and often power-seeking game, full of great rewards, not all of them material, but to be played succesfully only by the corrupted, or the corrupting, or at best the morally ambiguous. But on the other hand, we can detect something of the Transcendentalist dream – or James Senior's dream – of a complex, life-enhancing brotherhood of redeemed individuals in the novelist's refusal ever fully to reject the communal, the shared. One of James's richest themes is that of the two-edged nature of social living: manners seen not as mere Hawthornean oppression and falsity, but as a complex code for day-to-day living that extends and challenges the private self, that can achieve its own beauty and intelligence, and is capable – though only just capable, and in the teeth of opposition – of expressing a moral, as well as an aesthetic, ideal. James as an ambiguous novelist of manners – a tragic and comic novelist of manners, being both for society and against it – is once again expressing one of the deepest dichotomies in the intellectual traditions of his century.

If Henry James's life up to and in the year he became an author, 1864, should be seen as an individual life within the greater historical life of his surrounding culture, being shaped by it and also converting it into entirely personal shapes, it remains to look at certain of these highly personal shapes and events that led up to the personal watershed of 1864: the beginning of a literary life.

Much of our knowledge of these earlier years – impressionistic knowledge rather than details and facts – comes from James's two completed volumes of autobiography, *A Small Boy and Others*, and *Notes of a Son and Brother*, which cover his life no further than about 1865. The autobiography was written in 1911–13, in James's most sumptuously involved later style, and perhaps tells us as much about the style, the sensitivity, and the cast of mind of the writer at the end of his career as at the beginning. But through the linguistic mesh of gentle self-probing, proliferating qualifications, and half-abstract, half-sensuous evocation of the past, we catch sight of certain important images and outlines. One is that of the supersensitive and observant boy, obsessed by feeling himself different from and even cut off from others around him, and compensating by the very cultivation of his inner life: almost a stereotype of the creative artist in his earliest days. The small Henry James envied many of those around him – particularly his older brother William, who all his life was to be a much-loved example to him and a feared and gently resisted rod to his back. And what we have already touched on as the later James's creative principle of 'conversion' – extracting meaning, mental shapes, and beauty from the chaos of the world – is clearly prefigured in his memories of feeling excluded, of never fully belonging, of travelling and travelling, of envying the more worldly and glamorous of his contemporaries, and of drawing consolation – sometimes overwhelmingly satisfying consolation – from an inner and private vision. Other people, enviable people, were like 'the probable taste of the bright compound wistfully watched in the confectioner's window'. Yet on the other hand, by private compensation and by imaginative conversion:

> I remember ... how, creeping off to the edge of the eminence above the Hudson, I somehow felt the great bright harmonies of air and space becoming one with my rather proud assurance and confidence, that of my own connection, for life, for interest, with such sources of light.[5]

The purported reference in the latter is to his father as a 'source of light' – but in the ambiguity of the phrasing, and in the clear anticipation of the very similar vision, overlooking the Hudson, that inflames the native egotism of the young sculptor, Roderick Hudson, prototype of the beginning romantic artist, we can catch here a hint of something more than family piety: rather, a burgeoning and almost transcendent delight in the inner aesthetic resources of the self.

The autobiography, backed by external allusions, also gives us the significant shape of a boy reading omnivorously – too omnivorously, too unselectively perhaps, to reassure even such a liberal father as he had – and, importantly for his later writing life, hungrily consuming any theatrical and visual experience available to him. He remembers vividly the New York theatres and (less availably) the New York shows of paintings: pantomimes, crude and evanescent plays, panoramas and stage events of any kind (such as *The Cataract of the Ganges* and *The Rajah's Daughter*); and paintings, usually very large, of historical events such as Washington crossing the Delaware. James never lost his taste, almost an undiscriminating taste, for the theatre: a fact of great importance for certain aspects of his later style, as well as for his perpetual fascination with the function of appearance and role-playing in a complex social world. And the lure of the theatre was also to be crucial in one of the great crises and turning-points of his career and of his psychological life, in the 1890s. As for painting, having quickly progressed from enjoying Benjamin Haydon's imported narrative canvases, as a child, to a more refined passion for Tintoretto and Veronese (those most theatrical of painters), James was to remain a profoundly visual novelist, in whose work some overriding image of a building or an art-work often draws to a focus all the most inward suggestions of his fictional scenes and events.

The record of James's reading as a boy and as a young man is far from complete, but confirms the picture of hunger rather than of careful study. He seems to have read Scott, Dickens, and Thackeray – there is his account of himself (at seven) hiding beneath the family table in order to hear the adults reading aloud the first instalment of *David Copperfield*, just received, and being discovered and sent to bed because of the sound of his sympathetic weeping at the narrative. In France and elsewhere, under his various tutors, he began to read Balzac, Stendhal, George Sand (rather later), Turgenev (perhaps his favourite), Trollope, George Eliot, and presumably other unrecorded and more ephemeral writers. Most things that were read in his day seem to have passed his way. The older classics he knew, but only sporadically – Shakespeare, Cervantes, Dante, the Romantic poets. James experienced what he read, and he read and read. But he read nothing as a scholar or as a disciple. He used what he read, and, as always, *converted* it. T. S. Eliot's famous double-edged phrase about James's lack of philosophic or moral dogmatism – 'He had a mind so fine that no idea could violate it'[6] – could be adapted to fit his early reading and his education. 'He had a mind so avid, and so free, that no other author could possess it.'

The pages of James's autobiography are also filled with the sense of place, and the sensuous and imaginative enjoyment of place. Early memories of New York – of Washington Place, where he was born, and the more famous Washington Square (which *he* was to make famous, in his novella of that name) round the corner; and of West 14th Street where the family (inevitably) soon moved. Memories of Albany in New York State, where his maternal grandmother lived, surrounded (according to his memory) by the pervasive presence and flavour of peaches. Memories of streets, of visits and expeditions, the Staten Island ferry, the taste of ice cream, waffles, the smell of new books. Above all – in the light of what was to come – memories, amazingly early, of Europe, its inns, its picture galleries, its long coach journeys, beaches and Alps, its schools and tutors, its childhood illnesses, its glamour and glitter. Especially, and characteristically, this:

we had somehow waked early to a perception of Paris, and a vibration of my very most infantine sensibility under its sky had by the same stroke got itself preserved for subsequent wondering reference. I had been there for a short time in the second year of my life, and I was to communicate to my parents later on that as a baby in long clothes, seated opposite to them in a carriage and on the lap of another person, I had been impressed with the view, framed by the clear window of the vehicle as we passed, of a great stately square surrounded with high-roofed houses and having in its centre a tall and glorious column. I had naturally caused them to marvel, but I had also, under cross-questioning, forced them to compare notes, as it were, and reconstitute the miracle . . . Conveyed along the Rue St.-Honoré while I wagged my small feet, as I definitely remember doing, under my flowing robe, I had crossed the Rue de Castiglione and taken in, for all my time, the admirable aspect of the Place and the Colonne Vendôme.[7]

The Jamesian act of memory, as here, is a formidable and endearing one, and the medium through which it is brought to us – the late-James style of leisurely, self-indulgent to-and-fro – blends the distant past, the nearer past, and the present in a richly evaluative haze that provides its own answer to any scepticism one might feel. For all the humour, deliberate or inadvertent, of such touches as 'the lap of another person', or the waggling of the feet under the flowing robe, what stands out most in this typical evocation of remembered shapes is the fact that the Colonne Vendôme was impressive and romantically 'glorious' to his discriminating two-year-old eyes, that what he had taken in of things French and Napoleonic was to be 'for all my time', and that scene, memory, and the act of complex narration have become indistinguishable.

Certain other personal images and shapes demand to be picked out, partly from the Autobiography and partly from elsewhere, as part of the ground on which the literary life, in 1864, was to be launched, and which it was in turn to absorb and use. Important among these is the image of Newport, Rhode Island, where the wandering Jameses at last pitched their tent on returning from France in 1858, when James was fifteen, and where they then took up a more-or-less established residence between 1860 and 1864 (James himself leaving in 1862). Newport in James's artistic career means various things. It means social pleasure and complexity, burgeoning personal relationships, and a certain degree of sophistication; it means an encounter with painting and painters considered not in gallery terms but as a profession; and it means, on the other hand, a lifelong trauma.

James, whom we now look back on as perpetual exile and wanderer, a lonely sensibility always within yet never belonging to a

complex social life, found in Newport in these two years around
the outbreak of the Civil War his first experience of a reasonably
settled communal life. The town was still an unstressed and intimate watering-place for the reasonably well-off, rather than the
playground of yachting and mansion-building tycoons that it became – again as part of a culturally crucial change – soon after the
war. It seems at times to have been virtually populated by James's
cousins, half-cousins, and friends: the perfect environment for the
late-teenager seeking (we can easily imagine) a little consolidation
in life after the hectic peregrinations of the previous years. There
were endless visiting-calls, walks on the shore, talkative gatherings,
exchanges of ideas, growing perceptions of friendship and affection
– and shared excitement and grief as the news of battles came in
from Virginia, and as friends and relatives went to war (James's
own two younger brothers, Wilky and Robertson, were seriously
injured in action). But simultaneously with this growing personal
experience – experience of the sense and feel of fluctuating relationships: the very *donnée* of a novelist – there was the bracing discovery of an example of professionalism.

William James, the elder brother, something of a maverick till
later in his life, was at this stage thinking of becoming a painter,
and present at his painting lessons with William Morris Hunt in
Newport was Henry – as always, rather shyly in the rear. But Henry's experience of the bearded and velvet-jacketed Hunt – the dedicated professional, himself a pupil of Millet – was not only formative
in itself, in showing him aesthetic dedication and expertise in
operation; it also led on to the more impressive encounter with
another of Newport's artistic community, the painter John La Farge.
La Farge, an even more romantic figure than Hunt, can be seen as
the prototype of many of James's later portraits of the successful
artist. It is as though the young James's imagination had always
been searching, amid the endless unfocused talk and travel of his
family life, for one crystallising image of the successful creative
individual hard at work, untroubled by family anxiety or by self-
doubt. La Farge on his chestnut horse, or in his white suit, or at
work at his easel, or in his eloquent talk of artists and writers –
expressing his belief, like manna to his young listener, that the arts
were all one, and the pursuit of beauty and high craftsmanship one
of the greatest goals in life – became part of the gallery of types in
James's creative mind, and, more importantly, became a crucial
catalyst in James's own growing motivation to be a maker. James

writes movingly in various novels of the effect on the would-be
artist of ecouragement, of the sudden sense of external justification:
Rowland Mallett's crucial praise of Roderick Hudson, for example,
or, most memorably of all (in *The Tragic Muse*), the influence on
Nick Dormer, as a struggling painter, of Gabriel Nash's words of
praise (Gabriel, the announcing angel) and Nash's own example to
Nick not of artistic achievement but of the artistic sensibility incar-
nate. James at 17 found in his friendship with the 24-year-old La
Farge, in Newport, a shape for his own sensibility, and a specifically external direction to follow: that of hard work, concentration,
and professionalism. La Farge importantly linked the arts of painting and writing for James. He introduced James to Balzac, who
became James's novelist-hero, and to other French writers like
Mérimée and Gautier – so the external direction, once again, inclined towards Paris. And he also encouraged James to go ahead
and write, and when he had written to try to 'place' his manuscript.
This was another crucial piece of professional urging: not to be
content any longer with private exercises, or with the dilettante
delusion of writing only for a few friends. La Farge knew that
creativity at a certain point (for the user of words) required to become authorship. And his words were not lost on the very young
man who was to become one of the most professional of novelists,
and the one who more than any writer before him made out a
lifelong case for the full professionalism, theoretic sophistication,
and high role in human affairs of the writer of novels.

Two remaining images from the Newport days can be connected
by their opposition, and also by their ironic relationship: the figure
of Minny Temple, one of the brightest figures of James's Newport
group of friends; and secondly, James's traumatic accident in Newport in 1861. One is an image of a talented and spontaneous young
American woman, James's half-cousin, the very quintessence of
Isabel Archer and Daisy Miller and Milly Theale, who evoked his
strong affection, perhaps even the beginnings of love, and by dying
at 24 became an eternal Jamesian metaphor for loss and for the
tragic failure of relationships, of youth, of talent. The other, the
'obscure hurt' suffered by James in a crowd while watching a barn
fire, became a metaphor for personal withdrawal and disability,
even for loss of manhood. The memory of Minny's youthful vitality
and promise – the very epitome of Newport – energises in an imaginatively positive way James's future attitude to his fictional
heroines, and much of his romantic attitude to the promise of life.

And it also eventually functions as a reminder of failure and death: the equally romantic other face, the dark side, of life's promise, Minny's life being one long losing battle against consumption. And his own persistent physical problems in life – probably arising from some severe back strain incurred during the 1861 incident – became to his own ruminative, introspective imagination an image of disablement, of inability to commit the self fully to another or to others, and equally (though in slightly more positive terms) a helpful rationalisation of his instinctive isolation and watchful detachment. The famous 'obscure hurt' – on which many speculative pages have been written – was converted and used by James's mind: again, the principle of conversion, of imaginative transformation. It became something of a self-justification for not participating, like so many of his much-envied friends and cousins, in the trial and adventure of the Civil War. It almost became a professional badge, a badge of the pained sensibility, cut off from full physical experience but thereby increased in mental responsiveness to that experience, a peculiar and typically Jamesian variant on the other kind of professional justification of which La Farge was an example. Equally, and very revealingly, James was later to 'convert' the death of Minny Temple into something other than the straightforward grief and sense of personal bereavement which he also experienced. Hearing of her death, some years after the Newport period, in 1870, he wrote to William:

> Her image will preside in my intellect . . . The more I think of her the more perfectly satisfied I am to have her translated from this changing realm of fact to the steady realm of thought. There she may bloom into a beauty more radiant than our dull eyes will avail to contemplate . . . She lives as a steady unfaltering luminary in the mind rather than as a flickering wasting earth-stifled lamp.[8]

The tone of such phrases is a little over-effulgent, and the taste of being 'satisfied' by Minny's death is more than dubious: but the tendency of James's ruminative letter is clear. It grieves at death, but draws the strongest possible consolation from a highly subjective aesthetic idealism. Minny is 'translated' into an imaginative image, and thereby is given access to another and more permanent, because aesthetic, form of existence. The personal grief at the imperfections and brevity of life is in a state of interplay with James's

urge to glorify and convert: an imaginatively energising, and forever unresolved, dialectic of negative and positive.

Similarly, or at least analogously, we find in the image of his
traumatic accident in the crowd at the fire in Newport ('Jammed',
he tells us himself, 'into the acute angle between two high fences')
the encounter with a negative force, and the capacity of the mind,
the artist's mind, to draw strength from the negation: this being one
of the profoundest rhythms of James's creative imagination. He
writes of his injury – presumably a back injury – in extravagant
terms as 'a private catastrophe . . . the effects of which were to draw
themselves out incalculably and intolerably'; and indeed his later
years contain many references to a debilitating weakness of the
back. But in the irresistibly converting processes of his mind, albeit
many years later, he uses verbal sleight-of-hand to enlarge the
'catastrophe' until it embraces the surrounding national 'catastrophe' of the war – 'a huge comprehensive ache . . . one could scarce
have told whether it came most from one's own poor organism . . . or
from the enclosing social body, a body rent with a thousand wounds
and that thus treated one to the honour of a sort of tragic fellow-
ship.'[9] And by this 'conversion' it is clear that the disability, while
remaining only too real and negative, became also a symbol of
compensatory self-enlargment. So that the wound that would in a
way explain away his failure to enlist in the Union army like his
brothers and many friends thus became a peculiar way of mentally
participating in the war, as well as an image for his temperamental
need to withdraw (like Minny Temple in her death) from 'the changing realm of fact' to the 'steady realm of thought'.

These two Newport images of the lively girl dying young, and
the wounded young man of sensibility, can be seen as governing
shapes in the great novels and stories to come, in the form of characters that were to appear and reappear in the fiction and also, by
much larger extension, as general emblems of human power and
loss of power, of life's promise and life's betrayal. And they remind
us of how, as with many artists, James became a writer by transpos-
ing certain of his living weaknesses and flaws into what became, in
artistic terms, his most specific creative strengths.

When Henry James became a published writer in 1864 he had left
Newport behind for the very different world of Boston and Cambridge. It is a fact worth dwelling on that one of the most cosmopolitan and least nationalistic of American writers, and the most
famous of its great expatriates, began his career not only against a

background of unignorable national crisis and of family immersion
in most American realities of the time, but also from within the
still-dominant cultural centre of the nation, in or around Boston. It
is also notable that James, after his childhood of European travel,
should turn to writing during the most prolonged American phase
of his adult life. He left Newport in September 1862 to enrol for one
ineffectual (indeed, incongruous) year in Harvard Law School, then
settled in his parents' new home, first in Boston itself then in Cambridge, and did not make his first independent sortie to Europe till
1869, when he was 26 and already a prolific reviewer, essayist, and
short-story writer. And it was not until 1875 that he officially left
the family nest and settled definitely in Europe. What is of interest
in this important phase of his career is therefore not just the movement *out* of America to Europe, but the important presence of both
continents in his consciousness. As always with James, the pattern
is one of unresolved interplay, of not quite exclusive opposites,
rather than of clear-cut choice or of one value overcoming another.
All of the famous ambiguity of James's later style is rooted – and
therefore rooted firmly – in these detectable ambiguities and com-
plexities of his early mental life.

James seems to have begun writing criticism and fiction during
or immediately after his year at Harvard – his growing awareness
of his true vocation as a writer perhaps speeded up by his experience of the unsuitableness of the law. His first story, 'A Tragedy of
Error', appeared unsigned in February 1864 in the *Continental
Monthly* – *not* one of the weightier periodicals of the New England
establishment. Six months later, far more influentially in terms of
his half-chosen career, he had his unsolicited review of Nassau
Senior's *Essays on Fiction* accepted by the *North American Review*,
now edited by James Russell Lowell and Charles Eliot Norton, and
very much a pillar of the American literary scene both before and
after the war. From this point on, until James's definitive removal
to France eleven years later, his writing career was firmly set in the
day-to-day context of life in Boston and Cambridge, with, at the
very end, a period of six months in New York City. There were, it
is true, two very extensive and important trips to Europe during
these years – one in 1869 and one in 1872–4 – but the fact remains
that the writer was now officially and practically based in the
American scene, and in the publishing, as well as the social, conditions of the time.

James's sense of Boston and Cambridge comes across most

powerfully in *The Bostonians* (1885–6), and of a more rural and older New England in *The Europeans* (1878) and the opening of *Roderick Hudson* (1875). But in much of his fiction there are references and brief evocations – for example, the beautiful thumbnail sketch of Susan Stringham's Boston background in *The Wings of the Dove* (1902), or Strether's perpetual awareness of the nature (and weight) of Woollett, Massachusetts, in *The Ambassadors* (1903). The picture he paints is both affectionate and satirical, and his allusions in letters and elsewhere to his life in Boston are distinctly critical – 'this frigid, rigid town', where life in the family house in Quincy Street was 'about as lively as the inner sepulchre'.[10] Nevertheless, despite the provincialism that James deplored (particularly the later, fully Europeanised James, reminiscing without much nostalgia), he lived a fairly complex social life in these early years, a factor that must be placed against the idea (partly his own idea) that his sensibility was as isolated as Proust's. Life may have been unglamorous, but James began his writing life from inside a web of family activities and flourishing friendships: all of which provided his developing imagination with lasting images of social involvement, of the power and difficulty of personal relationships, and of the enriching stress of communal life.

As well as personal relationships – the continuing emotional friendship with Minny Temple, for example, or relationships such as that with Thomas Sergeant Perry, dating from his Newport days, or with his new Harvard friend, the young Oliver Wendell Holmes – James now also began to develop friendships that were professional as well as personal. His relationhip with Charles Eliot Norton, for example, began as that between a budding reviewer and an established Boston Brahmin who edited the *North American Review*, and grew into a fairly close lifelong friendship (typically of James, most of whose closest friendships were with women, he was even closer to Norton's sister, Grace). He also saw much of James Russell Lowell at Cambridge, a poet, critic, and essayist who completely embodied the older New England literary tradition. And more influentially for his own future – and more characteristic of his increasing commitment to the contemporary professional scene – James also met and at once responded to William Dean Howells, at first on the staff then editor of the newly-founded *Atlantic Monthly*, where James's first signed story, 'The Story of a Year', appeared in March, 1865 (he was also writing at this period for the *Nation* and the *Galaxy*, with professional acumen spreading his offerings across the spectrum of the periodical press). These were significant figures to offer guidance and praise to James, as well as space in their journals. Howells, for example, as early as 1866 wrote that the young James was 'gifted enough to do better than any one has yet done toward making us a real American novel'.[11] And Norton was so impressed that in 1868, when James was only twenty-five, he offered him the editorship of the *North American Review*, which James – perhaps fortunately – turned down. James can only have gained enormously in professional confidence from these contacts; but he also gained from the perpetual exchange of ideas about writing, about reading, and about the native as opposed to the European tradition. He discussed Hawthorne in particular with Howells, and also tapped the latter's knowledge of Italy and Italian writing. And with Norton – a more refined and intellectual figure than Howells – he could learn about Dante and offer in return (to both friends) his own growing familiarity with the works of Balzac, George Eliot, and George Sand (his early articles and reviews before 1875 also covered, among many others, Trollope, Dickens – reprovingly – Gautier, Dumas, Hugo, Flaubert, Stendhal, Goethe, Hardy, Thackeray, and – disparagingly – Walt Whitman).

The picture is of a young writer exploring other literatures (though, as always, not in any scholarly or systematic way) and sharing in a very active network of intellectual exchange and influence. There is also, as one would expect, evidence of James's partial detachment from those around him. Apart from his general criticisms of the provinciality and shallowness of American life, we find him able to be disconcertingly critical concerning a personal mentor like Howells. Typical of this completely two-way response by James to his contemporary scene are the two following contrasted accounts by him of Howells, both highly characteristic in style. The first, an open letter written on the occasion of Howells's seventy–fifth birthday in 1912, and celebrating Howells's long and influential career as the doyen of American letters, is nostalgically positive and evocative of that earlier period:

> you held out your open editorial hand to me at the time I began to write – and I allude especially to the summer of 1866 – with a frankness and sweetness of hospitality that was really the making of me, the making of the confidence that required help and sympathy and that I should otherwise, I think, have strayed and stumbled about a long time without acquiring. You showed me

the way and opened me the door; you wrote to me, and con-
fessed yourself struck with me – I have never forgotten the beautiful thrill of *that*. You published me at once – and paid me, above
all, with a dazzling promptitude; magnificently, I felt, and so that
nothing since has ever quite come up to it . . . you talked to me
and listened to me – ever so patiently and genially and suggestively conversed and consorted with me.[12]

And the second, from a letter written in 1871 to Grace Norton, is
almost alarming in its acute negations, its sense of an indebted
young writer nevertheless holding on firmly to his private judgement, and to his private discontents with America:

Poor Howells is certainly difficult to defend, if one takes a stand-
point the least bit exalted; make any serious demands and it's all
up with him. He presents, I confess, to my mind, a somewhat
melancholy spectacle – in that his charming style and refined
intentions are so poorly and meagerly served by our American
atmosphere . . . Thro' thick and thin I continue however to enjoy
him – or rather thro' thinner and thinner. There is a little divine
spark of fancy which never quite goes out. He has passed into the
stage which I suppose is the eventual fate of all secondary and
tertiary talents – worked off his less slender Primitive, found a
place and a routine and an income, and now is destined to fade
slowly and softly away in self-repetition and reconcilement to the
common-place. But he will always be a *writer* – small but genuine. There are not so many after all now going in English – to say
nothing of American.[13]

'Meagerly served by our American atmosphere': these ominous
words were written a year after James returned from a momentous
14-month trip to Europe which not only marked a significant inter-
regnum in his Boston and Cambridge years but can be seen to be
a turning-point in his writing life and in his private life. Recalling
it in 1905, in his most effulgent and honeyed manner, he fancifully
traces the origin of his expatriation – his 'vision-haunted migration'
– to one day in August 1866, when, calling on Oliver Wendell
Holmes's mother, in Charles Street, for word of his friend's '1st
flushed and charming visit to England', he 'got the news, of all his
London, his general English, success and felicity, and *vibrated* so
with the wonder and romance and curiosity and dim weak tender

(oh, tender!) envy of it, that my walk up the hill, afterwards, up
Mount Vernon St. and probably to Athenaeum was all coloured
and gilded, and humming with it.'[14] In the midst of his day-to-day
commitment to the social and literary life of Boston, the letters to
editors, the (usually) prompt delivery of manuscripts, the friendly
or dutiful visits and talks, the walks in the country, and in the
midst of an impressively prolific burst of review-writing and story-
writing (almost all of the stories being set in America), James fan-
cies that he hears the definitive call of Europe – although, perhaps
typical of the prevarications that were to mark the mental life of his
characters as well as his own, it was well over two years before he
answered the call, and took sail.

Having bade farewell (unknowingly for the last time) to Minny
Temple, James sailed from New York for Liverpool in February
1869. Two things call for emphasis about this first independent trip
to Europe (evocatively described by Leon Edel in his biography).
First, the way in which his own responsiveness to what he saw
prefigures the 'passionate pilgrim' aspect of his own travelling heroes and heroines and the romantic sensitivity to all fresh experience that never disappears from his fictional pages. And secondly,
the extraordinary degree to which James travelled not as the isolated, wandering sensibility one might have expected but as someone eminently provided with contacts and amenities wherever he
went. The passionate pilgrim came armed with letters of introduction, with helpful (though not excessive) notes of draft upon his
own and his father's bank accounts, and with a whole system of
friends and acquaintance already waiting to receive him. The sensibility was private; but his life in Europe (as in America) was intensely social and complicated from beginning to end – these two
things, once again, being the perfect recipe for the kind of fiction he
was to write.

For example, within a few days of his arrival in London – 'a
dreadful, delightful city' – James was called on by Leslie Stephen,
who had met him in Boston at the house of J. T. Fields, the editor
of the *Atlantic Monthly* (this being thirteen years before Stephen
became the father of Virginia Woolf). Stephen, a little surprisingly,
took James to the Zoo, then James dined with Charles Eliot Norton,
whom he accompanied after dinner to hear a public lecture by
Ruskin. Three days later, at the Nortons', he met Dickens's daughter. Then, after breakfast with the poet Aubrey de Vere, he visited
the William Morrises in Bloomsbury, and stayed to dinner (Jane

Morris, Pre-Raphaelitic in a long purple gown and 'some dozen strings of outlandish beads', had a toothache, and while Morris chanted his poetry aloud she lay stretched out on the sofa, her face under a handkerchief – 'this dark silent mediaeval woman with her mediaeval toothache'). A few days later, he dined with Ruskin and admired his Turners. Then he met Frederic Harrison, social philosopher, historian, critic, and editor of the *Fortnightly Review*. Then Burne-Jones, the painter; then lunched with Charles Darwin. And while admiring Titian's *Bacchus and Ariadne* in the National Gallery he became aware of a small man with red hair standing next to him: 'I thrilled . . . with the prodigy of this circumstance that I should be admiring Titian in the same breath with Mr. Swinburne – that is in the same breath in which *he* admired Titian and in which I also admired *him*.' Not long afterwards he called on George Eliot, who was friendly, and who, despite her 'low forehead, a dull grey eye, a vast pendulous nose, a huge mouth, full of uneven teeth', nevertheless made him fall in love with the inner beauty that spoke out through her voice, her features, her 'hundred conflicting shades of consciousness and simpleness'. Then he travelled, saw innumerable things and people, became rather ill (constipation and back trouble), partly recovered, spent £120 in eleven weeks – then headed across the Channel for Switzerland ('little else but brute nature') and, *sacrum sacrorum*, Italy. He responded with a long-saved-up ecstasy to Italy, and especially Rome: the buildings, the light, the crowded squares and cafés, the paintings (Veronese, Bellini, Tintoretto), the human faces and types. Rather less provided than in England with introductions in high places, he also now encountered the ordinary Americans abroad, and was scathing:

> the Englishmen I have met not only kill, but bury in unfathomable depths, the Americans I have met, A set of people less framed to provoke national self-complacency than the latter it would be hard to imagine. There is but one word to use in regard to them – vulgar; vulgar, vulgar. Their ignorance . . . their perpetual reference of all things to some American standard . . . our unhappy poverty of voice, of speech, of physiognomy – these things glare at you hideously.[15]

When he returned to Cambridge in the spring of 1870, it was to make his first attempt at a full-length novel. The novel, *Watch and Ward*, is only just readable, and can fairly safely be put into the same apprenticeship category as most of the short stories that preceded 'A Passionate Pilgrim' in 1871. But it is set – very vaguely, it is true – in Boston (as well as New York), a thin and unfleshed novel of manners and entangled love relationships revolving around a twelve-year-old adopted girl (the 'ward' in question) that weakly prefigures *What Maisie Knew* and *The Awkward Age*; and it can be seen as playing its role in James's hesitations during these years between America and Europe. It is almost as though the bareness of *Watch and Ward* was to prove James's own point that American society was too thin a material to stimulate successfully the imagination of the novelist – certainly of this particular novelist, at this particular time. At least it was a gesture towards Boston – as well as, in potential at least, towards James's growing interest in complex social and psychological relationships, in this case relationships dominated by (very diluted) sexual motives. This first novel – critics have traced in it influences of Prosper Mérimée and George Sand, Balzac and Dickens, and Oliver Wendell Holmes Senior (father of his friend) – is also a testimony to the importance of James's friendship with Howells. Howells had become full editor of the *Atlantic Monthly* only in July, 1871 (having been assistant editor up until then), and it was in those pages that *Watch and Ward* was serialised between August and December of that year. James had already published ten short stories in the same magazine, and clearly at this stage in his career owed an enormous amount to Howells's enthusiasm (Howells later said that he welcomed every one of James's contributions 'with [a] band of music'[16]), and also, probably, to his suggestions and criticisms. Howells was always a very supportive, though at times prudish, editor. But what James probably profited from most was Howells's strong sense of the practicalities and necessary compromises of periodical publication; and also from his strongly nationalist conviction that the American novel (rather than mere short story) was to be consciously nurtured in an attempt to break free from the domination of the contemporary English novel.

James's life between his return from Europe in 1870 and his final departure in 1875 – spent mostly in the family home in Cambridge, then during the winter of 1874–5 in New York – was extraordinarily prolific in terms of literary output: for example, forty-two published items in 1874 alone. But almost two of these five years were spent again in Europe, in his more extended, and even more seriously involving, trip of 1872–4. And our general sense of these five years is that they were an extended debate in his own thinking as to the claims of Europe and America: that is, the so-called 'International Theme' which he was about to explore in the major works that immediately followed between 1874 and 1881, *Roderick Hudson, The American, The Europeans,* 'Daisy Miller', and *The Portrait of a Lady.* It is another striking example of James fully living out his themes, in terms of personal experience, before dramatising them in his fiction. In the novels there may be no considered philosophy or prolonged abstract thinking – no over-cultivation of an idea, in T. S. Eliot's phrase, that could 'violate' 'so fine a mind'. But what we find is always debate and conflict: an interplay that goes beyond and behind ideas by examining contrasted human values as *experienced*, and ideas as revealed, enriched, and blurred in *action*. And these ideas were fully rehearsed and tried out in the felt experience – the inner action – that comprised the novelist's life.

So, feeling somewhat lonely, probably oppressed by the tensions of living *en famille*, especially with William in one of his own periods of psychological crisis and their sister Alice in permanent and highly demanding nervous invalidism, feeling somewhat nostalgic for European glamour, somewhat penned in by the parochialism of Cambridge and Boston, with the new post-war America booming westwards in a frenzy of commercial enterprise, James in these years nevertheless celebrates the challenge that America could still offer the imagination, writing to his friend Norton in 1871:

I conclude that the face of nature and civilization in this our country is to a certain point a very sufficient literary field. But it will yield its secrets only to a really *grasping* imagination . . . To write well and worthily of American things one needs even more than elsewhere to be a *master*. But unfortunately one is less![17]

Or again, rather more romantically, he evokes America as reality and as a metaphor for imaginative possibility in the following, where the opening phrase, 'hungry eastward [that is, European] thoughts', and the closing mild disparagement, 'honest Massachusetts', nevertheless 'frame' his evocation in true Jamesian fashion:

I lie there [in the hills outside Cambridge], often, on the grass, with a book in my pockets, thinking hungry eastward thoughts: but thinking too that we have very good things near us [at] home – witness these untrodden hills and woods – so utterly unhaunted

that I can people them with what shapes I will with this vast
outlook into purple distances and nameless inland horizons
fretted by superb undulations – which all simply mean honest
Massachusetts.[18]

In the play of tones in that passage, its subtle exaggerations and its
archly Johnsonian pomposities ('superb undulations'), we have a
fine example of the manner in which James's mental debate must
have been conducted – and a foretaste of how, in character, imagery, and stylistic nuances, it was going to be conducted in the
fiction to come.

He speaks at this time of Europe as his 'wound', a 'shaft', a
'bullet' in the body with the flesh grown over it; in Cambridge his
'sense aches at times for richer fare'; and the imagery of inner struggle is often added to that of pain and violence as testimony to the
nature of his inner debate – as in his famous cry: 'It's a complex fate
being an American, and one of the responsibilities it entails is fight-
ing against a superstitious valuation of Europe.'[19] Right through the
series of travel-sketches (mostly of North-Eastern scenes, like
Saratoga and Rhode Island) which he began writing for the *Nation*
in 1870 – partly to make money, and partly to do his imaginative
best by the American scene – there sounds out the involved
doubleness of his response. Even in one short phrase used for the
American landscape – 'the eloquent silence of undedicated nature'
– he manages to express a significant tension between 'eloquent'
and 'undedicated': that is, between the imaginative possibilities of
American space and grandeur, and the contrary perception that to
be 'undedicated' is to be blank to the point of inarticulacy.[20] And
when he describes American businessmen on holiday, lounging in
their hotel in Saratoga, he sets up a comic and apparently equal
tension between the images of 'fruit' and 'nut', in which, however,
we can detect without too much difficulty his own preference:

They [these men] are not the mellow fruit of a society which has
walked hand-in-hand with tradition and culture; they are hard
nuts, which have grown and ripened as they could. When they
talk among themselves, I seem to hear the cracking of the shells.[21]

The prolific writer of travel sketches – James the half-dedicated
journalist of these years, writing for the *Nation*, the *Atlantic*, and the
Galaxy – was soon writing back to America, describing the Louvre,

the streets of Berne, Milan, and Venice, as he accompanied his sister Alice and his Aunt Kate in a prolonged venture into the other side, the European side, of his intellectual dialectic, his personal international theme. Above all, it was his time in Rome that seems to have mattered on this occasion. Relieved of Alice (and her breakdowns), he was free to respond to Rome and the Campagna, and also to the Europeanised and highly agreeable American society he now met there, with an enthusiasm that allowed little space for reference to America and its claims. His time in Rome was a congested, almost frenzied, period of social activity, gallery and villa-visiting, horse-riding in the Campagna, wanderings through ruins, churches, back-streets, gardens: often in the company of attractive American women like Lizzie Boott, Alice Bartlett, and (perhaps with a hint of emotional involvement) Sarah Wister. In his small apartment in the Corso, in a warm spring, he had his thirtieth birthday in April 1873; and a month later, sitting down to do his accounts, was able to reassure his anxious mother that since he had earned about $740 that year from his travel-pieces and short stories, and spent just under that sum in his travels in France and Italy, he was virtually self-sufficient as a writer. Soon, after a not-untroubled visit to him in Italy by his ever-oppressive elder brother, who put pressure on him not to think of embracing a purely literary (or European) life, James nevertheless found himself – still from Italy – in the position of being able to dangle the project of an unwritten novel before two potential editors, Howells of the *Atlantic* and Josiah Holland of *Scribner's*, and offering it in the end to the better bid. Howells won the novel – for $1 200, at $100 per monthly instalment.

The novel was begun in Florence in the early summer of 1874, in James's apartment overlooking Piazza Santa Maria Novella; and was not completed until the spring of 1875, when he had returned to America and for the first time since his birth taken up residence, as a six-month experiment – his last American experiment – in New York City. The novel, *Roderick Hudson*, was his first major full-length fiction: and in the history of its composition, as in the new complexity and subtlety of its matter and manner, it marked more fully than anything that had preceded it the 'international' doubleness of James's life, the 'complex fate' of being one of the James family *and* an American, and the entry of its author into the maturity of his career.

2

American and Romantic

James's first four important works of fiction, all of which appeared in periodical form within a period of about three and a half years – *Roderick Hudson* between January and December 1875, *The American* between June 1876 and May 1877, 'Daisy Miller' in June and July 1878, and *The Europeans* between July and October 1878 – are all variably concerned with the clash of two cultures, American and European, that we have seen as prominent in their author's own experience in the immediately preceding years. But beyond personal biography they can also be seen as relating to certain larger cultural movements and concerns of their time.

In the Preface to *The American* (written thirty years later), James makes much of its 'romantic' qualities, by which he seems to mean, and with some disparagement, a certain distance from normal everyday experience, a deflection from the 'element of reality':

> The real represent to my perception the things we cannot possibly *not* know, sooner or later, in one way or another . . . The romantic stands, on the other hand, for the things that . . . we never *can* directly know; the things that can reach us only through the beautiful circuit and subterfuge of our thought and our desire . . . experience disengaged, disembroiled, disencumbered, exempt from the conditions that we usually know to attach to it.[1]

'Romance', in this limited view, is an affair of trickery, of sleight-of-hand – 'this hocus-pocus', as he says of his attempts to make Christopher Newman's affair acceptable to the reader, and to conceal its stylised, melodramatic differences from 'the way things happen'. And James's account points more to a local debate in the 1880s and 1890s (involving figures like Rider Haggard and James's friend, R. L. Stevenson) concerning the opposition of 'realism' and 'romance' in contemporary fiction than to Romanticism as a great intellectual and literary tradition. Yet it is to Romanticism – Romanticism direct, in the English and European mode, or Romanticism transmuted into Emersonian Transcendentalism in America from the 1830s onwards – that these four works so often refer us.

To begin with, each of the four draws its narrative energies and its emotional and intellectual content from the idea of possibility; change, development, discovery. *Roderick Hudson*, the most richly lyrical of the four, vibrates with a romantic concept of individual perfectability and creativity – qualified by an equally romantic perception of loss and imperfection. Roderick as a sculptor of potential genius is the romantic artist *par excellence*: destroyed in the end not by some clear and judgeable moral flaw but by some entropic quality in life itself that coexists with its vitality. Rowland Mallett, the cautious onlooker who is nevertheless empowered by money and taste to foster genius in others, is a man of repressed feeling and imagination who can only express himself vicariously – like so many of James's half-baffled romantics. And Christina Light, adventuress and *demi-mondaine*, is a *femme fatale* filled with a frustrated energy that is not all sexually manipulative but is as potentially creative, expressive, and world-moving as the inner energies of the sculptor in whom she arouses a debilitating passion. This psychology of romantic energy and romantic frustration is matched by the characteristic evocation of landscape in the book: and in particular the landscape and townscape of Italy, by means of which James expresses both his own personal passion for that land and the romantic archetype of an exotic, past-haunted place where full poetic and emotional expression can be assured.

Life seen as infinite promise, life experienced as a trap: so much of romantic poetry oscillates between these two poles, and finds in the tension between them the source of its energy and its tragic vision. *The American*, too, like almost any book James wrote, late as well as early, is driven by a basic motif of someone setting out on life, confronting life as a prize to be fought for – or, in various senses, to be bought. Its hero is Christopher Newman, the Californian – who is on three immediate counts, therefore, the American romantic hero, being named for America's discoverer, being the new man that America was intended to produce, and being from the West, America's newest and (after 1849) gold-filled frontier of possibility. And romantic energy (quizzically and subtly qualified, and at times withheld, by the hesitations of personal moral doubt and even fatalism) expresses itself in Newman's obstinate will as he challenges the inertness and self-protectiveness of the Old World in the form of the Bellegardes (the aristocratic Parisian clan who know

how to 'guard well' their dignity and their daughter, Claire de
Cintré). Newman's is not a directly imaginative and artistic energy
like Roderick's, nor is it even creative in a surrogate, distorted way
like Rowland's and Christina's. But even in his prosaic worldliness
– a man who would buy up art, and even buy a woman (whom he
also undoubtedly loves) – Newman is the romantic adventurer: the
archetypally Napoleonic young man from the provinces (as it were)
who comes arrogantly to the capital in order to express and to
achieve power. Nothing in James is more in the romantic tradition
than his fascination with power – and, in the case of *The American*,
his fascination with the battle that ensues between different varieties of power, the power of new money, a new race, a new energy,
in conflict with the power of established position, cold deviousness,
and self-esteem.

'Daisy Miller' and *The Europeans* modify these motifs wonderfully, and explore the possibilities and fluidities of personality in a
different way, but are still both lit through by the Jamesian principle that the individual is never fixed, always experimenting, always
discovering or inventing new selves, and being as much an artist by
the manipulation of a fan, a parasol, a mode of dress or a style of
living as by the making of sculptures (in Roderick's case) or the
expression of the free-ranging and sensitive private will against the
dead hand of social conservatism and personal fixity (in Newman's).
Daisy, too, romantically confronts the world's possibilities from
terraces overlooking the Alps or the Pincian Gardens in Rome; and
is watched, from *his* metaphorical terrace, by Winterbourne, who is
the over-hesitant and repressed appreciator of distances, of beauty,
of feeling, of the possibilities in a young woman's smile, a young
woman's (Minny Temple's?) American freshness and openness to
the chances of life. Winterbourne is the romantic artist *manqué* –
very, very *manqué* – and Daisy is his unwritten poem, his unde-
clared love, the formidable challenge to his moralistic preconcep-
tions. And Eugenia, in *The Europeans*, is very much the adventuress
and *femme fatale*, inventing her life and her self as she goes, as
creatively as any great actress or poet, and exposing on the way the
failure of will in others (Acton) or their non-romantic fixity, honest
provincialism, and irresponsiveness to self-expression and change
(the Wentworths – except for Gertrude, who embraces the romantic
and gets free). In 'Daisy Miller' and *The Europeans*, and also in *The
American*, we have the romantic (even the Gothic) syndrome of the
disturbing newcomer or stranger, who challenges a static or self-

protective society and situation, and thereby endorses the romantic principles of growth, mystery, and life-as-flux as against the oppressiveness of stale convention, petty rationality, and order.

These principles, however romantic, are very large, and to assert their importance in James's imagination in the late 1870s – or later – is not to claim that he was directly, or even consciously, under the influence of the earlier writers of Romanticism. There are various explicit references in each of the four works: in *Roderick Hudson*, for example, Roderick is overheard chanting a Byron-like couplet from Tennyson's *The Princess* as he prepares excitedly to leave Massachusetts for the promise of Italy; and his confession of his first collapse into over-romantic self-indulgence is ironically situated by the statue of Rousseau, father of Romanticism, in Geneva. In *The American*, Valentin, the attractive scion of the Bellegardes whose romantic but futile death in a duel is an ironic accompaniment to Newman's loss of Claire (death and defeat being the other side of the romantic coin), is seen by Newman's friend, Mrs Tristram, in the role of Keats's pale knight-at-arms in 'La Belle Dame Sans Merci'. *The Europeans*, in a clever trick of words, has Felix Young, Eugenia's brother who will rescue Gertrude Wentworth from her immurement in Boston fixity, step into her life straight out of the pages of *The Arabian Nights*. And in 'Daisy Miller', the Byronic associations of the Chateau de Chillon, and the fact that Winterbourne unromantically rejects Daisy just after himself reciting Byron's *Manfred* in the Colosseum by moonlight, are part of James's critique of timorousness and of the decay into mere aestheticism of the Byronic spirit. But these precise allusions, however interestingly they express something of the romantic qualities of inspiration, of elegy, or of irony that pervade the books, are almost incidental to the way in which this writing is steeped in an ongoing romantic tradition of a larger kind: an inheritance available to any writer of the time, and part even of the breathable air of the mid and later-nineteenth century, though only to a temperament, like James's, that chose, and was formed, to breathe it.

The tradition behind James's questioning, self-doubting characters has far too many constituents, extending over too great a stretch of a time, to be more than touched on here in a few of its aspects. From Rousseau, for example, comes the celebration of the individual's capacity to remake the self by struggle against the bonds of society, and through intuition and feeling – this emphasis on intuition as against intellect being transmitted, in the Anglo-Saxon world, through Coleridge and Carlyle, who also transmitted the ideas of German Idealist philosophy. The celebration of energy, often as expressed through the individual will, as the vital principle of all existence is pervasive in Romanticism – in Blake, for example, and in poetic imagery such as Coleridge's and Shelley's of the fountain, the river, and the wind. And in Carlyle the concept of the energised hero, making himself and the world around him, was given a particularly influential expression – long before Nietzsche later in the century, but along with, and feeding into, Emerson's powerful version of this romantic motif in the New England of the 1830s.

Two interestingly contrasted – though related – romantic versions of the self and its making are to be found in Wordsworth and Keats, both of whom we know James read (though that is of no great importance when dealing with something as intangible, yet as undeniable, as the spirit of an age). Just as we see in certain of James's heroes the struggle to shape the energies of personality in such a way as to express a particular talent, or to achieve possession and power of various kinds (sexual or aesthetic), so in such a seminal romantic work as Book One of Wordsworth's *Prelude* we have a 'narrative' of the baffled yet creative self in its search for full expression, seeking by a combination of travel and introspection to find the 'form' or theme that will remove the 'impediment' (such a Jamesian concept!) of loss of confidence, weakness of personal will, falsity to self ('That burthen of my own unnatural self'), and the 'heavy weight' of the everyday. The Wordsworthian self reaches its lowest point of despair when it falls into a paralysing guilt at having an unspent 'talent' that could define the self ('Like a false steward who had much received / And renders nothing back'), an experience of 'want of power', a 'timorous capacity' for 'circumspection' and 'subtle selfishness', all of which 'Doth lock my functions up in blank reserve'. Then Wordsworth suddenly finds the turning-point (between lines 271 and 304) in a specific memory of childhood: especially of childhood within the world of nature. And from that romantic visionary moment of the recovered past – the moment in which, through memory and through natural images the self finds its integrity in time, in memory of origins and of communication-in-nature – the self is re-made in its fullest energy and poetic self-confidence. Similar moments of release come to the locked-up artist, Nick Dormer, in *The Tragic Muse*, as well as to Strether in Paris, Hyacinth Robinson encountering his Princess in *The Princess Casamassima*, and Roderick Hudson being inspired by the same Princess, as Christina Light, in the earlier novel. These are the great turning-points when the creative self finds its necessary images: in Wordsworth's case the primary image of the running river of his childhood, the Derwent, symbol of romantic organicism and articulacy *par excellence*, which releases the sense of being reborn into full integrity, the child having truly become the father of the doubting man.

This Wordsworthian pattern became quite dominant in the nineteenth century: a pattern of personal alienation and fragmentation being healed by a recovered oneness with one's own past and with the surrounding world of nature (and sometimes, though less in Wordsworth himself, the surrounding world of human community). The motif was extremely powerful in George Eliot – for example, *Silas Marner*, in 1861, is almost a paradigm of the Wordsworthian experience – and not much less so in Dickens, whose middle-period and later novels, such as *Dombey and Son* (1848), *Bleak House* (1852–3), *Little Dorrit* (1855–7), *Great Expectations* (1860–1), and *Our Mutual Friend* (1864–5), are full of images of the oppressed self – either guilty or alienated by selfishness and cupidity – being restored to integrity and truth-to-self by processes of humiliation, physical illness, or revelation through encountering goodness and innocence in others, particularly in a child or a childlike nature. James is of course quite far from Dickens, though much less far from George Eliot. But there is a fundamental and recognisable kinship between his narrative of people cut off from life's promise, walled up in their own timorousness or in someone else's selfishness, seeking for a word that will release their energies and give a form to creative and passional impulses, and the great Wordsworthian prototype of the poet-hero struggling against 'impediment' to release in words and action (and through the medium of memory) the repressed true self. What the River Derwent and the 'mountain forms' of the Lake District were for the 'locked up' Wordsworth, the images of Italy, of Paris, of the 'mountain forms' of the Alps in 'Daisy Miller', of balconies and terraces and the personality of an alluring stranger or a suddenly intimate friend were for James and his fictional protagonists.

Very different from the Wordsworthian concept of selfhood, with its emphasis on development, learning, and organic relationship – and Wordsworth's was the model that spoke most to the subsequent Victorian mind – is Keats's more modern concept of openness, of perpetual drama, of relativism, and of unfinished, unfinishable, and potentially tragic process. The fragmentary 'narratives' of the self that one can detect in Keats's Odes, in particular, are full of unresolved opposites. The longing to transcend the self's limitations alternate with the realisation that time and space in the end must limit the self; the ecstatic search for the ideal collapses into the desire that the body, which is non-ideal, shall retain its senses; the dream-urge that moves towards self-loss and death clashes against the poet's all-too-human horror of death and vacuity ('to thy high requiem become a sod'). For Keats in his letters, life is 'a vale of soul-making', and he envisages in his own case a measurable process of development out of 'the chamber of maiden-thought' – two ideas that may seem quite Wordsworthian (and hence Victorian) in their acceptance of the notion of improvement. But the more predominant impression from the poems themselves is of an emotional and psychological process of selfhood that is not linear but even circuitous, and that finds in a foiled circuitousness its expression of energy and its own very Keatsian beauty – a concept that anticipates James's fine phrase about the 'romance' element of *The American*, 'the beautiful circuit and subterfuge of our thought and our desire'.[2] Keats explored that circuit and subterfuge more memorably than any other lyric poet, and provides us – and the nineteenth century – with a powerful and disturbing image of human character being a process rather than an entity, being fundamentally tragic in its imperfection and contradictory desires, and being heroic, too, in its destiny of self-achievement through hurling itself into the fullest possible experiencing of its own opposites, its own hesitations and expectations, its willed encountering with the 'veiled melancholy' that lies, and must be experienced where it lies, 'in the very centre of delight'. The Keatsian dynamic – as against the far more restrained and more progressive impetus behind Wordsworth's view of the individual – lurks more out of sight within the sensibility of the nineteenth century, but is nevertheless operative there. And with the early twentieth-century move towards a view of reality that is un-absolute and wholly relativist, enforcing fragmentation and unending, even chaotic, process, existential in its rejection of any attainable pure essence, the Keatsian insight can be seen to be prophetic: an insight that was to be developed very powerfully in the thinking and writing of James's brother William, perhaps the most modern and significant of American philosophers at the turn of the century.

Daisy Miller, ambiguously attractive and demanding, challenging her society and the half-attracted, observing Winterbourne by cultivating a Giovanelli who is so inappropriate to her innocence (though even he can appreciate that quality in her), and staring ambiguously at a stimulated but disapproving Winterbourne in the chiaroscuro of a moonlit Colosseum, where the fatal malaria lurks, dramatises the meeting-point of some of these Keatsian tensions. Christopher Newman, seething with frustration, and defeated by the blank wall of the convent that cuts off the woman he loves, tempted to take a revenge on her family that may be a mere waste of his energy, and confronting the arbitrary death of Valentin, is the Carlylean (and Californian!) hero trapped into a Keatsian aware-ness. Even the bitter-sweet ending of *The Europeans* leaves us with all the ambiguities unresolved concerning Eugenia as the bearer of the cup of promise or as the threatening adventuress, and Acton as the man who has scruples about truth (and truth-to-self) as against Acton the hesitant bystander who has watched life's possibilities drift away from him. Eugenia, who like the moon, we are told, has her dark unseen side, seems closer to the reality of multiple facets and perpetual change, of melancholy-in-delight, of life as drama, than any other figure in that book. And *Roderick Hudson*, even more clearly, bears everywhere in its pages the burden of Keatsian soul-making, of Keats's irreconcilable desires for the heat of human passion and for the cool unchangingness of art, and the Keatsian sense of outrage that life should be so desirable and in the same moment so betraying, so open yet suddenly so entombing – as in Roderick's rhetorical cry as he heads for the Alps and for his death, leaving behind the Italy that has seen the failure of both his talent and his passion:

'Dead, dead; dead and buried! Buried in an open grave, where you lie staring up at the sailing clouds, smelling the waving flow-ers and hearing all nature live and grow above you! That's the way I feel! . . . I don't know what secret spring has been touched since I have lain here. Something in my heart seems suddenly to open and let in a flood of beauty and desire. I know what I have lost, and I think it horrible! Mind you, I know it, I feel it! Remem-ber that hereafter. Don't say that he was stupefied and senseless; that his perception was dulled and his aspiration dead. Say that he trembled in every nerve with a sense of the beauty and sweet-ness of life; that he rebelled and protested and struggled; that he was buried alive, with his eyes open and his heart beating to madness; that he clung to every blade of grass and every wayside thorn as he passed; that it was the most pitiful spectacle you ever beheld; that it was a scandal, an outrage, a murder!'³

The romantic tradition which partly shaped James's sensibility, and within which all his books, but the early ones in particular, were both conceived by him and read by his readers, was also given a particular direction in America through the enormously influential figure of Emerson. Between 1836 and the Civil War, and to a considerable extent beyond the war, Emerson shaped and spoke for the mental life of his times. No matter that James, in his occasional encounters with the sage of Concord, spoke of him with irony and even some disparagement. Like his father, who knew Emerson well, James distrusted Emerson's facile dismissal of the problem of evil in human affairs (a mere temporary imbalance, according to Emerson, which by the principle of 'compensation' was always in process of being put right: each bad act being subsumed in some good consequence, somewhere, sometime). And James also noted, with restrained disapproval, the 'large allowance' one would have to make for a philosopher who was so provincial in his appreciation of literature ('the confession of an insensibility ranging from Shelley to Dickens and from Dante to Miss Austen and taking Don Quixote and Aristophanes on the way, is a large allowance to have to make for a man of letters'⁴). The general current that flowed through Emerson, however, could not be so easily dismissed, and especially relevant for the novelist was Emerson's refurbishment and celebration of the romantic notion of individuality. Transcendentalism, as initiated by Emerson, may have placed its ultimate faith in transcendence of the material world, as its name suggests; but the medium of transcendence was firmly that of the aspiring, self-questioning, independent individual. In this emphasis – though only in this emphasis – Transcendentalism was a return to the seventeenth-century Puritan tradition that eighteenth-century Deism, and Unitarianism its later variant, had overturned. It was even a return to the revolutionary, anti-institutional doctrines of the seventeenth-century Quakers, and of persecuted Antinomians like Anne Hutchinson, whose unbridled individualism was too much for the restrictive theocracy that was also a part, the conservative part, of Puritan thinking. Transcendentalism took Rousseau's doctrine that the individual personality was the fundamental datum and criterion of true knowledge, and grafted it to the strong American tradition (gone underground through the eighteenth century) of the power of the 'inner light' and the falsity of externally-enforced criteria, and thereby released on the nineteenth century the extraordinarily vital doctrine of self-reliance, self-development, and optimism about the possibilities of life: the new man (Christopher *Newman*) in a New (and benignant) World. In seminal works like his essay 'Nature' in 1836, like his Phi Beta Kappa address, 'The American Scholar', at Harvard in 1837, and his 'Divinity School Address', also at Harvard, in 1838, Emerson emphasised the national elements in this process of self-improvement and spiritual sublimity, and (significantly for the Jamesian motif of the two cultures of America and Europe) famously challenged the relevance to America of European literary and philosophical models, and indeed of all traditional dogmas of the past. The individual, and especially the newly-confident, newly-enfranchised American individual, having thrown off the shackles of Europe and of self-doubt (and even of any too prolonged and debilitating worry about the problem of evil), would go on to activate the divine spark that was within him, taking him – as one constituent of the infinite spiritual principle or 'Oversoul' that pervades the Universe and lies behind all merely physical phenomena – into a universal brotherhood of individual men. To cultivate the self, and especially the feelings of the self, is to fulfil the divine purpose and to be in accord with all other cultivators of the self. Emerson's philosophy, to put it mildly, is open to question; and with its vaguenesses, its self-contradictions, its half-hearted and neo-Oriental mysticisms, and its blithe dismissal of evil or even of any significant human conflict of interests, it calls for at least the 'large allowance' that James mentioned on other grounds. But what matters most, for the present purpose, is that the general tendency of Emersonian thinking – aided by Emerson's brilliant phrase-making and gleams of genuine prose-poetry in his writing and lectures – matched exactly the cultural and politico-economic mood of the time. As always in that strange subject called intellectual history, it is impossible to decide whether the age invented Emerson, or Emerson invented the age. All that can be certain is that for the age – and for writers like James, and the readers of James's works — Emerson gave highly influential verbal shapes to what was already happening or about to happen in many areas of the nation's awareness. In this way Transcendentalism spoke for America's strongly-rooted democratic experiment, based on belief in the individual. It consciously turned its back on

Europe in order to match, and foment, the new republic's self-confidence. It preached idealism and self-advancement as a kinetic force that sustained economic and political expansionism, the 'self-reliance' that fuelled capitalism, the growth of industry immediately after the war, and, from the 1840s onwards, the push westwards. The Mississippi Basin, the plains of the North-West, and the Pacific Coast were developed and conquered in order, no doubt, to make money, create a market, and achieve power – but at the same time the movement west, like the development of capital and of the railroads, can also be seen as another expression (a far more lasting one, of course) of Transcendentalism's transmission of the romantic cult of the individual and the releasable energies of the inner self.

What these early novels of James provide, and what indeed his later fiction goes on providing in only slightly less evident form, is an intelligent, subtle, and not unsympathetic critique of Emersonian Romanticism. Since James is almost never a dogmatic or didactic writer, but a dramatiser of the complexity of the human scene, his *mise-en-scène* is almost bound to provide various sides to any question. And in this way, un-Emersonian though his own cast of mind may have been in so many ways, and even anti-Emersonian in its essential scepticism, it is clear that the Emersonian scenario for human possiblility is one of the important constituents of the scene he paints, even when scrutinised sceptically or opposed, in action, by its opposite. The narrative and emotional energy of *Roderick Hudson* and of *The American* and *The Europeans*, for example, is determined by the sense of *possibility* being opposed by the force of *obstacle*: that is, a fully Emersonian energy being released into a world, inconceivable to Emerson (though not to Wordsworth or Keats), that thwarts it. The dream of self-development, of an almost infinite self-extension through art, through passion, through personal power confers romantic status on Roderick as artist-lover, on Newman as entrepreneur-lover, on Eugenia as actress-*femme fatale*. And the baffling presence of the *wall* – the wall of Claire de Cintré's convent and the 'Chinese wall' of Old World duplicity-through-manners for Newman, the wall of humiliating paralysis for Roderick, the 'cliff' of a hostile and unworkable America turned against Eugenia as 'swimmer' – is what gives these figures, by opposition, their tragic or their near-tragic status. James, as much as any American or post-Romantic of his times, can share in the romantic dream of self-fulfilment and self-transcendence through an achieved harmony wih some larger, even cosmic, reality, or with a lover, or with the creative force of the mind. And it is only to the degree that he can express the force of that desire that he can convey to his readers the power of what opposes it, and the grievousness of the clash between them. The romantic mind is almost always binary in its operations. Even Emerson, for all his avoidance of the pessimistic and the tragic, expresses his world-view through a patterning of opposites: the one leaf that has two sides, the darkness that in his case is always exactly balanced by its brightly-lit opposite, both of them being facets of the One. And James too, long before the later development of his famous radical ambiguity, thinks in a mode that is essentially binary and romantic: setting the urge of possibility against the pressure of impediment, and releasing immediate intimations of fear and melancholy within the Keatsian moment of delight.

The passive bystander-figure in these works of James – the hesitant and vicarious Rowland Mallett, the over-scrupulous and timorous Acton and Winterbourne, and even much later variants of the type, like Ralph Touchett or Merton Densher – belong to this romantic binary principle and to the drama of opposites. They are moving to the reader for the very reason that they have an intuition of a life that is the opposite of their own: that is, the freer, less rational, and far more dangerous world of Roderick, or Eugenia, or Daisy (or of Isabel, or of Kate Croy). Their frequent appearance in James's work is one mark of how he goes beyond Emerson, and how he inscribes within his fiction the non-Emersonian element of the reality-principle. It is realistic of the algebra-loving Acton to consider the gamble of marrying Eugenia, with her combination of the predatory, the sexual, and the sophisticated, simply too great: one that threatens his reality-principle of self-restriction and prudence. It is realistic, if pathetic and unadmirable, of the stirred Winterbourne to adhere to the conventional world represented by the elderly expatriate ladies around him in Geneva and Rome, and by the deadening formulae of their judgemental language. And Rowland Mallett, for all that he seems pale and even furtive as the half-jealous moral critic of his protégé, the romantic artist Roderick in his full flight and tragic fall, also represents those pragmatic survival-qualities and sceptical reticence that are the opposites of high Romanticism (and are found, if not very clearly in Emerson, in that other very American variant of hard-headed individualism, the ideas and example of Thoreau: very much the pragmatic, even mathematical, bystander at the far edge – the least nebulous edge – of Transcendentalism).

The bystander-figure also points to another distinctive trait of these early novels that connects them to certain dominant ideas of their time. That is the fear of loss of will and loss of feeling – derived precisely from the romantic exaltation of those faculties. In the James household, amid all that talk and encountering and travelling, there was also a cultivation of feeling – not Rousseauesque or sentimental overflow, by any means, but an emphasis on the need to respond emotionally and with full consciousness to any event. This personal background of an emphasised expressiveness, for James, would have added to it the strong nineteenth-century fear of emotional hypertrophy. We have already noted, as only one example, how for Wordsworth the drying-up of feeling is expressed in terms of 'frost' and 'impediment' – as it is, similarly, in Coleridge, whose 'Dejection: an Ode' is a key text in the literature that explores loss of language and loss of responsiveness to the external world. George Eliot and Dickens both centre their moral view on the disastrousness for the moral self of hypertrophy of feeling: the heart turned into stone, into ice – or into any of the inhuman machines of a machine-age – by some obsession or some narrow egotism or cupidity (for example in *Silas Marner* and in *Dombey and Son*). John Stuart Mill's *Autobiography*, published after his death in 1873, is a classical nineteenth-century account of an acute personal crisis of loss of feeling – in his case, in youth – resolved only by the discovery of music and poetry (fittingly, it was Wordsworth's poetry) as keys to unlock the fixity of the heart. And nearer at hand for James, the nineteenth-century fear of the frozen heart is expressed with an almost neurotic single-mindedness throughout the work of Hawthorne, whose short story 'Ethan Brand' (1851) is one characteristically powerful study, among many, of the ossifying effects of a scientific curiosity and egotism that cuts off its victim-villain from the redeeming warmth of human community.

So when Roderick Hudson cries out in tragic outrage against the dulling of his perceptions and his aspirations, and his fate of being 'buried in an open grave', he is expressing for James not only the great romantic theme of frustrated energy but the subsequent Victorian terror of emotional atrophy. And less theatrically, this is the same private devil, the same death, that Rowland and Winterbourne and Acton, and their successors, have to fight against, for all the reasonableness, the normality of their unheroic selves. One of James's greatest achievements as a novelist is the way he can uncover the most profound and threatening gulfs lurking not just in the textures of day-to-day life but also inside the very strategies that are adopted for our survival as average, cautious human beings.

The romantic and American-romantic syndrome which seems to be so influential as a context to James's opening career, and so operative within his work despite the innumerable singularities that any artist imposes on the material and thought of his age, can roughly be summarised then as comprising the following motifs and themes (many of them contradictory, or at least binary). The concern with the individual personality in its subjective nature. The emphasis on energy and the personal will, on the need to assert the self against a resistant world of otherness, the surrounding 'not-me'. The frequency with which these energies are thwarted by 'impediment'. The urge to express the self, especially through art, the imagination, and through passion – contrasted not only with the failure to do so, but with the actual dangers of such expression, and the opposing virtues of pragmatism, doubt, and self-protection. The idea that the self is not given, but is perpetually to be made and re-made, with the consequent emphasis on life as an endless vista of offered possibility: either for good or ill. That the self has an organic connection with the world outside, and with its own roots in time, especially in childhood. The casting-off of what is past, what is inherited, and the dangers of such a rejection. The at best ambiguous quality of a life determined by any preordained principles other than those of renewal and revolution. The cult of the self-reliant individual, accompanied by the fear of isolation and emotional petrification. The need, therefore, to continue to cultivate the heart and the heart's language, often in community with others. The distrust of philosophic materialism, and the belief that reality, both for the individual and for all men, is fundamentally spiritual. And therefore that the material world of nature – including its landscapes – is an affair of signs and symbols: itself a language for underlying spiritual facts. That the physical world, in its colour and details, is a proper home for the creative mind, which finds pleasure and meaning in responding to these signs and symbols. The sense that art and everyday life may be often in conflict, but that art is both the language of an ultimate reality and the activity of all men when thinking and feeling at their utmost: and that an ongoing creativity, therefore, is the basis of life. The hostility to fixed forms and to completeness: the belief that life, like a work of art, is more like process than stasis. That judgement is a dangerous activity, like over-rationality; and spontaneity and intuition powerful (if also dangerous) faculties. The cultivation of self-consciousness as that which allows for creativity. The accompanying fear of excessive introspection as leading to paralysis and self-doubt. The recognition that the world, for all its language of spiritual reality and its closeness to the human, is all too often a prison, a wall, a constriction of the self.

These possible formulations are not only inadequate in themselves as an overall picture of the spirit of Romanticism, they also have to be played against one another, since interplay and drama – binary or not – are an essential aspect of the romantic notion of process. And there is at least one further formulation, arising out of several of those already given, that remains to be looked at, since it has particular significance for understanding James, whether James as romantic, or James as American, or James (as we shall come to later) as realist, as moralist, and then as Modernist: that is, the key concept of role-playing.

The romantic concept of the self not as a fixed entity but as something to be made and re-made, when added to the romantic emphasis on life as process and drama, inevitably leads to the corollary that the self discovers itself through the theatre of personal gesture, guise, and even social manners. The Keatsian stress on the 'chameleon poet', taking on the nature of everything he sees outside himself, is a pointer in this direction. And so is Whitman's later celebration of the protean poet 'seeking types' with whom (and with which) to identify passionately in an act of universal self-extension – and though Whitman can move only too easily into the ecstatic realm of the One, in which individual identity is subsumed and all roles become the same, his poetry is nevertheless filled dazzlingly with the perception of the precise outlines of other people and phenomena through which the self-discovering, self-inventing poetic sensibility can theatricalise itself. Closer perhaps to James's obsession with the unfixed nature of the individual self, as displayed and performed in its progress through the world of relationships and manners, is the specifically French strain that runs from Diderot in the mid-eighteenth century to Stendhal in the 1830s. Diderot's influential 'Paradoxe sur le Comédien' is a proto-Jamesian account of the unsteady relationship between self and role, self and theatrical mask, on the stage of both art and life. Closer at hand James certainly found in Stendhal, whom he read and appreciated, particularly *La Chartreuse de Parme*, a brilliant enactment of how the self, to its own hurt as well as its gain, can radically change its shape and signs. Character is never a fixed entity in Stendhal, rather a force and energy, a source of potentiality rather than of knowable qualities and categories: something that we can respond to, as to a charisma or a menace, rather than tabulate or morally judge. James's Eugenia, in *The Europeans*, is the most sustained example of this, one of his own most basic and lasting tenets. She is a walking tissue of potentialities, some of them merely rapacious, others sexually liberating or aesthetically and imaginatively enhancing – and for James the self is as much an aesthetic creation, a creation of the whole consciousness of the subject, as it is either genetic or circumstantial. Eugenia (like Chad Newsome in *The Ambassadors*, much later) knows how to enter a room: how to impinge upon others, retain her own privacy, and at the same time enact something of her personality in physical gesture, in pauses, and – in the largest sense of the word – in style. At a street corner in Boston she can simultaneously respond spontaneously to the beauty of the American sunset and know that in so responding, publicly, she will be an object of interest to the passers-by. Her house (as so often in James) becomes an emblem of herself: it is a cottage loaned her by Mr Wentworth, her distant relation and host, and to the puzzlement and excitement of the non-theatrical Wentworths her abode is both more private and enclosed than anything they have ever known *and* more public, in its quality of extreme decoration and thought-out display.

Even in the character of Daisy Miller, apparently far less sophisticated than a Eugenia – indeed, in her American spontaneity and thoughtlessness the very opposite of a Eugenia – we nevertheless also detect James's fascination with what we might call, after Diderot, the paradox of the actress. Where is the 'real' Daisy? Where, behind all the shifting possibilities for the spectator – and transmitted to us, the ultimate spectators, through the hesitations of Winterbourne, the fictional spectator – can one be confident about judging or knowing such a girl, who seems more and more conscious of her own situation and who at times seems to manipulate her own naivety for ends not totally naive? She is at the same time too 'innocent' for the worldly apparatus of sceptical (and ossified) judgement wielded by Mrs Walker, Mrs Costello, and (in part) by Winterbourne, *and* too blatantly self-aware for any purely intuitive, 'open', or 'American' response. The two worlds of response – 'American' and 'European' – are in a perpetual process in our minds, and in James's presentation of her. Neither is totally 'wrong'. But Daisy's 'reality' is not available to either 'world' on its own, and seems to exist only in fluidity and multivalency: the real self, that is, as a tantalisation and a perpetually unfinished drama, energising an ambiguous narrative and taunting and exposing the other equally fictional 'selves' around her.

The concept of life and of character as theatre, which is crucial to an understanding of James, is probably best seen as mediated through a romantic-European rather than any native American tradition. Even though Whitman, who is Emerson's poetic offspring, describes the growth of the self in an imagery that tends towards the dramatic, the mystic extension and multiplication of the self through natural objects, for Emerson himself character is in the end both more integral and more transcendental than in James's between-two-worlds mode of thought. Emerson is more conservative, potentially more distrusting of the radically aesthetic (and Stendhalian) view of the self. And he is also more absolutist and idealist in the strongly Platonic tendency of his thought towards the all-unifying One, the Oversoul. James is no Platonist. For him, reality – reality of the self, reality of the world – is hardly at all to be conceived in terms that transcend the temporal and the phenomenal, and for him the aesthetic is more a temporal than an idealist mode. He has, it is true, something of a left-over religious sensibility in his romantic urge towards harmony and beauty (always quickly contradicted by his perception of what everyday truth is like, and the pressures of the quotidian). But basically James is a relativist, not an absolutist, for whom reality is a shifting thing, depending on its context and, above all, on its actors. Character depends on consciousness, and consciousness is not something given but something achieved, and perpetually to be re-achieved, within a changing world.

Hawthorne, too, on whom James was writing at this very time, as we shall see, is conservative in his emphasis – his tragic emphasis – on the inability of character to re-make itself. His characters remain trapped in certain postures of the past: that is their specific fate. And if they have to strive in a new direction, it seems most often to be in a direction that is only delusively fluid and open. The wish of Hester Prynne or of Arthur Dimmesdale to be other than they are, to escape the fixed conventions of their Puritan world and their Puritan selves, is short-lived and essentially self-deluding. And while James's tragic cast of mind, his partial sense of the futility of human effort, may owe something to Hawthorne's scepticism and social/historical determinism, James's concept of the self remains nevertheless far more open and encouraging. James's famous 'complaint' against (or on behalf of) Hawthorne – that Hawthorne's America provided none of the complex texture of social manners necessary to most novelists – is in fact a strong testimony to James's own quite un-Hawthornean, but Stendhalian and romantic, belief that character could be extended and re-made by using the varying roles that social manners, especially European social manners, made possible.

From Emerson, then, James might be seen as drawing some of his belief in the individual consciousness as the focus and as the energy of reality; but from the tradition of Diderot and Stendhal, and from the variable novelistic examples of Thackeray, Balzac, Turgenev, George Sand, and George Eliot (though, significantly, not consciously from Jane Austen) he drew his conviction that the individual consciousness cannot develop free of the social medium in which it exists and through which it moves wearing many masks and in many shifting postures of relationship. For James, as for his great mentor, Balzac, this is specifically the glory as well as the tragedy (and tragi-comedy) of the self: that it is not free and unaccommodated, but an entity forced into dependency and interchange – in short, into drama.

By the time that *The Europeans* and 'Daisy Miller' had run their course as serials in 1878, this European tradition we have spoken of – the tradition of Balzac, Turgenev, George Sand, Stendhal – had become a living reality for James. Within the three-year period that saw their publication and that of *Roderick Hudson* and *The American* before them, James had made his crucial decision in favour of Europe over America as providing his best medium as an artist, and his future home as a man: the man, in James, being almost always the same as the artist. The six months spent in New York, beginning in January 1875, a period of frenetic hard work, mostly in the field of weekly articles, book reviews, art reviews, theatre reviews (especially for the *Nation* but also the *Galaxy* and *Atlantic* – a total of seventy over that year), but also including the completion of *Roderick Hudson* and the seeing into print of his first collection of short stories, *A Passionate Pilgrim*, and his first collection of travel pieces, *Transatlantic Sketches*, can be seen as James's last attempt to make America work for him as a place to live. But the effect was to turn him temporarily into something of a literary hack, assiduously counting his monthly takings (about $200), complaining at the absence of serious company for him in the city, and studding his letters with nostalgic references to Florence and Rome. To return for a while from New York to Cambridge was in fact to take stock of his growing professional success – *Transatlantic Sketches* sold particularly well, and *A Passionate Pilgrim* and *Roderick Hudson* were receiving appreciative, if qualified, notices – and, with his eyes already turning to Europe, to write his first truly important piece of criticism: significantly enough, an essay for the *Galaxy* on the achievement of Balzac, whom he was later to call 'the father of us all'. It was as a now well-established professional writer of fiction and reviews, a practical journalist with an agreement to send back a weekly letter to the *New York Tribune* at $20 each letter, and not least as a 'son' of the great Balzac that James left America definitively in October 1875, and within two months was in the company of Turgenev, Flaubert, Zola, Daudet, Maupassant and de Goncourt in Paris. And it was in that ambience, the ambience of Paris as a place, and of the *confrérie* of such distinguished and very un-American writers, that he was very soon at work writing *The American*.

The first of these, the great Russian writer now mostly living in Paris, was the one closest to James in cast of mind and in the atmosphere of his books, as well as the one he got to know best during the year of intense literary contacts that followed in Paris. James knew the other's writing well already (even James Senior had corresponded friendlily with him), and in the previous year, 1874, had published in the *North American Review* an appreciative essay in which he brought out features in Turgenev that seem to emphasise the resemblance between the two men's creative temperaments. The points James makes in that essay tell us much about the literary tradition that he was now consciously seeking out (and simultaneously modifying by his own contribution to it) at this moment of his arrival in Europe, and as he began to write his first important group of novels. And early though the essay is, in date and style, with here and there a touch of immaturity, it remains nevertheless one of the most self-revealing pieces of criticism he ever wrote.

He picks out in Turgenev his extreme care as an artist and an observer, contrasting him favourably with the 'rapid, passionate, almost reckless improvisation' of Scott, Dickens, and George Sand. He admires Turgenev's habit of taking notes, and his grasp of precise detail for its own sake; the particularity, not generality, of his characters; and, especially, the treatment of his heroines, 'radiant with maidenly charm', non-English spontaneity, and independence:

If his manner is that of searching realist, his temper is that of an earnestly attentive observer, and the result of this temper is to make him take a view of the great spectacle of human life more general, more impartial, more unreservedly intelligent, than that of any novelist we know.[5]

Turgenev avoids the tendency, found in almost every novelist except George Eliot (and she is far from perfect in the matter), to sacrifice 'moral unity' and seriousness for 'a rounded plot' and 'mechanical episodes'. 'He believes in the intrinsic value of "subject" in art' as opposed to mere effectiveness or entertainment value – a 'subject' that intrinsically allows 'a greater amount of information about the human mind'. He has 'a minutely psychological attitude', and finds new ways of revealing the mind by placing grotesques, 'simpletons and weak-minded persons', on the sidelines of his plots – 'the opportunity of watching the machinery of character, as it were, through a broken window-pane'. And in one particularly resonant phrase, a Turgenev tale is 'moving, not in the sense that it makes us shed easy tears, but as reminding us vividly of the solidarity, as we may say, of all human weakness'. He is 'universally sensitive'; modulates everything with imagination; and while 'his merit of form is of the first order', and his sensuousness is powerful, he nevertheless surpasses the formal cleverness and the sensuousness of the French by his very different 'apprehension of man's religious impulses, of the *ascetic* passion, the capacity of becoming dead to colours and odours and beauty.' His Russianness is particularly singled out, but also his being an exile and having 'a poet's quarrel' with his native land. 'American readers will peculiarly appreciate this state of mind; if they had a native novelist of a large pattern, it would probably be, in a degree, his own' – since the fluidity of Russian society resembles that of America, and 'the Russian character is in solution, in a sea of change.'

There is very much more throughout the essay to give us phrases and ideas about James himself, especially James in the late 1870s and those romantic aspects of James at which we have just been looking: the characteristic mixture in Turgenev of realism and poetic idealism; the complete identification of form with 'moral meaning'; the 'after-sense of sadness that sets his readers thinking'; the characters in his novels who show 'natures strong in impulse, in talk, in responsive emotion, but weak in will, in action, in the power to feel and do simply'; his 'dramatic form' and power of

concretisation; his avoidance of 'unembodied ideas' and all abstraction; the mixture of bitterness and sweetness in his imagination; the
irony, the 'lurking meanings'. James describes the charm but 'oddity' of Turgenev's Hélène (in *On the Eve*) almost as though she was
Isabel Archer – 'some quaintly-feathered bird brought from beyond
the seas' – and makes Schubin, the young sculptor, and Bersenieff,
the bystander, into Roderick Hudson and Rowland Mallett: 'If [these
two] . . . are born to suffering, they are born also to rapture. They
stand at the open door of passion, and they can sometimes forget.'
Christopher Newman, imagining his Claire walled away from him
in her convent, is prefigured here in Turgenev's Lavretzky (in *A
Nest of Gentlefolk*) catching a glimpse of his love through the barred-
off grating of her convent: 'a pair of lovers accepting adversity
seem to [Turgenev] more eloquent than a pair of lovers grasping at
happiness.' His heroines 'have to our sense a touch of the faintly
acrid perfume of the New England temperament – a hint of Puritan
angularity'; and it is his women 'who mainly represent strength of
will – the power to resist, to wait, to attain.' Lisa's 'love for Lavretzky
is a passion in its essence half renunciation', and contains 'the dusky,
antique consciousness of sin' (the hint here is of Fleda Vetch, in *The
Spoils of Poynton*). James worries at large about the possible wanton-
ness of Turgenev's pessimism, which he takes more seriously, more
critically, than Hawthorne's 'innocent' and more guileless play with
'dusky subjects', and expresses his preference for 'elegists who have
an ideal of joy'. The essay ends with a wonderfully eloquent cry,
Jamesian through and through, that like everything else in this most
personally revealing essay seems to set a key-note for his own
ambitions, for what he has already written and is writing, and for
the whole writing career ahead of him that is to be devoted to the
uncovering of human tragedy and to the power of wakeful human
consciousness:

> [Turgenev's] sadness has its element of error, but it has also its
> larger element of wisdom. Life *is*, in fact, a battle. On this point
> optimists and pessimists agree. Evil is insolent and strong; beauty
> enchanting but rare; goodness very apt to be weak; folly very apt
> to be defiant; wickedness to carry the day; imbeciles to be in
> great places, people of sense in small, and mankind generally,
> unhappy. But the world as it stands is no illusion, no phantasm,
> no evil dream of a night; we wake up to it again for ever and
> ever; we can neither forget it nor deny it nor dispense with it. We

can welcome experience as it comes, and give it what it demands, in exchange for something which it is idle to pause to call much or little so long as it contributes to swell the volume of consciousness. In this there is mingled pain and delight, but over the mysterious mixture there hovers a visible rule, that bids us learn to will and seek to understand.[6]

'. . . swell the volume of consciousness . . . learn to will and seek to understand': it is as though James, almost on his way to Paris (and to Turgenev in person) at the age of thirty-one, is making a statement of artistic intent, and at the same time pointing to what is incumbent on the protagonists of his novels: on figures like Rowland Mallett, like Christopher Newman, like Acton and Winterbourne, who are all placed in a specific problematic relationship to consciousness and to the will. Those very phrases could well be a credo from Keats's letters – or even (especially in the mostly iambic pentameter of the concluding phrase) a climactic line from Book One of Wordsworth's *Prelude*. In everything James writes about Turgenev, with its effect of his own sensitivity being laid, and fitting perfectly, on top of that of his subject, one can detect what made the others to whom Turgenev introduced him in Paris – Flaubert, Zola, Maupassant – so much less close to his own romantic-ironic-elegiac spirit, despite his admiration for their craftsmanship and their artistic self-confidence.

Helped by Turgenev and by others, James had a crowded year in Paris: providing his letters for the *Tribune* with great difficulty, and recognising more and more clearly his own unfitness for regular journalism, at least of a newspaper kind; writing and finishing *The American*, after some financial haggling, for his friend Howells at the *Atlantic*; visiting the great early Impressionist exhibition at Durand-Ruel's and concluding (lamentably) that 'the "Impressionist" doctrines strike me as incompatible . . .with the existence of first-rate talent. To embrace them you must be provided with a plentiful absence of imagination'[7]; writing his second major article on Balzac, of significance for his work in the decade to come; then, after travelling in the provinces, deciding on an impulse to try settling in London, where, unlike Paris, he might not feel 'an eternal outsider'. In London, he was to find his true ambience. Installed by December 1876 in his lodgings in Bolton Street, just off Piccadilly, and quickly inscribed by Motley, the historian, as an honorary member of the Athenaeum, James was drawn at once far more deeply than was ever possible to him in Paris into the full social whirl of the capital, dining at his new friend Lord Houghton's alongside Tennyson and Gladstone, then with Browning, then Pater, then Meredith, then Arnold – the list is endless – and, in a famous statistic, being recorded as dining out 140 times in one winter, 1878–9.

He began writing 'Daisy Miller' on returning from one of his visits back to the Continent in early 1878, drew together his recent critical essays and had them accepted for publication as *French Poets and Novelists* (published in February, 1878), and quickly finished *The Europeans* before even 'Daisy Miller' had appeared, only to go on at once to another, and slighter, novel, *Confidence*, which began publication in *Scribner's Monthly* in August 1879. *The Europeans* was successful, if not outstandingly; *The American* much discussed, though with reservations. Short stories, like 'An International Episode' and 'The Pension Beaurepas', many of them on his now-established International Theme, flowed from his pen with new depth and subtlety – as did the usual reviews and essays. But 'Daisy Miller', his first work to be initially published in England – in Leslie Stephen's *Cornhill* – was by contemporary standards a sensation. It was pirated at once in America, where it sold 20 000 copies (without any gain to James) in a few weeks. It became a talking-point on both sides of the Atlantic, exciting some censure from Americans for its not uncritical portrayal of American girlhood but also receiving lavish praise. Daisy as 'the American girl' suddenly became a new literary and cultural type – even a hat was named after her. James was at last – and with extravagant suddenness – launched on a tide of reputation, if not quite of popularity (as he complained to William, 'The aforesaid fame, expanding through two hemispheres, is represented by a pecuniary equivalent almost grotesquely small'[8]). He was even able in his new confidence to ride out imperturbably the genuine furore of acrimony that broke out in America on the publication late in 1879 of his *Hawthorne*, in the English Men of Letters series, saying 'I hold it a great piece of luck to have stirred up such a clatter. The whole episode projects a lurid light upon the state of American "culture" '.[9]

James's *Hawthorne*, therefore, can virtually be taken as the sign – almost his conscious gesture – of farewell to the American scene. Only four years after his departure from New York (and after the serialisation of *Roderick Hudson*) he could now write in his *Hawthorne* an affectionate, sensitive, yet clearly disparaging account of the only American writer of the past with whom he might conceivably have felt some affinity. Hawthorne may have been – in his rather stiff and even eighteenth-century way – one of the expressions of the romantic tradition in America. But James could pay only a kind of reluctant half-justice to Hawthorne's 'beautiful, natural, original genius'. What he brought out most – what in 1879 mattered most to him – was not Hawthorne's partially romantic depths but the inevitable thinness of his American material, the mechanical quality of his symbolism, the 'charm', 'modesty', 'delicacy', 'lightness of conception' that resulted not in great work of human warmth and profundity (like Turgenev's) but only in 'a splendid piece of silver-smith's work' like *The Scarlet Letter*. And always at hand, as the focus of James's interest and the suggested cause of Hawthorne's limitations, was America itself – 'the crude and simple society in which he lived'. With only a certain amount of irony, James fa-mously – in the eyes of his American reviewers, infamously – listed 'the items of high civilization . . . which are absent from the texture of American life', ranging from the lack of a sovereign, an aristoc-racy, a church, and an army to the absence of cathedrals, universi-ties, and public schools: 'no literature, no novels, no museums, no pictures, no political society, no sporting class.'[10] James, surveying English society with whatever scepticism from within the well-pad-ded depths of the Athenaeum, or across his 140 dinner tables in one season, is evidently releasing something in the pages of *Hawthorne*. With an elegant and light-handed arrogance, at the age of 36, he is covering his tracks and, like many an artist, doing a necessary vio-lence to his place of origin and to his younger self: his self as American and Romantic. London was now his home. Turgenev and Balzac were to be his masters. And he had already, as the American outrage at his *Hawthorne* flooded in, begun work on *The Portrait of a Lady*.

3

Victorian and Realist

The Portrait of a Lady – which most critics have come to see as James's first great novel – began its serial publication in *Macmillan's* in October 1880, just two months before the death of George Eliot. In a way both events marked the end of an epoch for the novel in England. In the same year Trollope, perhaps the last of the mid-Victorians, published his penultimate novel, *Dr. Wortle's School*, and was to die two years later. Meredith and Hardy had just established their commanding reputations with *The Egoist* (1879) and *The Return of the Native* (1878), and, however unlike one another, were both writers of a radically different kind from George Eliot. George Gissing and George Moore, very much the new Realist voices of the 1880s, published their first novels in 1880 and 1883 respectively, Gissing with *Workers in the Dawn* and Moore with *A Modern Lover*. And – just about as far as one could get from the George Eliot tradition – the so-called New Romance, in the hands of Stevenson, Rider Haggard, Hall Caine, and others, was just about to come into prominence, for example with Stevenson's *Treasure Island* in 1881–2 and Haggard's *King Solomon's Mines* in 1885.

James's relation to George Eliot, however, was more complex than one of simply supplanting her by a style of his own; and his four major novels of this new decade – *The Portrait of a Lady* in 1880–1, *The Bostonians* and *The Princess Casamassima* both in 1885–6, and *The Tragic Muse* in 1889–90 – can all be seen as in certain ways a highly modified continuation as well as a critique of the George Eliot mode of High Victorian realism and moral seriousness. James, as we have seen, was an American and a Romantic; he was also, even now, in the 1880s, something of a pre-Modern; he was above all a highly individual writer who, like any great writer, properly challenges the applicability of such categories. But in so far as he also offers the aspect of having been a Victorian, among so many other aspects, it is probably in his relation to George Eliot that his Victorianness can best be seen – especially in this, the most Victorian period of his writing life and of his personal life, when he found himself at last, from 3 Bolton Street, just off Piccadilly, firmly ensconced in Victoria's England, an unexiled *habitué* of its clubs, its country houses, its galleries, its dinner-tables, its literary soirées, its Casaubons, its Dorothea Brookes, its Gwendolen Harleths.

A few days after George Eliot died, James found himself literally occupying her place – sitting in her usual chair in her study – when he visited to offer condolences to John Cross, whom she had married only seven months before:

> He, poor fellow, is left very much lamenting; but my private impression is that if she had not died, she would have killed him. He couldn't keep up the intellectual pace – all Dante and Goethe, Cervantes and the Greek tragedians . . . several hours a day spent in reading aloud the most immortal works.[1]

This irreverent Jamesian testimony to the high seriousness of the late occupant of the study chair lends a shade of authenticity to the anecdote about James's reply when asked what Cross, twenty years her junior, must have felt at the moment of bereavement:

> James considered [the question] intensely, and answered slowly: 'Agony . . . Dismay . . . Amazement . . . Fear . . .' Then suddenly his face lighted. He threw up his hands and almost shouted: '*Relief!*'[2]

Much earlier, in 1869, James had described very touchingly the general impression of 'sagacity and sweetness' he gained from one of his first meetings with the author of *Felix Holt*, which he had reviewed (with qualified admiration) on its publication three years before. There must have been other visits after James settled in London to what he referred to as the 'literary temple' of The Priory, by Regents Park, where George Eliot and G. H. Lewes lived, and where they famously held intellectual court every Sunday (Eliot, according to James, conversing in a low, harmonious voice, and only on 'the highest themes'). And most ironically of all, in the winter of 1878–9 there was the awkward and perceptibly unwelcome visit paid with a mutual friend, Mrs Greville, to the Eliot–Lewes country villa in Surrey where, on leaving the 'chill desert' of the sitting-room, unrefreshed by any proferred tea ('a conceivable feature of the hour, but which was not provided for'), James had the humiliation of seeing Lewes return to Mrs Greville with much vehement hand-waving the two loaned volumes (apparently unread and unrecognised) of James's own just-published *The Europeans* ('The vivid demonstration of one's failure to penetrate there had been in the sweep of Lewes's gesture, which could scarce have been bettered by his actually wielding a broom').[3]

In accord with the quizzical tone of these reports, there is always something less than adulation in James's published reviews and articles – ten in number – on George Eliot's writing. He criticises her discursiveness and tendency to excessive analysis, while admiring the rare qualities 'of thought, of generalizing instinct, of *brain*'. In *Romola* there is 'too much reflection . . . and too little creation' – a serious criticism which he expands in his quite acerbic review of Cross's *The Life of George Eliot* for the *Atlantic Monthly* in 1885: 'the novel . . . for her was not primarily a picture of life, capable of deriving a high value from its form, but a moralised fable, the last word of a philosophy endeavouring to teach by example'.[4] And *Middlemarch*, which is 'a very splendid performance', and 'sets a limit to the development of the old-fashioned English novel', is over-crowded, and lacks what James clearly implies he himself would have liked to give it: 'the form . . . of an organized, moulded, balanced composition, gratifying the reader with a sense of design and construction.' Two other points in James's review of *Middlemarch* – which he wrote in either Paris or Rome during his 1872–4 trip, and published in the *Galaxy* in 1873 – point ahead revealingly to *The Portrait of a Lady* and its underlying ambitions. One is his almost wilfully personal response to the concept of George Eliot's Dorothea, whom he evokes in a language and tone very similar to his sympathetic praise – indeed his imaginative appropriation – of Turgenev's heroines, and who clearly prefigures his own Isabel Archer:

> An ardent young girl . . . framed for a larger moral life than circumstance often affords, yearning for a motive for sustained spiritual effort and only wasting her ardour and soiling her wings against the meanness of opportunity . . . To render the expression of a soul requires a cunning hand; but we seem to look straight into the unfathomable eyes of the beautiful spirit of Dorothea Brooke. She exhales a sort of aroma of spiritual sweetness, and we believe in her as in a woman we might providentially meet some fine day when we should find ourselves doubting of the immortality of the soul.

The second point is equally personal, and with the hint of an unconscious self-portrait:

we maintain that to relish [*Middlemarch*'s] inner essence we must
– for reasons too numerous to detail – be an American. The author has commissioned herself to be real, her native tendency
being that of an idealist, and the intellectual result is a very fer-
tilizing mixture.[5]

It is hard not to deduce from these phrases a picture of James,
seven years later in 1880, as an American idealist and romantic,
consciously commissioning himself to be real in just the same way
– and hoping for at least as fertilising a result.

James's ambivalence towards George Eliot – or in the following
case his trivalence, perhaps – is perfectly expressed in the witty
three-voice dialogue, 'Daniel Deronda: a Conversation', in the *Atlantic Monthly* for 1876. Most of the various possible dislikes and
enthusiasms that James could have felt for that novel are elegantly
bandied about among the three imaginary speakers, varying from
the aesthetic Pulcheria's 'a very ponderous and ill-made story' to
the more solemn Theodora's 'She is simply permeated with the
highest culture of the age'. But in the tactful middle position of
their male friend Constantius we find a particularly resonant
summing-up which has the ring of James himself, never putting the
demands of form out of mind but consciously girding himself,
slightly against the grain, for an Eliot-like fullness of observation
and mimetic rendering:

'Yes, I think there is little art in *Deronda*, but I think there is a vast
amount of life. In life without art you can find your account; but
art without life is a poor affair. The book is full of the world.'[6]

There are three main 'worlds' in *The Portrait of a Lady*: the American world, which we hardly see but which is present in the nature
and values of most of the characters; the Italian and Italianate world,
in the dusky intricacies of which Isabel Archer's Americanness comes
to grief; and the English world, which James now recreates with the
authority of a committed Victorian denizen of Bolton Street and a
realist who has figuratively, as well as actually, sat in George Eliot's
vacated chair. Its famous opening – assuredly and wittily ponderous,
full of a perceived time and place, rich with the sense of human
confrontation and unfolding – is James's tribute to the fullness of
his own new-found world:

Under certain circumstances there are few hours in life more agreeable than the hour dedicated to the ceremony known as afternoon tea. There are circumstances in which, whether you partake of the tea or not – some people of course never do – the situation is in itself delightful. Those that I have in mind in beginning to unfold this simple history offered an admirable setting to an innocent pastime. The implements of the little feast had been disposed upon the lawn of an old English country house, in what I should call the perfect middle of a splendid summer afternoon. Part of the afternoon had waned, but much of it was left, and what was left was of the finest and rarest quality. Real dusk would not arrive for many hours; but the flood of summer light had begun to ebb, the air had grown mellow, the shadows were long upon the smooth, dense turf. They lengthened slowly, however, and the scene expressed that sense of leisure still to come which is perhaps the chief source of one's enjoyment of such a scene at such an hour. From five o'clock to eight is on certain occasions a little eternity; but on such an occasion as this the interval could be only an eternity of pleasure.

No other Victorian writer conveys more confidence to his readers than does James, in such openings as this – or, indeed, in such continuations, as his narrating eye goes on to focus more closely on the precise shadows cast on the lawn at Gardencourt by three differing men, on the very particular teacup held in one hand by the oldest of the three, on the tell-tale gesture of one of the younger men watching the older man with concern, while the latter's own eyes are turned (as ours must now follow them) towards the 'rich red front' of his Tudor home and all the details of its structure and history:

> Privacy here reigned supreme, and the wide carpet of turf that covered the level hill-top seemed but the extension of a luxurious interior. The great still oaks and beeches flung down a shade as dense as that of velvet curtains; and the place was furnished, like a room, with cushioned seats, with rich-coloured rugs, with the books and papers that lay upon the grass.[7]

The Jamesian act of narrating is far from invisible: it seems to become part of the very scene that it makes us witness, unrolling its physical details and its atmospheric and psychological nuances in a way that is both tangible – something out there – and, paradoxically, part of the inward abstract process of consciousness, of self-aware narrating and commenting. The Victorian fondness for the technique of the omniscient narrator – such as George Eliot herself used, as part of her belief in the novel as a genre of edification and moral judgement – is taken over here by James and at the same time emended. For all his well-known criticism of the 'terrible crime' of the self-revealing and illusion-breaking narrator[8] he himself never completely abandoned the 'our heroine' or the 'those that I have in mind' approach, though also introducing into it a serious playfulness and liberating ambiguity of tone very different from George Eliot's high seriousness. The impression of belief in himself and in his task as a narrator gives powerful authenticity to the whole fictional 'ado' about Isabel Archer (his own phrase in the Preface), and becomes a part of its 'realism'. Realism is of course never the same as reality, and is itself no more and no less than an application in art of special conventions and tricks. And the felt presence of a watchful, self-indulgent, highly intelligent, and highly involved narrator like James can be precisely one of these effective tricks. If he succeeded in getting 'the world' into his fiction with a new thoroughness and a new personal rootedness, through the 1880s, it was partly by placing himself so interferingly yet so validatingly inside the fictional process of representing that world.

What James himself emphasised in writing his Preface to *The Portrait of a Lady*, more than quarter of a century later, was not so much questions of narration, however, as questions of character. In this interest, too, his Victorianness declared itself. It is tempting, in the light of so much that is modernist and anti-traditional in James's writing, to look there for evidence of the twentieth-century loss of belief in stable character: to find in James's proliferating nuances some fundamental dissolution of personality and a foretaste of Ezra Pound's modernist image of the self as 'a broken bundle of mirrors'.[9] But it is striking how even in the Preface (written in Pound's own time) James characteristically uses Turgenev's example to highlight his own creative first principle of having 'the vision of some person or persons, who hovered before him, soliciting him, as the active or passive figure, interesting him and appealing to him just as they were and by what they were.'[10] It is not the obliquity or the instability of character that seems to touch James when he is writing about his own art, but rather the need to show the consciousness of any such character in its relationships with the consciousness

of other characters – in the case of *The Portrait of a Lady* this is how
he aimed to overcome the apparent disadvantage of having to deal
with the 'frail vessel' of one young woman's temperament. Relationships (always a key word in James's theory of fiction) are the
means by which character is to be presented and made interesting
– as interesting, he hopes, as George Eliot's Dorothea Brooke and
Gwendolen Harleth and Maggie Tulliver, those other 'frail vessels'.
But there is little question, at least in James's explicit critical thinking, of such a modernist concept as 'character' being a purely provisional and even delusive notion, or of any philosophic doubt that
there may not be a core of personality that antedates and is detached from relationships. That is, in the writing of *Portrait*, James
seems very consciously to be attaching himself to a tradition of the
English novel – only one of its traditions, after all – that used sympathetic solidity of psychological representation as its main mode
of rendering, and the felt 'reality' of its characters (especially when
conveyed through their relationships with others) as its source of
interest to both writer and reader.

In thematic terms, too, *The Portrait of a Lady* has vital links with
the classic Victorian novel and with traits of English thought that
were still dominant – though under challenge – in the 1880s. Almost as much *The Mill on the Floss* or *Middlemarch* – or the fiction
of Charlotte Brontë or Mrs Gaskell from the 1840s and 1850s, for
that matter – James's middle-period novels revolve around clear
moral crises: crises of personal choice and personal judgement. In
the classic High Victorian mode, the crisis often takes the form of
a choice between duty and passion: like Maggie Tulliver in *The Mill
on the Floss* (1860), tempted egotistically by the attractions of Philip
Wakem and Stephen Guest as against her sense of duty towards
her family or her cousin Lucy. The question of individual moral
choice was almost an obsession in nineteenth-century English writing, and became not only a focus for the Victorian writer's (and
reader's) powerful emotionality, even to the extent of melodrama
and sensationalism of effect, but also a guiding structural principle
in the deployment of plot: the positioning of climax, turning-point,
complication, and denouement. Choice between two modes of action, one dutiful and the other passionate or self-regarding, was not
only the moment in which the Victorian personality was seen to
express its most important powers and to declare its inner essence;
it was also, complicatingly, the moment in which the larger drama
between free will and destiny found its flashpoint within the life of

the individual. What we decide, as between duty to others and the urgent demands of the self, especially the pleasure-loving self, defines personality and, in literary terms, determines the shape of a fictional plot. But it also releases a chain of events which take on the form of an ineluctable destiny: created by an individual's decision, but thereafter acting with the force of Calvinist predestination or the pattern of Greek tragedy. Chillingworth's words to the sinning Hester, in Chapter 14 of Hawthorne's *The Scarlet Letter* (1850), are a *locus classicus* of this strange nineteenth-century amalgam of free, responsible individualism and helpless submission to fate: 'By thy first step awry, thou didst plant the germ of evil; but since that moment, it has all been a dark necessity ... Let the black flower blossom as it may!' And in Chapter 16 of *Adam Bede* (1859), George Eliot has the Reverend Mr Irwine enunciate a similar sombre warning to Arthur Donnithorne, whose own moral choice – in this case the easy choice of thoughtless gratification – will create a dark necessity and the tragic plot-structure of the novel: 'Consequences are unpitying. Our deeds carry their terrible consequences ... consequences that are hardly ever confined to ourselves' – a warning later endorsed by George Eliot as omniscient (though enigmatic) narrator: 'Our deeds determine us, as much as we determine our deeds' (chap. 29).

In many ways *The Portrait of a Lady* fulfils, even while it strongly modifies, this classic Victorian model of a plot built around choices, and of an intellectual pattern that interweaves free will and determinism. Isabel Archer is a masterly study in the complex ways in which the individual makes his or her own destiny at the same time as being impelled by uncontrollable factors of culture, of inheritance, and of circumstance, and is then further impelled by a new situation which is created by that personal decision becoming entangled with circumstance – the doer and the deed each determining the other. Isabel is very much a girl of her type, her era, her place – even a girl of Albany, N. Y., to be precise:

She had had everything a girl could have: kindness, admiration, bonbons, bouquets, the sense of exclusion from none of the privileges of the world she lived in, abundant opportunity for dancing, plenty of new dresses, the London *Spectator*, the latest publications, the music of Gounod, the poetry of Browning, the prose of George Eliot.[11]

And yet the keynote of her early behaviour is her wish to free herself from any determining circumstances of social (and sexual) convention, as in the episode where her aunt, Mrs Touchett, instructs her as to the impropriety of a young woman sitting up late with gentlemen:

> 'You're too fond of your own ways' [Mrs Touchett tells her].
> 'Yes, I think I'm very fond of them. But I always want to know the things one shouldn't do.'
> 'So as to do them?' asked her aunt.
> 'So as to choose', said Isabel.[12]

And so Isabel goes on to choose and to choose, turning down Lord Warburton, turning down Caspar Goodwood, ignoring Ralph Touchett's advice – thus not only challenging her world but, when the choices go wrong, succumbing fatally to the world's imprisoning conventions, in the form of marriage with Osmond. Her final choice – not to run off with the ever-waiting Goodwood but to return to her sterile and deadly marriage – is an almost classical one, in the mould of Hester Prynne or Maggie Tulliver, between the temptation of individual passion and the will to submit, by abnegation, to the destiny that her own earlier decision had set in train. On the last page of the novel she chooses imprisonment in order to be true to her own earlier 'free' choice, however mistaken it had proved: producing the ultimate cruel paradox of the book, as Jamesian as it is Victorian, that the final assertion of personal freedom can resemble a willed submission to external circumstances.

The novel is a tragedy of the Victorian dream of freedom – the human dream of freedom – struggling under the pressures of society and of marriage, and in an age where industrialisation and new social and economic complexity seemed to have brought such pressures to a new head. John Stuart Mill's 'On Liberty' and 'The Subjection of Women', in 1859 and 1869 respectively, had struck a new and liberal keynote for the whole mid-Victorian age, as had Matthew Arnold's *Culture and Anarchy*, also in 1869, in another mode; and the themes of *The Portrait of a Lady* are conceived in that tradition of liberal anxiety and desire. Chapter 42, in which Isabel sits up alone all night staring with retrospective clarity into the terrible trap of marriage she has fallen into – 'the house of darkness, the house of dumbness, the house of suffocation' – was seen by James himself in the Preface as 'obviously the best thing in the book . . . a supreme illustration of the general plan.' It is often compared with Dorothea's vigil of introspection and self-assertion against the tyranny of a dead marriage in Chapter 80 of *Middlemarch*. And at the heart of both novels is an intense vision of the tragically complicated interrelationships of freedom, choice, duty, and convention: a vision which seems to catch the anguish not just of two fictional heroines but of a whole social culture pained by the peremptoriness, and averse to the solitariness, of the individual consciousness:

> [Osmond] had his ideal, just as she had tried to have hers; only it was strange that people should seek for justice in such different quarters. His ideal was a conception of high prosperity and propriety, of the aristocratic life . . . Her notion of the aristocratic life was simply the union of great knowledge with great liberty; the knowledge would give one a sense of duty and the liberty a sense of enjoyment. But for Osmond it was altogether a thing of forms, a conscious, calculated attitude. He was fond of the old, the consecrated, the transmitted; so was she, but she pretended to do what she chose with it . . . She had resisted of course . . . She had pleaded the cause of freedom, of doing as they chose, of not caring for the aspect and denomination of their life – the cause of other instincts and longings, of quite another ideal.
> . . . The real offence, as she ultimately perceived, was her having a mind of her own at all. Her mind was to be his – attached to his own like a small garden-plot to a deer-park.[13]

James wrote this, his first extended dramatisation of the perils and self-delusions of the free spirit, not only from within the contemporary English tradition of liberal self-scrutiny and exhortation. He was also writing about freedom from his new personal vantage-point of maturity in years and of having at last found a settled home from which he could contemplate the search for freedom that had been, if anything, excessive in his own upbringing. Freedom, from 3 Bolton Street, must have seemed less like the mere rootlessness and alienation that it had threatened to become; and though the heaping-up of dinner invitations on the mantelpiece, the pervasiveness of English philistinism, and the intrusions on his privacy of family and friends brought increasing pressures of their own, it was far from being the 'house of suffocation'. It allowed him a security that in turn lent narratorial confidence to his patiently-deployed tale of Isabel in her trap, and allowed a new breadth of

treatment, analytic and social detail, a perpetual weave of commentary, a dovetailing of minor characters, a build-up of atmosphere
and a variable sense of place, that together made *Portrait* James's
major response to the challenge of the classic mid-Victorian novel.
It was also, of course, a development out of his earlier fiction, with
some of the earlier romantic and American lyricism, and much of
his perpetual elegiac sense of life itself being a trap. Isabel may
enact a freshly-articulated Victorian drama of personal freedom
caught in the web of circumstance and personal error; but the plot
of choices gone wrong (hers and those of others), of youthful promise imprisoned within the egotism of another personality, of wrong
people matched and lovers kept apart, is stamped throughout with
the younger James's intuition, as he had written to Howells in 1877,
that 'We are each the product of circumstances and there are tall
stone walls which fatally divide us . . . I suspect it is the tragedies
in life that arrest my attention more than the other things and say
more to my imagination.'[14]

It is also worth recalling that *The Portrait of a Lady*, for all its
George Eliot-like solidity and its broad-based composure of treatment in the English tradition, was characteristically Jamesian in
having been begun in Florence and finished – or almost finished –
in Venice. Bolton Street was so far from becoming a personal 'house
of suffocation' that it was a springboard for frequent trips to his old
and to some new haunts south of the Alps. He took a year-old
'fragment' of his new novel to Florence in April 1880, having first
signed contract to have it serialised by Howells in the *Atlantic
Monthly* in the second half of 1880 and simultaneously – this for the
first time – in England, in *Macmillan's* (the terms he struck were
$2500 from the *Atlantic* and £250 from *Macmillan's*). During the
writing of it there were brief but socially congested visits to Rome
and Naples from Florence; more work on it during the autumn and
winter spent in London (after working expeditions to Brighton and
Dover); and in February, 1881, when the novel's serialisation was
well under way, a memorable visit to Venice (via Paris, San Remo,
Genoa, Milan, Rome, and Ancona), where, despite the distractions
of the 'ceaseless human chatter' that he described in the Preface as
coming in at his windows on the Riva Schiavoni he brought Isabel's
tragedy of immurement to its last stages. James often writes with
great vividness about the relationship, helpful and unhelpful, between his task of writing and his insatiable pleasure in travelling.
In the case of the final writing of *Portrait*, in Venice, he expresses

the double-edged quality of that relationship with particular clarity, and in a way that speaks for his long-lasting combination of travel and composition, a particular creative phenomenon more marked in James's writing career than in that of any other nineteenth-century novelist in English (perhaps Dickens comes nearest):

> romantic and historic sites . . . offer the artist a questionable aid to concentration when they themselves are not to be the subject of it. They are too rich in their own life and too charged with their own meanings merely to help him out with a lame phrase; they draw him away from his small question to their own greater ones . . .
>
> There are pages of the book which, in the reading over, have seemed to make me see again the bristling curve of the wide Riva . . . The Venetian footfall and the Venetian cry – all talk there, wherever uttered, having the pitch of a call across the water – come in once more at the window, renewing one's old impression of the delighted senses and the divided, frustrated mind. How can places that speak *in general* so to the imagination not give it, at the moment, the particular thing it wants? . . . one finds one's self working less congruously, after all, so far as the surrounding picture is concerned, than in presence of the moderate and the neutral, to which we may lend something of the light of our vision. Such a place as Venice is too proud for such charities; Venice doesn't borrow, she but all magnificently gives . . . Such, and so rueful, are these reminiscences; though on the whole, no doubt, one's book, and one's 'literary effort' at large, were to be the better for them. Strangely fertilising, in the long run, does a wasted effort of attention often prove.[15]

'Strangely fertilising' the visit to Venice in 1881 was certainly to prove, not only for the concluding of *Portrait* – which, incongruously, is about imprisonment in Rome, and death and abnegation in England – but also for 'The Aspern Papers', set in Venice and written six years later, and for the latter part of *The Wings of the Dove*, long after that. And even more immediately 'fertilising' was the effect on James's imagination of travelling back to America only a few months later, in the autumn of that same year, 1881: his first visit back for six years, and one that ushered in both a new novel and, on another plane, significant personal changes in his life. Within a few months of his arrival in the bosom of his family, in Cambridge, and while he was on a visit – his first – to Washington, James's mother died. Her death occasioned a characteristically effusive and hyperbolic elegy in his notebook journal, dated 9 February 1882:

> She was patience, she was wisdom, she was exquisite maternity. Her sweetness, her mildness, her great natural beneficence were unspeakable . . . there seems not to be enough tenderness in my being to register the extinction of such a life . . . It was a perfect mother's life – the life of a perfect wife.

Only three months before, not long after being reunited with his mother in Cambridge, he had written in the same journal a long, meditative résumé of his European life, and his newly-confirmed Europeanness: 'My choice is the old world – my choice, my need, my life . . . Heaven forgive me! I feel as if my time were terribly wasted here!'[16]

The two notebook entries are significant in a related way. One month of Cambridge and Boston was enough to make James wonder why he had come back; and the sudden death of his mother seems to have evoked in him a compensating exaggeration of lament and personal eulogy which was only to confirm his sense of having definitively said farewell to his American youth. And as if to add a further symbolic knell to the passing of the old America where he was brought up, he found himself attending the funeral of Emerson in Concord that April, 1882: a grave, beside the grave of Hawthorne, which clearly marked the ending of an era in American letters. Less than a year after his mother's death, in December 1882, James's father died, only seven months after James had returned from Boston to England – then not long afterwards his younger brother Wilky, in Milwaukee (and at the same time his old friend and mentor, Turgenev, in France). So that James, on a second American journey of bereavement – this time he stayed for eight months, until August 1883, arranging the family's financial and other affairs – found himself taking stock of the Bostonian scene with a self-consciousness now heightened by his sense of a major turning-point: the death of both parents, the winding-up of a family home, the settlement of a modest inheritance (he gave his own share over to his invalid sister, Alice), and, not least, in April of that year, while in New York, the sobering event of his fortieth birthday. Clearly here was a period of concentrated disturbance and even of potential crisis; but it all sharpened James's eye, as usual, for the American scene around him – despite his boredom and partial distaste at what he saw. And though he continued while in America to work on several new short stories, a dramatised version of 'Daisy Miller', some travel-pieces, and the first collected edition of his fiction (the Macmillan Edition), he was also closely observing the very Boston and New York – Boston's Beacon Street, seemingly inhabited mostly by ladies; a week-end escape to Cape Cod; New York's crowded midtown and Central Park – that were about to become the setting for his next major novel. His first recorded note on the writing of *The Bostonians* – a transcription into his notebooks of a plot-synopsis just sent to J. R. Osgood the publisher – was set down in Boston itself, in April 1883, and ended significantly:

> I wished to write a very *American* tale, a tale very characteristic of our social conditions, and I asked myself what was the most salient and peculiar point in our social life. The answer was: the situation of women, the decline of the sentiment of sex, the agitation on their behalf.[17]

By the late summer of 1884 – back in London again, where amid his usual overcrowded social life he was developing quite new friendships, for example with Edmund Gosse, Mrs Humphry Ward, and John Singer Sargent the painter – James was trying to get *The Bostonians* under way, having signed an advantageous contract with Osgood to have it serialised in the *Century*. He had already contracted to provide another novel for the *Atlantic* for the following year, and clearly was under pressure. And yet, in *The Bostonians* and *The Princess Casamassima*, written under such pressure in less than two years, and totalling over 400 000 words between them, James produced two of his most concerned, leisurely-paced, and certainly his two most realist novels.

James had noted, as regards *The Bostonians*, his wish to write about 'social conditions'; and more clearly than in anything else he had ever written we now find him consciously dramatising a whole culture in crisis – a crisis defined by him very personally and idiosyncratically. *The Portrait of a Lady*, in which he had combined his own characteristic subtlety of evaluation along with a George Eliot-like focus on moral crisis and loss of freedom, remained essentially a study of specific individuals, no more than touched by typicality, locked into their personal fate. And even the more consciously

'International' works of the 1870s like *Roderick Hudson* and *The American*, had shown certain broadly national and human types without conveying a very strong sense of historical turning-point or cultural struggle. But in *The Bostonians*, from beginning to end, we are shown a nation, at a fateful moment in its history, divided in hostility between men and women, between North and South, and between, on one hand, the values of privacy, feeling, and truth-to-self and, on the other, public exposure, abstraction, and commitment to dogma. The whole, slow-moving thrust of the narrative draws its energy from social concussion and social oppressiveness, and – as in *The Princess Casamassima* – from a classically nineteenth-century grasp of the modern city as being itself an inhumane incubus: 'the heavy and the weary weight' (in Wordsworthian phrase) of institutionalised falsity and power-seeking. Boston is a place, and a weight, of vapid public meetings and endless talk, of manipulative deals – deals empty of real human content but heavy with self-delusion – being struck in seedy drawing-rooms and in lecture-halls. Boston resists the sensibility and will of the isolated Southern hero, Basil Ransom, and – like the sex-war which the plot concentrates on – its resistances and hostilities are added to the memory, throughout the book, of the recently-concluded Civil War, which becomes a metaphor for cultural wars of another kind. The burden of the social – the impenetrably social – is rendered almost physically in the narration, always through Ransom's alienated response. For example, in this account of his arrival (impecunious, provincial, resentfully Southern) at Mrs Burrage's fashionable Wednesday Club in New York:

By the time he had crossed Mrs Burrage's threshold there was no doubt whatever in his mind that he was in the fashionable world. It was embodied strikingly in the stout, elderly, ugly lady, dressed in a brilliant colour, with a twinkle of jewels and a bosom much uncovered, who stood near the door of the first room, and with whom the people passing in before him were shaking hands. Ransom made her a Mississippian bow, and she said she was delighted to see him, while people behind him pressed him forward. He yielded to the impulse, and found himself in a great saloon, amid lights and flowers, where the company was dense, and there were more twinkling, smiling ladies, with uncovered bosoms. It was certainly the fashionable world, for there was no one there whom he had ever seen before. The walls of the room were covered with pictures – the very ceiling was painted and framed. The people pushed each other a little, edged about, advanced and retreated, looking at each other with differing faces – sometimes blandly, unperceivingly, sometimes with a harshness of contemplation, a kind of cruelty, Ransom thought; sometimes with sudden nods and grimaces, inarticulate murmurs, followed by a quick reaction, a sort of gloom. He was now absolutely certain that he was in the best society.[18]

The rendering of Olive Chancellor is a wonderful, unfunny parody of the Jamesian heroine up to this point in his *oeuvre* – the 'free spirit', like Isabel, of scrupulous, conscientious self-testing – who has turned parodic because of cultural malaise and the absence of a properly sustaining structure of human relationships: in particular, the relationships that James, in his social conservatism and private sexual timidity, located within the conventional terms of domestic affection, privacy, and female marital dependence. *The Portrait of a Lady* had been a sympathetic, even tragic study of a woman of spirit 'ground in the mill of the conventional' – the conventions that her husband incarnates. *The Bostonians*, by a kind of reversal, is a study of a passionate, spirited woman, Olive Chancellor, locked into psychological perversity by a failure of affection-within-convention and by a new milieu that has rejected personal warmth (and the subjection of women to caring men) in favour of abstract causes and public exposure. Olive's personal taste is always at war – a state, once again, of civil war – with her theories of social reform, her instincts with her principles. A theory of equality makes her travel by street-car – but 'in her heart she loathed it.' She is full of intensity and, at a remove, of implied sexual feeling; but her eyes have 'the glitter of green ice'. Her desire to 'reform the solar system if she could get hold of it' means that 'she always felt more at her ease in the presence of anything strange. It was the usual things of life that filled her with silent rage.' For James, in this instance, 'the usual things of life' certainly mean traditional domestic and marital relationships, and he clearly, even over-clearly, endorses them in this book in a way that runs counter to his celebration of Isabel Archer's heroic and doomed search for freedom. But underlying his personal committedness to an unexpectedly conventional ethic and a conventional psychology in *The Bostonians* is something more than his mere conservatism and his own apprehensiveness towards the New Woman (only just appearing in the

1880s). What gives the book its moral energy, and redeems some aspects of its one-sided propagandistic quality, is a larger issue that we have already seen at work in his 'American and Romantic' phase: that is, his characteristic nineteenth-century terror of the drying-up of feeling under the deadening influence of mechanical, abstract thought – reformism in this case seen as the tyranny of the Idea, and as the *damnosa hereditas* of a century of utilitarianism and materialistic science.

Equally significant for the way that *The Bostonians* became one of James's most contemporary works – a novel filled by his sense of several of the issues of his age – was its concern with the will to power. James had always been fascinated by personal power, and by the power-hunger of the artist, but in *The Bostonians* we have his most fully developed acount of how a social grouping can be ener-gised by contending personal wills in search of aggrandisement. The importance of the concept of will in nineteenth-century think-ing is generally associated with the name of Nietzsche. But although Nietzsche's writings were well known to and influential on William James, and were being read and reviewed in America from the mid-1870s (Henry James's friend T. S. Perry wrote the first review of Nietzsche in 1875), it is more helpful to see *The Bostonians* in the context of a general nineteenth-century obsession than in terms of anything specifically Nietzschean. Behind James's thinking – as indeed behind Nietzsche's – was the whole Romantic cult of the self-willed individual, emblematised for many by the phenomenon of Napoleon, and most influentially promulgated in the writings of Carlyle (of whom Basil Ransom is an admirer). Lionel Trilling iden-tified Napoleon as the image behind the character of Hyacinth Robinson in *The Princess Casamassima*; but in Basil Ransom and in Olive Chancellor we have an even more convincing re-enactment, in each case, of the phenomenon of the would-be conqueror, the asserter of self over others and over circumstances, the angry de-fender and aggressor, the ambitious seeker and manipulator, within a system of other people's driving wills and desires. Olive, for example, though an idealist and a battler for other women's free-dom, becomes enslaved by her own will in pursuit of an idea, and exercises a constrictive personal authority over Verena that is purely self-aggrandising and destructive of Verena's freedom: 'Verena was completely under the charm ... The fine web of authority, of dependence, that her strenuous companion had woven about her, was now as dense as a suit of golden mail'.[19] Ransom, too – like Napoleon an ambitious young man from the provinces – has the will to oppose Olive, to seize the woman he wants, and to make good. His will to power is as economic as it is sexual – and as it is philosophical, moral, and political. He is very much the post-war refugee from a defeated and conservative society, the South, who simply must succeed as a lawyer in New York in order to live – and James brilliantly combines these motives in Ransom against a back-drop of an American society, both in the back parlours of Boston and the glittering drawing-rooms of New York, that knows how to exclude and resist the will of the outsider.

The book is about failure and success, social fragmentation and personal delusion, displaced passion and dreamed-of warmth, and is illuminated by James's acute awareness of how, in America's post-war Gilded Age, the failure or success of a whole society, like that of individuals within it, was hanging in the balance. That society comprises power-seekers like Mrs Burrage, who wants a particular wife for her son, and will buy or subtly bully her way to success; like Olive's sister, Mrs Luna, whose sexual predatoriness – unlike Olive's – is all aimed at Ransom; like Matthias Pardon, the hollow journalist hungry for 'copy' and eager to 'manage' Verena; and like Selah Tarrant, most grotesque of them all, charlatan mes-merist and faith-healer, who preys like a jackal on this society of freaks and misfits, and when he cannot manipulate his own daugh-ter, Verena, is prepared to sell her into the manipulative control of someone else, Olive. And yet, by a characteristic Jamesian irony, the focus of all these contending wills to power, Verena Tarrant, is herself without will: a figure of feminine (as opposed to feminist) pliancy and red-haired charm whom everyone manoeuvres to pos-sess or to hide away from others – and is so will-less, indeed, as to be something of a troublesome blank at the centre of the book. Her one talent is the dubious gift of tongues: an emotion-tinged regur-gitation of the ideas of others, disguised as inspirational speaking. James's very partial diagnosis of a culture in turmoil and decay – such as he had just re-witnessed from within its Boston and New York strongholds during his two death-centred visits of 1881–2 and 1882–3 – is expressed in the final irony that the futile, perverted energies of that whole frustrated culture are directed at possessing someone else's false talent for words. Words, on the lips of Verena (deprived as she is, for James, of a validating, traditional relation-ship with men until 'rescued' by Ransom), have themselves become as nebulous, as hollowed-out of human significance, as the abstract hunger of the Bostonians who fight to possess her.

The overlapping in time of *The Princess Casamassima* and *The*

Bostonians is very striking – the latter appeared in the *Century* between February 1885 and February 1886, and the former in the *Atlantic* from September 1885 till October 1886 – and confirms the impression given by both books that however different in their settings, and in much of their tone, they both emerge from essentially the same creative matrix: James's new perception, in the mid-1880s, of historical crisis and of how a society can be grasped, through the novel form, in some crucial posture of self-betrayal. His sense of America for the writing of *The Bostonians* – 'I wished to write a very *American* tale, a tale very characteristic of our social conditions' – had been dramatically heightened, and darkened, by his return there after an absence of six years. And his homecoming to London in August 1883 seems to have plunged him equally into a newly critical and depressed view of England and the English. He felt a new social unrest on every side, political violence at hand, increasing misery and frustration among the working classes, and a strident and uncontrollable jingoism in England's ruling – but only just ruling – class:

> The ministry is still in office, but hanging only by a hair, Gladstone is ill and bewildered, the mess in the Soudan unspeakable, London full of wailing widows and weeping mothers, the hostility of Bismarck extreme, the danger of complications with Russia imminent, the Irish in the House of Commons more disagreeable than ever, the dynamiters more active, the income tax threatening to rise to its maximum, the general muddle, in short, of the densest and darkest.[20]

In February 1886 James witnessed the aftermath of the Trafalgar Square riots, finding damage and broken windows all around him in Bolton Street (he had recently signed a lease on 34 De Vere Gardens, in Kensington, which was to be his London home for years to come, but had still not moved out of Piccadilly). The Dilke scandal and other prominent divorce cases seemed to be exposing the cracks in the facade of Victorian society. And James, in a letter to Charles Eliot Norton in 1886, gave expression to his personal sense of social apocalypse that underlay the whole writing of *The Princess Casamassima*:

> The subject of the moment, as I came away, was the hideous Colin Campbell divorce case, which will besmirch exceedingly

the already very damaged prestige of the English upper class. The condition of that body seems to me to be in many ways very much the same rotten and *collapsible* one as that of the French aristocracy before the revolution – minus cleverness and conversation. Or perhaps it's more like the heavy, congested and depraved Roman world upon which the barbarians came down. In England the Huns and Vandals will have to come *up* – from the black depths of the (in the people) enormous misery, though I don't think the Attila is quite yet found – in the person of Mr Hyndman [a new Socialist leader].[21]

By far the most eloquent attempt to link *The Princess Casamassima* to the historical facts of its time is Lionel Trilling's essay in *The Liberal Imagination*, which sees James's picture of superficial, plotting anarchists in London as a completely accurate representation of 'the political development of a large part of the working class of England at the beginning of the eighties', with even Hyacinth Robinson's craft of a bookbinder as entirely typical of the skilled workers who were drawn towards anarchism (the German-born Johann Most, perhaps the original for James's Hoffendahl, the Bakunin-like anarchist leader in the novel, was himself a bookbinder). Trilling sees Hyacinth Robinson's tragic indecision, caught between his wish for revolution and his reluctance to see art and civilisation destroyed, as a perfectly contemporary response to anarchist belief, and suggests that Bakunin's and Nechayev's *The Revolutionary Catechism* 'might be taken as a guidebook to *The Princess Casamassima*'. He lists the number of terrorist associations and assassination attempts of the late 1870s and 1880s, and establishes that even James's apparently romantic notion of having a princess play at being an extreme radical is perfectly substantiated by the number of aristocrats who became involved with the anarchists of the time. 'Quite apart from its moral and aesthetic authority', Trilling sums up, '*The Princess Casamassima* is a brilliantly precise representation of social actuality.'[22]

James's portrayal of Hyacinth's London is of a place 'rotten and collapsible', and of a population as essentially isolated from one another and as locked into delusion and falsity as the reformers, charlatans, and hangers-on of *The Bostonians*. It is paradoxical that in these two novels James should scrutinise two societies, American and English – the first of which he criticises elsewhere for its provincialism and conservatism, and the second for its depravity and

conventionality – by focusing on the presence of a reform movement active within each society. The effect is one of a double indict-
ment. Boston and London are exposed as a deadening weight of
inertia and injustice; and the impulse to reform, from within each,
is only another part of that dead weight, being self-delusive, futile,
and essentially an expression of conventional self-seeking. Reform-
ist feminism in one case, and terrorist anarchism in the other, are
seen by James as similarly perverse emanations of decadence and
despair. Ransom's alternative reformism is Carlylean and individualistic – a return to the private life and to private affections – and
has to be hedged around with irony on James's part (though with
hardly as much irony as a modern reader might expect). And
Hyacinth, caught in an equal but more violent dilemma – between
a desire for revolutionary justice and an aesthetic admiration for
the achievements of civilisation – identifies with both, and can re-
solve his impasse only by suicide. The effect is strangely more like
late Dickens than it is like George Eliot – partly from the strongly
urban nature of the subject-matter and the highly-coloured mode of
characterisation, combined with melodrama of incident, that sometimes approach Dickensian caricature and theatricality (for example, Miss Birdseye and Selah Tarrant in *The Bostonians*, Rose
Muniment and Captain Sholto in *The Princess Casamssima*). As in
Little Dorrit and *Our Mutual Friend*, James's cities – Boston, New
York, London – are seething masses of displaced energy, guilt, and
oppression, places without coherence or structure, populated by
wanderers, plotters, people in false roles, the frustrated, and the
guilty. Only here and there does some disconnected and ineffectual
bearer of truth shine out: truth for both Dickens and James in this
instance meaning truth-to-heart, charity, and anti-revolutionary
intuition (plus, in James's case, the equally vital, equally conservative impulse towards the aesthetic).

The Princess Casamassima is a striking instance of how an author,
while being faithful to his very individual imaginative interests,
can nevertheless substantiate these individual concerns in a social
and historical way. It is as though at the very mid-point of his
writing career James suddenly found that some of the themes he
had been developing out of his very private, even withdrawn sensibility were after all the most crucial issues of his era. He had
made his decision to live in Europe, and, more exactly, in London:
the move to De Vere Gardens was a confirmation of that decision,
a more confident claiming of space, rather than a continuing

expression of restlessness. He had just looked bleakly, though with some affection still, into the culture where he had grown up, and had seen his old home and his family dispersed by age and death. He was in his early forties, intent on making each novel better than the last, and on expressing his talent to the full. And now, almost unexpectedly, not fully recognised as such by the readers and reviewers of his time, his fictional pattern of the lonely, life-hungry sensibility coming up against the trap or the wall that life constitutes had been boldly projected outwards into the complex pressures of the times: the atmosphere in which he moved, went to his dinners, and walked the streets of London.

The Princess herself, who in *Roderick Hudson* was the type of the dangerously bored passionate woman living vicariously through Roderick the artist, is now even more convincing as the high-born *capriciosa* living out her own half-understood frustrations by identifying, partly in sexual terms, with the 'awakening revolution' – and accidentally frustrating at least one act of that revolution by giving Hyacinth, the tyro revolutionary, access to the culture of her class, and thereby to his own eventual paralysing indecision. The princess's self-deluding search for personal power (like Olive Chancellor's) is the Jamesian search for psychological fulfilment written large into the power-game of politics, social influence, and money – where fulfilment and reality prove to be as ungraspable as anywhere else. Paul Muniment, the pragmatic working-class revolutionary, is James's type of the worldly, properly ambitious person within whose very efficiency the possible betrayal of others lies coiled up in wait like a snake. Where the other revolutionaries are hopelessly ineffectual, Muniment is probably the only real hope of the revolution – but just as probably will be the one to sell it short (as Lionel Trilling said in 1948: 'today Paul Muniment sits in the Cabinet and is on the way to Downing Street'). Lady Aurora, contrasted with the Princess, is the genuine aristocrat unconscious of 'slumming' in her humanitarian work among the dispossessed – but is even more enfeebled as a personality, and as an effective force, than Dickens's Little Dorrit herself. In James's sardonic, post-Dickens view, it is never the meek who shall inherit the earth. And Hyacinth, who is too meek by far – despite, or perhaps because of, his significant genetic mixture of aristocratic father and homicidal proletarian mother – becomes not a simple re-enactment of some Winterbourne or Acton poised timorously (and aesthetically) on the verge of life's challenge to action but a hero of his time, caught and destroyed at the perfect Arnoldian flashpoint between culture and anarchy. It is a rare achievement in the English novel, and one that confirms the crucial change in James's scope of writing in the 1880s, that the question of taste – Hyacinth's taste, as he discovers in Venice and at Medley, the Princess's country house, the long-concealed beauty of the civilised world, instead of preparing for the act of assassination that is his revolutionary duty – should be so fully developed in the direction of tragedy: public as well as private tragedy. James's own too-easy identification with such a figure – 'some individual sensitive nature or fine mind . . . condemned to see these things [of civilisation] only from outside – in mere quickened consideration, mere wistfulness and envy and despair'[23] – might easily have limited the book to being a study in self-pity or aesthetic fatalism. But Hyacinth's world is too rich in detail, and too peopled, to be merely a field for lyrical elegy. He extends into, and is at the centre of, a whole web of influence, affection, indifference, and power: would-be parental and guiding figures for Hyacinth like Amanda Pynsent, the dressmaker who has brought him up, and Mr Vetch, the old violinist who has instructed Hyacinth in radical scepticism towards Queen and Government; the revolutionary circle who fill 'The Sun and Moon' with their circuitous talk (as aimless and imprisoning as the talk of Conrad's anarchists in *The Secret Agent*, to represent which the listening Stevie Verloc drew meaningless, intersecting circles on his page); and the almost-lover, almost-sister for Hyacinth, the vividly proletarian shopgirl, Millicent Henning, who for all her warmth abandons him readily in the end, pressured by class and (through Captain Sholto) by the sexual exposure of her class. The very expansiveness and breadth of James's writing – as with *The Bostonians* – underline how he has transposed his old themes into a new mode of interconnection that takes on the shape of a collective destiny. Trilling sums up with an appropriate resonance:

> Hyacinth's death, then, is not his way of escaping from irresolution. It is truly a sacrifice, an act of heroism. He is a hero of civilization because he dares do more than civilization does: embodying two ideals at once, he takes upon himself, in full consciousness, the guilt of each. He acknowledges both his parents. By his death he instructs us in the nature of civilized life and by his consciousness he transcends it.[24]

Just as in *The Bostonians*, with his local knowledge and expatriate perceptiveness, James had caught the crisis – or a crisis – of the time, so in *The Princess Casamassima* this American and Romantic plunged his readers into a richly textured sense of the 1880s in England. It was a book to match the time – the rise of Socialism being perhaps the most important single historical feature of that decade, partly as a result of the 1870 Education Act combining in its effect with the great agricultural collapse and economic crisis of the 1870s. It has been said that modern Socialism – after the failure of Chartism in the 1840s – began in England only with the publication of *Progress and Poverty*, by the American Henry George, in 1879. The Social Democratic Federation was founded in 1881 by H. M. Hyndman (whom James, as we have seen, suspected was not quite cut out to be the Attila to lead the Huns), and included William Morris among its early leaders. The Fabian Society began in 1883, and 1889 saw the publication of *Fabian Essays in Socialism*, including essays by Sidney Webb, Annie Besant, and Bernard Shaw. The 1884 Third Reform Act and the 1888 County Councils Act both began a swing in the balance of power towards the lower middle classes; and the 1889 Dock Strike at last galvanised the somnolent trade union movement into new militancy. To fuel the new political groupings came the statistical enquiries into the physical living conditions of contemporary London by Charles Booth, in 1886. And William Booth's Salvation Army and the founding of the Christian Social Union and of Toynbee Hall all brought a new light of social concern and education into the very areas where Hyacinth Robinson wandered and listened, and which William Booth in 1890, parodying the Imperial ethic and clichés of the time, was to call 'Darkest England'.

But however apt *The Princess Casamassima* was as a novel – perhaps even *the* novel – of the mid-1880s in England, and however apt *The Bostonians* (though rather more blurredly) as a novel catching the moment where the old liberal Bostonian establishment succumbed to the commercial ascendency of the Gilded Age in America, another important aspect of both books remains to be mentioned. In subject-matter and in type and application of moral concern the two together marked a major development of James's art in the direction of social and historical awareness: a movement of focus from individual lovers and artists (or would-be in both cases) to a whole community, or even nation, caught in the toils. But in February 1884 James had also made a brief trip to Paris, where he renewed his acquaintance with the dominant group of French writers whom he had frequented nine years before: Zola, Daudet, Edmond de Goncourt (Flaubert was now dead, as was Turgenev, and Maupassant he would not meet again until a visit by the latter to London in the following year). The short visit reawakened old ideas rather than brought new ones, and can be seen to have had more a catalytic or even symbolic value than to have set James on a new path. His account of it is very like his first impressions of years before. He wrote to Howells on 21 February 1884:

> I have been seeing something of Daudet, Goncourt and Zola; and there is nothing more interesting to me now than the effort and experiment of this little group, with its truly infernal intelligence of art, form, manner – its intense artistic life. They do the only kind of work, today, that I respect; and in spite of their ferocious pessimism and their handling of unclean things, they are at least serious and honest.[25]

By the autumn of the same year, clearly under the stimulus of Parisian talk, Parisian theories of realism, James wrote one of his most famous essays, 'The Art of Fiction', a realist credo – a very local and temporary credo – which established a theoretical tone for the writing and reading of *The Bostonians* and *The Princess Casamassima*. The 1880s was not only the period in which James most clearly embraced the social in the sweep of his fiction but the one in which he most explicitly endorsed the tenets of realism, a realism which in its French proponents, from Balzac to Maupassant, went considerably beyond the moralised verisimilitude of a George Eliot.

The aspects of *The Bostonians* and *The Princess Casamassima* that might strike the reader as being Balzacian or even – to stretch a point – Zolaesque are fairly straightforward, but important in their simplicity. As in the example of the French, James gives a new attention to the piling up of physical detail – particularly detail of setting – and to the careful establishing of the social class and type of character. He gives attention to lifelike dialogue, to details of daily work and other routine, and to the points of contact between social institutions and individuals. Very roughly, there is an effect of conscious narratorial observation and of a self-conscious presentation of the data of observation, with the novelist taking the position of 'historian' (as James occasionally said) – or even of 'secretary' or 'scientist' (as Balzac and Zola had said respectively) – rather than of poet or stylist or melodramatist. One critic, writing of James's whole *oeuvre* and not just of the fiction of the 1880s, suggests a threefold 'systematic realism' shared by him and Balzac:

> James and Balzac both work methodically (systematically) to present a convincing picture of life in the world. Their realistic intentions naturally lead them to describe and analyze systems of behavior, communication, exploitation, and so on, that structure the world, and to rely, consciously and unconsciously, upon these systems to help structure their texts and to provide them with figurative language. Finally, their desire to create literary analogues for life in the world leads them to elaborate textual systems of great complexity, of purposeful particularity, and of ample power both to reproduce something like the density and the texture of experience and to involve the reader in an active process of reading and interpretation.[26]

Apart from the obvious shared interest – always there in James, but certainly intensified in his realist writing of the 1880s – in the nature and use of power, the role of class, gender, and money, the organisation and the use and abuse of group-interests, and social manners of every kind, the kinship between James on one hand and the French realists or Naturalists on the other comes out most obviously in the attention to significant physical detail. This becomes interestingly strained in its excessiveness, and verges at times on a mannered and even nervous expressionism that in itself is reminiscent of Zola. For example, there is some significant excess in the long description of Basil Ransom's lodgings:

> Basil Ransom lived in New York, rather far to the eastward, and in the upper reaches of the town; he occupied two small shabby rooms in a somewhat decayed mansion which stood next to the corner of the Second Avenue. The corner itself was formed by a considerable grocer's shop, the near neighbourhood of which was fatal to any pretensions Ransom and his fellow-lodgers might have had in regard to gentility of situation. The house had a red, rusty face, and faded green shutters, of which the slats were limp and at variance with each other. In one of the lower windows were suspended a fly-blown card, with the words 'Table Board' affixed in letters cut (not very neatly) out of coloured paper, of

graduated tints, and surrounded with a small band of stamped
gilt. The two sides of the shop were protected by an immense
pent-house shed, which projected over a greasy pavement and
was supported by wooden posts fixed in the curbstone. Beneath
it, on the dislocated flags, barrels and baskets were freely and
picturesquely grouped; an open cellarway yawned beneath the
feet of those who might pause to gaze too fondly on the savoury
wares displayed in the window; a strong odour of smoked fish,
combined with a fragrance of molasses, hung about the spot; the
pavement, towards the gutters, was fringed with dirty panniers,
heaped with potatoes, carrots, and onions; and a smart, bright
waggon, with the horse detached from the shafts, drawn up on
the edge of the abominable road (it contained holes and ruts a
foot deep, and immemorial accumulations of stagnant mud) im-
parted an idle, rural, pastoral air to a scene otherwise perhaps
expressive of a rank civilization.[27]

That concluding phrase, 'otherwise perhaps expressive of a rank
civilization', is pure James and none other; but the rest of the description is something new in James's work, and might well have
gained restrained approval in the talkative soirées at the Goncourt
house at Auteuil or in Daudet's apartment by the Jardin du Luxembourg. And even more characteristic of the whole mode of *The
Princess Casamassima* – certainly the more Zolaesque of the two – is
this description of Hyacinth at his familiar activity of walking the
London streets:

It was a long walk from Lomax Place to the quarter of the town
in which (to be near the haberdasher's in the Buckingham Palace
Road) Miss Henning occupied a modest back-room; but the influences of the hour were such as to make the excursion very agreeable to our young man, who liked the streets at all times, but
especially at nightfall, in the autumn, of a Saturday, when, in the
vulgar districts, the smaller shops and open-air industries were
doubly active, and big, clumsy torches flared and smoked over
hand-carts and costermongers' barrows drawn up in the gutters.
Hyacinth had roamed through the great city since he was an
urchin, but his imagination had never ceased to be stirred by the
preparations for Sunday that went on in the evening among the
toilers and spinners, his brothers and sisters, and he lost himself
in all the quickened crowding and pushing and staring at lighted

windows and chaffering at the stalls of fishmongers and huck-
sters. He liked the people who looked as if they had got their
week's wage and were prepared to lay it out discreetly; and even
those whose use of it would plainly be extravagant and intem-
perate; and, best of all, those who evidently hadn't received it at
all and who wandered about, disinterestedly, vaguely, with their
hands in empty pockets, watching others make their bargains
and fill their satchels, or staring at the striated sides of bacon, at
the golden cubes and triangles of cheese, at the graceful festoons
of sausage, in the most brilliant of the windows. He liked the
reflection of the lamps on the wet pavements, the feeling and
smell of the carboniferous London damp; the way the winter fog
blurred and suffused the whole place, made it seem bigger and
more crowded, produced halos and dim radiations, trickles and
evaporations, on the plates of glass.[28]

Once again the special Jamesian addition to the scene is irrepressible – 'graceful festoons of sausage', 'halos and dim radiations' –
but the effort at reportage is so honest and sustained, the attempts
to catch working-class London speech sufficiently successful (he
laboured at recording 'phrases of the people' in his notebooks), and
the note at times of a restrained, factually-based outrage so authentic that the general result more or less justified what he promised
T. S. Perry in a letter of December 1884, as he was about to begin
the novel: 'I have been all the morning at Millbank prison (horrible
place) collecting notes for a fiction scene. You see I am quite the
Naturalist. Look out for the same – a year hence.'[29]
    By the time James was paying his remarkable visit to Millbank
prison, Naturalist's notebook in hand, he had already entered into
the lists of mild public controversy with his 'The Art of Fiction',
published in *Longman's Magazine* for September 1884. And only one
week before he wrote to Perry about his prison visit he was also
writing to Robert Louis Stevenson in Bournemouth about the public dispute over the realism of fiction that had just then broken out
between the two of them. James's credo, 'The Art of Fiction', was
in the first place a reply to a published lecture by Walter Besant on
'Fiction as One of the Fine Arts' in which Besant, after arguing for
the formal and social status of the novel and for its accessibility to
technical analysis (with all of which James warmly agreed), went
on to argue for the novel's moral duty and for the need of the
novelist to have first-hand experience of everything he or she was

going to describe (with which James did not at all agree). But what
then transpired between James and Stevenson was in fact much
more interesting and more revealing than Besant's original pro-
nouncement. Stevenson published 'A Humble Remonstrance', also
in *Longman's*, in December, as a rejoinder to James's realist position
that the novel competes with life. The result was not only a *locus
classicus* of disagreement (though also of partial agreement) on the
central issue of fiction as representation but also a lifelong friendship between the two writers: the American realist and the Scottish
romancer.

James's emphasis, partly brought about by his wish to go beyond
Besant's unsubtle advocacy of the basic 'ingenuity' and even teach-
ability of novel-writing, fell strongly on the mimetic:

> the air of reality (solidity of specification) seems to me to be the
> supreme virtue of a novel . . . Many people speak of [the novel]
> as a factitious, artificial form, a product of ingenuity, the business
> of which is to alter and arrange the things that surround us, to
> translate them into conventional, traditional moulds. This, how-
> ever, is a view of the matter which carries us but a very short
> way . . . Catching the very note and trick, the strange irregular
> rhythm of life, that is the attempt whose strenuous force keeps
> Fiction upon her feet. In proportion as in what she offers us we
> see life *without* rearrangment do we feel that we are touching the
> truth; in proportion as we see it *with* rearrangement do we feel
> that we are being put off with a substitute, a compromise and
> convention.[30]

This is the nub of James's essay, apart from some valuable commentary on the English novel's need for theory and for confidence
as a major art form, on vivid impressions being more valuable than
full practical experience for the budding writer, on the unreliability
of formal categories like 'character' and 'plot', 'novel' and 'romance',
and on the only appropriate 'morality' of fiction being no more and
no less than 'the quality of mind of the producer.' What Stevenson
at once took issue with – and very eloquently, in 'A Humble Remonstrance' – was James's insistence that the novel aimed at 'correspondence with life'. He argued that the novel, like any art, aimed
at 'a certain figmentary abstraction . . . neat, finite, self-contained,
rational, flowing, and emasculate'. And in a striking peroration,
Stevenson takes the very line which most readers today would

rightly associate with James the formalist, the first great theoretician of the novel, the later champion of technique and formal coherence, rather than the James of the 1880s, the James of 'The Art of Fiction':

> Our art is occupied, and bound to be occupied, not so much in making stories true as in making them typical; not so much in capturing the lineaments of each fact, as in marshalling all of them towards a common end. For the welter of impressions, all forcible but all discrete, which life presents, it substitutes a certain artificial series of impressions, all indeed most feebly represented, but all aiming at the same effect, all eloquent of the same idea, all chiming together like consonant notes in music or like the graduated tints in a good picture ... The novel which is a work of art exists, not by its resemblances to life, which are forced and material, as a shoe must still consist of leather, but by its immeasurable difference from life, which is designed and significant, and is both the method and the meaning of the work.[31]

No wonder that James in his letter to Stevenson of 5 December 1884, concluded (perhaps a little lamely after all): 'we agree, I think, much more than we disagree ... Excellent are your closing words, and no one can assent more than I to your proposition that all art is a simplification.'[32] And if there is a distinct contradiction between James's advocacy of 'correspondence with life' in the essay and his 'all art is a simplification' in the letter, it is no less amusing to find Stevenson in the following year (by now a very real friend of James) contradictorily writing to the author of *The Princess Casamassima*, just beginning its serialisation, to welcome his bold new realism:

> yes, sir, you can do low life, I believe. The prison was excellent; it was of that nature of touch that I sometimes achingly miss from your former work: with some of the grime, that is, and some of the emphasis of skeleton there is in nature. I pray you to take grime in a good sense; it need not be ignoble; dirt may have dignity; in nature it usually has; and your prison was imposing.[33]

It is not surprising that James and Stevenson, having each for the moment endorsed the opposite sides of the art-as-reality, art-as-convention dispute, should be found apparently on the brink of reversing roles. James was in the process of writing his two most realist novels, and needed to establish his credentials as a realist in his own theoretic terms (Zola is given a half-respectful mention in the essay – 'solid and serious work' – but only as having achieved 'an extraordinary effort vitiated by a spirit of pessimism on a narrow basis'). And clearly James's equal, and more famous, commitment to the shaping and excluding side of art is always waiting in the wings to declare itself. Because what lies around the James–Stevenson debate, fully known to both men and forcing both of them into some dialectical overstatement, is yet another general feature of literary life in the 1880s that must be added to the already dense context of ideas within which James's new novels were being produced, justified, and criticised. This is the whole critical debate on realism as against idealism in fiction (to use the terms of the time). The debate, though it was taking place in England throughout the Victorian period, actually came to a head in the periodical press during the 1880s, due to three almost simultaneous events: the coming into prominence of French Naturalism, the novels of James himself (he was often linked with W. D. Howells as comprising a new school of 'American realism'), and the sudden *éclat* of the 'Romances' of Rider Haggard and others which were seen to constitute a rival school.

James had begun 'The Art of Fiction' with this assertion, unduly flattering to the French:

> Only a short time ago it might have been supposed that the English novel was not what the French call *discutable*. It had no air of having a theory, a conviction, a consciousness of itself behind it . . . there was a comfortable, good-humoured feeling abroad that a novel is a novel, as a pudding is a pudding, and that our only business with it could be to swallow it.[34]

In fact, one of the most striking features of the literary milieu in England at any time between the advent of Dickens and the close of the century is the sea of words that filled the periodical press on the subject of the novel. Undoubtedly, the general standard of criticism was fairly low, and its ventures in the direction of theory very limited, but in countless thousands of novel-reviews and large comprehensive review-articles in those weekly, fortnightly, and monthly journals that virtually comprised the regular intellectual life of the nation the origins, function, and basic principles of fiction were endlessly debated. On one side the naive belief that the novel was

and should be a 'slice of life' drew strength from the realist example and arguments of George Eliot and Trollope, the former setting
a keynote in her review of Ruskin's *Modern Painters* in 1856:

> The truth of infinite value that he teaches is realism – the doctrine
> that all truth and beauty are to be attained by a humble and
> faithful study of nature, and not by substituting vague forms,
> bred by imagination on the mists of feeling, in place of definite,
> substantial reality.[35]

Trollope's credo (written in the mid-1870s) was even more
forthright:

> I have always desired to 'hew out some lump of the earth', and
> to make men and women walk upon it just as they do walk here
> among us, – with not more of excellence, nor with exaggerated
> baseness, – so that my readers might recognise human beings
> like to themselves.[36]

Most readers were only too pleased to recognise what they took
to be themselves, and to disparage – from about 1850 onwards – the
earlier melodrama and exaggeration of Dickens. So that between
1850 and 1880 the simple doctrine that dominates the reviews is
that the true mark of any novelist 'is the capacity of representing
human nature, of creating any figure without life, which to all who
see it shall seem to have life, and life of the vivid kind' (a mid-
Victorian platitude interestingly echoed throughout 'The Art of Fiction' – for example, 'the air of reality . . . seems to me to be the
supreme virtue of a novel . . . the illusion of life. The cultivation of
this success, the study of this exquisite process, form . . . the beginning and the end of the art of the novelist . . . It is here in very truth
that he competes with life').[37] Nevertheless, even before 1880 the
tenets of mimetic realism were always under pressure from various
directions. First, there was the strong demand that the novelist must
transmute inherently unpleasing material so as to give pleasure or
to respect the traditional decorum of art – typical being a hostile
review of Trollope in the *Fortnightly Review* for 1869 which pronounced that 'no amount of skill can make common-place men and
common-place incidents and common-place feelings fit subjects of
high or true literary art'.[38] Many reviewers in this vein continued to
affirm the novelist's right, or duty, to transcend the everyday in

order to please and entertain. Secondly, the transforming subjectivity of the artist's imagination was stressed by others – the *Westminster Review* complaining in 1873, 'Our painting is mere photography,
and our descriptive writing is mere topography. Mind is not seen.
The play and grace of imagination are lost'; and one enthusiastic
reviewer in the *British Quarterly Review* for 1879 finding in early
Meredith an example of the kind of subjectivity that 'achieves its
loftiest triumph in so moulding all conceivable relations, be they
natural or supernatural, fact or dream, into the ideal form of their
own all-fusing imagination'.[39] Thirdly, a vague transcendental
idealism was another alternative principle used to combat realism,
stressing 'essence', or 'higher truth', or 'beauty'. Meredith again
provides an example, this time a review of *Diana of the Crossways* by
W. E. Henley in the *Athenaeum* for 1885: 'This is indeed the merit
and distinction of art: to be more real than reality, to be not nature,
but nature's essence. It is the artist's function not to copy, but to
synthesize'.[40] And in 1888 Thomas Hardy disparaged contemporary
'novelists of social minutiae' and their 'photographic curiousness'
as being false to fiction's principle of being 'more true, so to put it,
than nature or history can be.'[41] Fourthly, there was also some faint
recognition in places that even 'realism' of effect might be itself a
convention and not a matter of pure imitation. Leslie Stephen argued strongly against the theory of 'actual illusion' when writing
on Defoe and on Richardson in the *Cornhill* in 1868; and in the
following year a writer in *Once a Week* anticipated Stevenson's main
argument against James by criticising the majority belief of the day
that the aim of art is to reproduce faithfully, and the failure to
recognise that all 'naturalness' is achieved by non-natural and highly
selective devices: 'Realism is reached by unreal means; naturalness
by artificial aids; simplicity by what may be called the necessary
exaggeration of art'.[42]

By the mid-1880s all of these contending emphases entered into
a new extreme phase under simultaneous pressure from, as it were,
America, France, and the land of Romance. When James wrote to
his friend Perry in 1884, half-ironically, half-boastfully, 'I am quite
the Naturalist' only a week after he had agreed with Stevenson that
'art is a simplification' he was only keeping in play the dialectic
that had broken out in the previous few years over the merits and
demerits of the so-called American school of realists. Apart from
the minority who complained of James's novels that 'the sense of
reality is never established. He cannot invest his characters with the

flesh-and-blood attributes which lay hold of simple sympathies'
(*British Quarterly Review*, 1880), or who actually praised Howells for
his 'unique photographic genius' (*Pall Mall Gazette*, 1885), by far the
most characteristic comment is this, by George Saintsbury on James,
in 1877:

> He has read Balzac, if it be possible, just a little too much; has
> read him until he has fallen into the one sin of his great master,
> the tendency to bestow refined dissection and analysis on char-
> acters which are not of sufficient intrinsic interest to deserve such
> treatment.[43]

W. E. Henley laments the vulgarising cultivation of the common-
place by the two Americans, resulting in 'such an incarnation of the
ephemeral as Daisy Miller' (*Academy*, 1882); and in 1883 the *Quarterly Review* expressed boredom at James's 'tea-pot style of conversation'.[44] Both novelists come under fire for their pessimism, their
tendency to loose endings, their lack of sympathy and of emotional
commitment to their characters, their over-analysis, and their 'small-
beer chronicles of the soul' (*Temple Bar*, 1884). Underlying most of
the hostility is the vague sense that James's (and to some extent
Howells's) use of analysis is clinical and over-scientific, and to that
degree a part of Zolaism – since the general attack on French Naturalism in the 1880s is based far less on any anti-mimetic principle
of representation than on a moral fear of experimental science (a
fear justified later for British reviewers by Zola's quasi-scientific
credo, *Le Roman expérimental*, in 1880) and above all on an almost
hysterical disapproval of the corrupting squalor of the Naturalists'
basic material. George Moore, himself the most confessedly Zolaesque of English novelists in the 1880s (with *A Modern Lover* in 1883,
A Mummer's Wife in 1885, and *A Drama in Muslin* in 1886), was one
of the few not only to praise Zola but to do so in terms not of the
Frenchman's realism but of his poetry, abstraction, and high idealism. He wrote of the English translation of Zola's *Pot-Bouille* in 1885
in words that strangely echo Stevenson's idealist view of art in 'A
Humble Remonstrance' (and even James's own much later emphases
in the Prefaces to the New York Edition):

> Émile Zola has then done no more than to exaggerate, to draw
> the strings that attach the different parts a little tighter than they
> would be in nature. Art, let there be no mistake on this point, be

it romantic or naturalistic, is a perpetual concession; and the character of the artist is determined by the selection he makes amid the mass of conflicting issues that, all clamouring equally to be chosen, present themselves to his mind.[45]

If Zola could not be seen – except by George Moore – as an idealist and poet, but by the majority of reviewers and readers as the central menace of godless science and demoralising realism, with the two Americans as only slightly feebler, greyer versions of the same mimetic degeneracy, the alternative was dramatically there to hand in the early and mid 1880s. Haggard's *King Solomon's Mines*, *She*, and *Allan Quatermain* appeared in 1885, 1886–7, and 1887; and Stevenson's *Treasure Island*, *Prince Otto*, and *Kidnapped* in 1881–2, 1885, and 1886 (to be joined by writers like Marie Corelli, G. A. Henty, Hall Caine, and Anthony Hope). In 1890 the *Scots Observer* applied the new school of romance as a criterion, and fulsomely attacked Howells for straying 'from the highway of art, from the road that leads by Greek temples and spired mediaeval cities to the purple hills and the bountiful plains of the land of New Romance'.[46] In terms of criticism, 1887 was the year of recognition for what was seen as a virtually new genre on the literary scene (though Hawthorne was often praised at this time as a pioneering Romancer), that same year seeing breathtakingly ambitious pronouncements on its behalf from Saintsbury ('The Present State of the Novel', in the *Fortnightly*); from Haggard himself, sneering at the 'laboured nothingness' of the emasculate American novel ('About Fiction', in the *Contemporary*); and from Andrew Lang, unhesitatingly choosing Romance over 'the dubitations of a Bostonian spinster' ('Realism and Romance', in the *Contemporary*). And finally, Hall Caine's 'The New Watchwords of Fiction' in 1890 (again in the *Contemporary*) came as a wild and even Messianic climax to the whole decade-long controversy, pouring scorn on Zolaesque realism and on any belief that valued 'the real facts of life' or saw the novelist as a mere historian:

And I would add for myself as the essence of my creed as a novelist: *Fiction is not nature, it is not character, it is not imagined history; it is fallacy, poetic fallacy, pathetic fallacy, a lie if you like, a beautiful lie, a lie that is at once false and true – false to fact, true to faith.*[47]

Within this Babel of contradictory critical debate and discussion – contributing to it in his own criticism, and occasioning it by two such momentously American-Realist novels as *The Bostonians* and *The Princess Casamassima* (both appeared in book-form in the same year, 1886, in February and October respectively) – James pursued his equally congested personal life, further complicated by the permanent move to England of his sister Alice (with her intimate companion and nurse, Katharine Loring). There were frequent visits to stay – and to talk – with the Stevensons in Bournemouth, where Alice also moved for a while (almost bedridden for the remaining seven years of her life, and suffering from a variety of acute physical and nervous symptoms which her doctors could diagnose only as 'neuraesthenia'). The summer of 1885 was spent in Dover working on *The Princess Casamassima*, with autumn outings to Broadway in Worcestershire and to Paris, ending in a threatened financial crisis when James's American publisher, Osgood, went bankrupt, leaving him with apparently almost no return from *The Bostonians*. There was the problem of setting up a much more complex domestic ménage in De Vere Gardens, where he moved early in 1886, taking with him a married couple, the Smiths, as his new servants (both of them already showing disturbing signs of being hard drinkers, and continuing to do so for the next sixteen years), and an equally new (but perfectly sober) dachshund named Tosca. There were visits to Leamington, where Alice eventually settled; and the usual influx of summer visitors from America and Europe – including one notable visit from Maupassant, scandalously colourful in personality and already ill from syphilis, but for James, his host, a figure nevertheless of exemplary professionalism, powers of observation, and enviable concision in writing style. Although the reviews for neither *The Bostonians* nor *The Princess Casamassima* were reassuring – the Americans greatly disliked the former but quite favoured the latter, partly for its compensating criticisms of English society; the English reviewers, inevitably, being entertained by the anti-American satire of the former, but unconvinced by the verisimilitude and gloom of the latter – James eventually did rather better financially by *The Princess*. After the financial disaster of *The Bostonians* (which brought him a derisory £492 for serial and book sales combined), he was paid $6000 for the serialisation of his new work and an advance of £550 against book sales, and so was able to make his first trip to Italy for six years, in December 1886. Ensconced at Bellosguardo, outside Florence, and living there in continuous close proximity to

his friends the Bootts and also to Constance Fenimore Woolson
(about whose possible emotional attachment to James much has
been speculated, though little established), James responded to Italy
and to the sudden removal of the pressures of his last two years in
London by writing 'The Aspern Papers'. It is one of his most suggestively symbolist and even Gothic novellas, and in its poetic
evocation of Venice and its brilliantly stylised and witty dramatising of a treacherous obsession with the conjoined powers of poetry,
sexuality, and history was about as far as James could get from the
milieu of Millbank Prison and from the prosaic detailing of his mid-
period realist mode.

He had spent seven weeks in Venice, going from Florence, in the
early part of the year (1887), then again for five weeks in the summer; and was back in London by the end of July. But in 'The Aspern
Papers' he had achieved one of his richest expressions not only of
the Italy he always loved like nowhere else, but, in symbolic terms,
of the drama between intimacy and exclusion, promise and loss,
aggrandisement and desolation, that was somewhere at the centre
of his creative imagination – and which had been expressed, in
such a different fictional mode, in Olive Chancellor's 'stations' of
anguish, deprived of Verena, on the beach at Marmion, and in
Hyacinth Robinson's final walks, haunted by the reality of what he
had seen in Venice, through the ungraspable shadows – the 'battered scenery' – of contemporary London. Equally haunted and
deprived, but far more self-deluding, the ironised narrator of 'The
Aspern Papers', in one moment of truth, sees that Venice has withheld from him its supreme gift of human intimacy. Suddenly – on
the phrase 'And somehow' – Venice taunts him with its ungraspable,
receding reality, the rich world shrunk down tantalisingly for him
into the mere figments of theatre:

> I don't know why it happened that on this occasion I was more
> than ever struck with that queer air of sociability, of cousinship
> and family life, which makes up half the expression of Venice.
> Without streets and vehicles, the uproar of wheels, the brutality
> of horses, and with its little winding ways where people crowd
> together, where voices sound as in the corridors of a house, where
> the human step circulates as if it skirted the angles of furniture
> and shoes never wear out, the place has the character of an im-
> mense collective apartment, in which Piazza San Marco is the
> most ornamented corner, and palaces and churches, for the rest,

play the part of great divans of repose, tables of entertainment, expanses of decoration. And somehow the splendid common domicile, familiar, domestic and resonant, also resembles a theatre with its actors clicking over bridges and, in straggling processions, tripping along fondamentas. As you sit in your gondola the footways that in certain parts edge the canals assume to the eye the importance of a stage, meeting it at the same angle, and the Venetian figures, moving to and fro against the battered scenery of their little houses of comedy, strike you as members of an endless dramatic troupe.[48]

During and immediately after his seven-month visit to Italy in 1886–7, James wrote and wrote in one of his periodic fits of especially high productivity, finishing 'The Aspern Papers', 'A London Life', and *The Reverberator* – two novellas and a short novel – as well as 'The Lesson of the Master', 'Louisa Pallant', amd a number of other short stories, plus the usual critical or biographical essays. At least twelve significant new items came into print in 1888 alone. And to crown everything, by September of that year he had already begun to send off to the *Atlantic Monthly* the first instalments of yet another ambitious, full-length realist novel which he had been planning for the past two years and which was to bring quite abruptly to an end this significant, crammed decade of his writing career.

In certain ways, *The Tragic Muse* is the summation of James the realist and Victorian, the man of his time writing within and for his time. It may be about 'the conflict between art and the world', as he himself was to describe its basic conception in the later Preface, and thus an elaboration on a theme that had concerned him from at least as early in his career as *Roderick Hudson*. But what he achieved in *The Tragic Muse* more than any other of his novels (or his short stories about artists), early or late, was to dramatise that theme within a conveyed sense of what constituted the 'real' in terms of practicality, of compromise, of work, of contemporary issues, and of committed human feeling. This enables him to render 'art' to us, the other element in the conflict, as a complex, fully-fleshed part of the 'world', and the 'world', in turn, as the matrix, rather than the simple enemy, of art. For all that James began the decade of the 1880s as the heir to George Eliot, this richly open-ended book with which he concluded that period – it was serialised in the *Atlantic* between January 1889 and May 1890 – demonstrates the degree to which his art of nuance had developed away from her far more categorical, more cut-and-dried art of philosophic commentary. *The Tragic Muse* has been criticised by many readers for being too essay-like and discursive. But on the contrary it could be argued that it even points ahead to the dramatised and ambiguous fiction of James's later period in the way that its ideas emphasise interplay rather than category.

Two images from the Preface (written almost twenty years later), one describing how he began writing the novel in his high fourth-floor apartment in De Vere Gardens, the other how he ended it, wrestling with the usual tendency of his material to ramify beyond control, in a hotel room in Paris, provide a linked metaphor for this important Jamesian idea of interplay. Describing his search to find 'a deep-breathing economy and an organic form', a 'complete pictorial fusion', for the complicated material of *The Tragic Muse* that threatened always to burst apart, he recalls his task as being 'lighted mainly ... by a wide west window that, high aloft, looked over near and far London sunsets, a half-grey, half-flushed expanse of London life' – that is, by metaphoric implication, a threateningly rich 'expanse' of 'life' that pressed against the shape designed to contain it. And at the end of the long struggle for composition, while visiting the Centenary Exhibition in Paris at the end of 1889, he experienced the even 'sharper pressure' of expansive life (its 'confounded irreducible quantity') against the necessary but imperfect restraints of art, the conspiratorial 'plot' of reality against the formal 'plot' of his narrative. Again the image is of a city seen and heard through the framing shape of a window, in this case the window in the Hôtel de Hollande:

> I catch again the very odour of Paris, which comes up in the rich rumble of the Rue de la Paix – with which my room itself, for that matter, seems impregnated ... to an effect strangely composed at once of the auspicious and the fatal. The 'plot' of Paris thickened at such hours beyond any plot in the world, I think; but there one sat meanwhile with another [that is, 'plot'] on one's hands, absolutely requiring precedence ... there being so much of the confounded irreducible quantity still to treat.[49]

This is the very same interplay that the novel explores in the parallel plots of Nick Dormer and Julia Dallow, Peter Sherringham and Miriam Rooth: the pressure, paradoxically both 'auspicious' and 'fatal', between the world of action, practicality, and compromise on one hand, and on the other – in a suggestive phrase from the novel – the 'cold passion of art'. Just as 'The Art of Fiction' in 1884 – itself the fruit of a visit to Paris – surprises us by its celebration of 'the air of reality', and offended Stevenson by its setting up of the novel as a rival of real life, so in *The Tragic Muse* what strikes the reader more familiar with the common notion of James the formalist and aesthete is the degree to which it offers a fundamental critique of aetheticism, and establishes art – the art of portrait-painting, the art of acting – as an activity very much of and in the world: uncomfortably so, no doubt, but always drawing its sustenance from the world's philistine and formless multifariousness.

From so crammed and ambitious a novel it may be allowable to pick out one tiny but characteristic episode that illuminates some of these general features. In Chapter 9 Nick Dormer, torn between the worldly call of politics (represented by the handsome Julia Dallow, who is the Muse of politics) and the almost equally worldly call of portrait-painting (in which alone he might realise his 'real' self), discusses art and life with Gabriel Nash, the Pateresque aesthete, as they cross the Seine towards Notre-Dame, itself a Muse of another kind:

It greeted Nick Dormer and Gabriel Nash with a kindness which the centuries had done nothing to dim. The lamplight of the great city washed its foundations, but the towers and buttresses, the arches, the galleries, the statues, the vast rose-window, the large, full composition, seemed to grow clearer as they climbed higher, as if they had a conscious benevolent answer for the upward gaze of men.

'How it straightens things out and blows away one's vapours – anything that's *done!*' said Nick; while his companion exclaimed, blandly and affectionately:

'The dear old thing!'

'The great point is to do something, instead of standing muddling and questioning; and, by Jove, it makes me want to!'

'Want to build a cathedral?' Nash enquired.

'Yes, just that.'[50]

The cathedral is a great artefact, a 'large, full composition'. But within its 'wide and bright domain of art' it subsumes, rather like James's own window in the Hôtel de Hollande, 'the perpetual click on the neat bridges', 'the lamplight of the great city', and, not least, the voices of the two friendly Englishmen drinking their beers and arguing about style and action. Even more implicatingly – that is, showing even more powerfully how art is implicated in life, and vice versa – the very sight of Notre-Dame enters into Nick's life, moves him strongly away from the idea of a political career, and encourages the 'reality' of his temperament to declare itself: declare itself for art, which is more real for him than the delusive theatricalities of the House of Commons. What is so significant about Notre-Dame is its *achieved* quality – 'anything that's *done*', and again, 'The great point is to do something.' Art that has been fully rendered, and has therefore entered into the world of *doing*, reduces the mere aesthete, Nash, to a kind of impotence. 'The dear old thing!' is a self-defensive piece of facetiousness on the part of a mere talker and theoriser. Nash will always be an amateur; Nick – like Miriam, the Tragic Muse herself – aspires after professionalism, the supreme doing. And though Nick falls short in the end, and Miriam's future as an artist of the stage is not quite assured either and is fraught with compromises on every side, the novel seems clearly to endorse the heroic act of attempted professionalism, which is an act, a real act in the real world, of self-commitment.

Running right through *The Tragic Muse*, sustaining its theme, is the sense of James's own commitment, through acquired knowledge, to the world of the 1880s it portrays: the world of people arguing outside cathedrals or in gardens in St. Johns Wood, dinner-parties redolent of political gossip, studios, galleries, country houses, cafés, and notably the world of the London and the Paris stage – its endless vulgarising compromises, but equally its capacity, as something supremely and professionally *done*, to 'straighten things out and blow away one's vapours'. The actual life of politics – the career, running in his family, that everyone expects and tries to pressurise Nick Dormer to follow – is not given in any detail in the book, but is recreated in certain important ways: especially the ways that it exists, both negatively and positively, within the imaginative response to politics and to history of Nick himself, and of Julia, his determinedly anti-artistic fiancée. But it is given a sufficient external presence in the plot in the form by which it was vividly known to James at first hand: not the division-lobbies but the gossip and the anecdotal dinner-parties, unforgettably summed up in the person of old Mr Carteret, Nick's family confidant, would-be political patron, and ceremonious entertainer of committee-men:

[at a certain hour] the conversation would incline itself to public affairs. Mr Carteret would find his natural level – the production of anecdote in regard to the formation of early ministries. He knew more than any one else about the personages of whom certain cabinets would have consisted if they had not consisted of others. His favourite exercise was to illustrate how different everything might have been from what it was, and how the reason of the difference had always been somebody's inability to 'see his way' to accept the view of somebody else – a view usually, at the time, discussed, in strict confidence, with Mr Carteret, who surrounded his actual violation of that confidence, thirty years later, with many precautions against scandal. In this retrospective vein, at the head of his table, the old gentleman always enjoyed an audience or at any rate commanded a silence, often profound. Every one left it to some one else to ask another question; and when by chance some one else did so every one was struck with admiration at any one's being able to say anything. Nick knew the moment when he himself would take a glass of a particular port and, surreptitiously looking at his watch, perceive it was ten o'clock. It might as well be 1830.[51]

Far more dominant in the book, and obviously far more intimately known by James, is Miriam Rooth's world of the stage. Behind James's deeply felt and vivid representation of her struggle to perfect her art – to impose 'composition' on the 'confounded irreducible quantity' of dramatiseable life by the 'cold passion of art' – lies his lifetime of devoted playgoing, and, more particularly, his involvement throughout the late 1870s and 1880s in public debate and controversy over the nature of acting and the practice of the French, as opposed to the English, theatre. Rather unexpectedly, it was Matthew Arnold who ushered in this debate with his article, 'The French Play in London', written on the occasion of the Théâtre Français performing in London in 1879, a visit which James had also recorded in one of his articles for the *Nation*. But discussion in the periodicals concerning the theory and practice of acting was further stimulated by the controversial début on the London stage of the American actress, Mary Anderson, in 1883, and in 1884 by the topical and popular novel *Miss Bretherton*, by James's friend, Mrs Humphry Ward, which was partly based on the Mary Anderson episode and on the relation of public acting to private life, and which clearly influenced the conception of *The Tragic Muse*. In June

1884 James recorded in his notebooks having discussed 'a study of the histrionic character' with Mrs Humphry Ward in a way that draws together his friend's chosen subject, what the London newspapers of that season and for seasons to come were full of, and what *The Tragic Muse* developed out of four years later (the reference to Mrs Kemble is a reminder of James's long-standing friendship with Fanny Kemble, retired doyenne of the London stage; and to Rachel, a reminder of the almost legendary French actress whose image lies behind that of Miriam Rooth):

> Mrs H. Ward mentioned the other day to me an idea of hers for a story which might be made interesting – as a study of the histrionic character ... The interest, I say, would be as a study of a certain particular *nature d'actrice*: a very curious sort of nature to reproduce. The girl I see to be very crude, etc. The thing a confirmation of Mrs Kemble's theory that the dramatic gift is a thing by itself – implying of necessity no *general* superiority of mind. The strong nature, the personal quality, vanity, etc., of the girl: her artistic being, so vivid, yet so purely instinctive. Ignorant, illiterate. Rachel.[52]

From the beginning of the 1880s articles and books on the art of acting were suddenly everywhere. Diderot's *Paradoxe sur le Comédien* was translated in 1883, Mrs Kemble herself published on Shakespeare and the stage, William Archer's *Masks or Faces? A Study in the Psychology of Acting* came out in 1888, and James's admired acquaintance, the French actor Coquelin (who visited him in De Vere Gardens), published controversial articles of his own on acting and was the subject of an essay by James in the *Century* for 1887. James also wrote significant review-articles on the stage in 1881 ('The London Theatres', in *Scribner's*), in 1882 ('London Pictures and London Plays', in the *Atlantic*), in 1883 ('Tommaso Salvini', the great Italian actor, on a visit to Boston, in the *Atlantic*), again in 1883 ('A Poor Play Well Acted', in the *Pall Mall Gazette*), in 1887 ('The Acting in Mr Irving's "Faust" ', in the *Century*), and very importantly in 1889, while writing *The Tragic Muse*, an imaginary dialogue full of debate and wit, 'After the Play', in the *New Review*.[53]

All of this confirms what a sympathetic reading of James's novel might suggest: that it is imbued with the real debating issues of the day, that even its discursive, argumentative quality as a novel links it to reality and topicality, and that its underlying theme of the interdependence – as well as the tensions – between art and the world is explored within an already-established and demonstrated commitment to the everyday and the pragmatic. Miriam Rooth, as the devoted artist (less crude than James originally envisaged in his Notebook), may strike some of those around her in the story as a 'priestess of harmony', a Notre-Dame of the stage. But she is also earth-bound: the stage and indeed all art being no religion but a perpetual hard-working encounter between artist and the stuff of experience:

> To say she was always acting suggests too much that she was often fatiguing; for her changing face affected this particular admirer at least [Peter Sherringham] not as a series of masks, but as a response to perceived differences, an intensity of sensibility, or still more as something cleverly constructive, like the shifting of the scene in a play or a room with many windows. Her incarnations were incalculable, but if her present denied her past and declined responsibility for her future, it made a good thing of the hour and kept the actual very actual.[54]

Such questions are precisely those that James and so many others had been discussing, with reference to Diderot, Mary Anderson, Henry Irving, and all the London and Paris stage through the 1880s. But they clearly develop out of James's characteristic investigation in much of his fiction of the whole question of role-playing in social and in private life, of personal identity as a dramatic and always-changing entity, and of the whole life of social manners being a theatre of self-invention and self-obfuscation, of enhancement and of betrayal. If such questioning as to the fluidity of the self – 'something cleverly constructive' – was seen earlier as part of James's make-up as a Romantic, it is now transposed fully, in his mid-career, into the mode of realism and contemporaneity. Peter Sherringham – torn between his career as a diplomat and his attraction to Miriam, and himself a development of James's earlier character-type of the hesitant, divided observer – cannot fully recognise this quality of transposition and reality in the Tragic Muse herself. Rather like Gabriel Nash, Sherringham wishes to remain something of an amateur – which is perhaps the worst fate of the aesthetic mind. He is a dabbler, a snob, a theorist of the theatre, who draws the line at actually – realistically – marrying into it. He cannot compromise, whereas in this book compromise seems to belong to the essence of the real artist, the artist of the real: struggle, professional self-education and self-testing, but in the end the acceptance of compromise. This is the lesson for Miriam as much as it is for Nick, whose portrait-painting will probably never achieve artistic greatness – but will at least express the 'truth' of his own commitment to it, as well as some of the 'truth' of the world it portrays. The actress, the creature of disguises, who strikes the doubting Peter Sherringham, the Jamesian tragi-comic man, as a taunting, desirable mountebank and 'an embroidery without a canvas', is in fact the most balanced, dedicated, and pragmatic person in the book. She is the one who maintains the most living dialectic between her public roles and her private self, and who offers to Peter Sherringham, to Nick Dormer, and all the others a lesson in how to maintain, at whatever cost in perfection, a nevertheless vivifying interplay between 'form' and 'life', between 'art' and 'the world', between 'idea' and 'conditions': 'the application, in other words, clear and calculated, crystal-firm as it were, of the idea conceived in the glow of experience, of suffering, of joy.' The following is how she describes her necessary commitment to the life of the streets, which is so necessary to her life of acting and to the 'cold passion' of her chosen art:

> 'I have learned a great deal that way; sitting beside mamma and watching people, their faces, their types, their movements. There's a great deal goes on in cafés: people come to them to talk things over, their private affairs, their complications; they have important meetings. Oh, I've observed scenes, between men and women – very quiet, terribly quiet, but tragic! Once I saw a woman do something that I'm going to do some day, when I'm great – if I can get the situation. I'll tell you what it is some day; I'll do it for you. Oh, it *is* the book of life!'[55]

In many ways *The Tragic Muse* is the climax to James's decade of commitment to the imperfect but real 'conditions' of his English world, both personally and through the artistic mode of realism. The book champions art, as one would expect, and finds much that is valid even in Gabriel Nash's Pateresque extravagances; and there is no doubting James's distaste at the vulgarities that comprise so many of the 'conditions' of Miriam's 'book of life' in the London theatre – among others, the shallow little actor-manager, Basil Dashwood, whom she finds it practicable and (in something of

Nick's and Peter's sense of the word) 'politic' to marry in the end.
But the novel also puts art quite firmly to the test – more firmly
than in most of the more schematic short stories of that period and
later which also explore the 'life versus art' theme, such as 'The
Lesson of the Master' and 'The Death of the Lion'. 'Oh anything for
art!', Biddy, Nick's sister and quietly in love with the infatuated
Peter, is made to exclaim bitterly as she is asked to hold up, for
Peter's pleasure, Nick's painting of her rival, the Tragic Muse – a
cry that is ironically echoed in Peter's almost-final 'Art be damned!',
as he rages at his failure to persuade Miriam to leave the stage and
marry him in *his* 'daily life of man'. Art is no easy transcendence.
It is based on sacrifice and on niggling compromise, on ongoing
struggle and negotiation rather than an achieved ideal – like the
struggle with his own recalcitrant material that James described, in
the Preface, from his memory of the 'fatal' richness of the sounds
of Paris at his window above the Rue de la Paix.

This is the final gesture which *The Tragic Muse* offers to its decade. The 1880s were not only a period of debate, as we have seen, on
the nature of theatre: far more, it was a decade in which the tenets
of literary realism seemed at times to be outfaced by the fantasy-
extravagance of the New Romance in fiction, and by the growing
influence of Pater and the doctrines of 'Art for Art's sake', herald-
ing Oscar Wilde and the 1890s. James himself was on the point of
moving away from the literary mode he had first grown into in *The
Portrait of a Lady*, then mastered in *The Bostonians* and *The Princess
Casamassima*. His own decade of personal crisis and stylistic experimentation with symbolism and the conceits of a personal mannerism was at hand. But in 1890, in one of the humanest, yet also most
art-centred novels he ever wrote, he was able to express his faith
both in art and in the contingent. Even philistinism, against which
the Yellow Book and its sort were soon to fulminate, and of which
he provides memorably comic examples in figures like Nick's
mother, Lady Agnes, or in Mr Carteret and his sister, is allowed its
sustaining virtue: 'The goodness of these people was singularly
pure: they were a part of what was cleanest and sanest and dullest
in humanity'. Philistinism even underpins the artistic: Nick and
Miriam laughingly agree that they are both 'awful Philistines' in
the degree to which their respective practices of art will continue to
simplify, to follow the contingent, and to cut corners. Above all, the
activity of art is upheld as being the utterance of what is most real
and solid in the mind and temperament of the developing artist;

and as being a vital part of the world's movement. On the verge of
a new and dangerous decade – the decade of *fin de siècle* – with his
own career marked by the prodigious achievements of the 1880s
and yet suddenly put at risk by his newly undermining sense of
having no public, no sales, no culture to sustain him, James for
perhaps the last time managed to complete a major novel on a note
of the broadest reconciliation, in which the style of patient unfolding, knowledgeable exposition, and detailed nuances of gesture,
scene, and dramatic encounter which he had perfected over the
previous ten years seem by the end completely in harmony with
the stance taken about the intrinsic place of art in the world. For
James, artistic form is always a matter of relationships: pattern,
interplay, pressure, give-and-take. And *The Tragic Muse*, in the way
it enacts the complexity of the central relationship that is its *idée
mère* – 'the conflict between art and "the world" ', as the Preface
announces it – offers in its dramatised way as profound a theory of
form and realism, of art and its conditions, as James ever formu-
lated. It is as though James as realist, as Victorian, and equally as
dedicated formalist, had amended that half-admiring remark of four-
teen years earlier about the not-quite-artistic realism of George Eliot's
Daniel Deronda: 'The world is in the book.' In *The Tragic Muse*, by
celebrating art and its struggles – the always-imperfect arts of acting, of painting, and of his own fiction – he was also, paradoxically,
celebrating everyday experience, and placing the book of art firmly
in the world.

4

Crisis and Experiment

In his fiftieth year, in 1893, James wrote a masterly brief tale with the revealing title of 'The Middle Years'. It is about a novelist in crisis – and who is cheated by illness and death of the chance to 'experiment' into a new 'last manner' that would have been the consummation of his career. The style of the tale – romantically rich, but still some distance from the baroque convolutions with which this decade of James's writing was to end – expresses an extraordinary complexity of contradictory emotions, tones, and stances. All emanating from the protagonist, there is a languorous, even swooning self-pity, a witty yet orotund world-weariness, a shrewd acerbity and intelligent self-scrutiny, anxiety yet profound complacency, baffled exhaustion yet a longing for change and struggle, a lucid arrogance and bitterness, an over-sweet self-indulgence, eventually a self-transcending sense of elegy. 'Poor Dencombe', as the narrative so often calls him, is apparently convalescent, but in fact dying, by the sea. His latest novel, *The Middle Years*, just published, arouses in him all of these emotions. There is a recognition-scene. A passing young doctor is also carrying a copy. He is an admirer, one of the very few. Perhaps Doctor Hugh will save the master's life as well as confirming his artistic self-regard. The young doctor sacrifices a worldly opportunity – a suggestion of money and marriage, like a miniature novel-plot – in order to stay by Dencombe's side. He is a self-sacrificing, scientific acolyte at the death-bed – or perhaps, more hopefully, at the altar – of art.

Typical of these rich combinations, and of the way James's style was now tending in the 1890s, is this:

> He should never again, as at one or two great moments of the past, be better than himself. The infinite of life was gone, and what remained of the dose a small glass scored like a thermometer by the apothecary. He sat and stared at the sea, which appeared all surface and twinkle, far shallower than the spirit of man. It was the abyss of human illusion that was the real, the tideless deep.[1]

There is the characteristically rhetorical gap between 'never again' and 'be better' in the first sentence. Then in the second, 'the infinite of life' is James the Romantic, the slightly grandiose, suddenly deflated by the mixed metaphor-and-simile that follows, in which the finite remaining 'dose' of life – the apothecary's medicine – is measured on the graduated glass of a 'thermometer'. Next, there is an unexpected half-levity in the word 'twinkle' as applied here to the sea. Then a strange movement from the apparently optimistic invocation of 'the spirit of man' to the very opposite, 'the abyss of human illusion' – both concepts, that of human spiritual richness and human spiritual poverty, forming apparently the one 'reality', so much deeper than the mere sea.

There is a new melodramatic extremism in the images, both the negative and the positive: a new personal urgency, as well as a new stylistic enamelling. Dencombe discovers to his dismay that he can barely remember what he has written in his new book:

> He uttered a low moan as he breathed the chill of this dark void, so desperately it seemed to represent the completion of a sinister process. The tears filled his mild eyes; something precious had passed away . . . This was the laceration – that practically his career was over: it was as violent as a grip at his throat. He rose from his seat nervously – a creature hunted by a dread . . .

The mannered excess is startling: 'moan', 'chill', 'dark void', 'desperately', 'sinister', 'tears', 'passed away', 'laceration', 'violent', 'grip at his throat', 'nervously', 'hunted', 'dread'. And just as extreme is the way the very opposite kind of perception is voiced, only a few lines later, as Dencombe dips into his own book, and recovers:

> Everything came back to him, but came back with a wonder, came back above all with a high and magnificent beauty . . . it was extraordinarily good. He dived once more into his story and was drawn down, as by a siren's hand, to where, in the dim underworld of fiction, the great glazed tank of art, strange silent subjects float. He recognised his motive and surrendered to his talent. Never probably had that talent, such as it was, been so fine.[2]

The story hardly ceases to vibrate at this high pitch between the extremes of anguish – the characteristic Jamesian longing for the

impossible second chance – and a kind of honeyed pride and composure, the pleasure, which is almost a sexual pleasure, of letting
oneself literally swoon in the arms of a youthful, panting admirer,
then drawing sustenance from the idea of a splendid 'last manner'
and the heroism of all artistic struggle: 'the precious metals he would
dig from the mine, the jewels rare, strings of pearls, he would hang
between the columns of his temple.'

The whole tale is a fascinating counterpart to Thomas Mann's
Death in Venice, which was to appear twenty years later; and though
its view of art is far less touched than Mann's by the idea of the
unconscious and the Dionysiac, and on the whole less ambiguous,
it leaves us, in Dencombe's dying words, with a grandiloquent credo
that could almost have been Mann's and that of his artist-hero,
artist-victim, Aschenbach, dying in imaginative and sensual self-
abandon on the beach at Venice: 'We work in the dark – we do
what we can – we give what we have. Our doubt is our passion and
our passion is our task. The rest is the madness of art.'[3] 'The Middle
Years' oscillates between feverish despair and feverish confidence
in that 'task' and 'madness' of art. But in that same year in which
he wrote it, 1893, James, the most prolific of writers, wrote no other
single piece of fiction, and was in the middle – the middle year –
of one of the strangest interregnums of his career: six years without
a novel, with only several collections of stories, and a prolonged
attempt, and humiliating failure, to make himself into what he could
not be, a dramatist.

It had all begun before the completion of the writing of *The Tragic
Muse*, the indifferent reception of which was to confirm his growing sense of failure as a full-length novelist. In July 1888 he wrote
to R. L. Stevenson in Samoa:

'I have just begun a novel which is to run through the *Atlantic*
from January 1st . . . After that, with God's help, I propose, for a
longish period, to do nothing but short lengths. I want to leave
a multitude of pictures of my time, projecting my small circular
frame upon as many different spots as possible and going in for
number as well as quality, so that the number may constitute a
total having a certain value as observation and testimony.'[4]

That is one view – one of James's own various views – of what was
to happen between 1890 and 1896. It suggests the positive and creative aspect to his abandonment of the novel. For James's crisis was

as double-sided as Dencombe's in 'The Middle Years' – and so was
the experimentation that in some ways caused and in some ways
healed that crisis. The crisis, being double, came positively from the
highly creative desire to do new things – in particular, theatrical
things – and negatively from deep despondency and loss of confidence. The despondency and its causes had already come out clearly
in a letter to Howells in the same year as he wrote to Stevenson,
1888:

> I have entered upon evil days ... I am still staggering a good
> deal under the mysterious and [to me] inexplicable injury wrought
> – apparently – upon my situation by my two last novels, the
> *Bostonians* and the *Princess*, from which I expected so much and
> derived so little. They have reduced the desire, and the demand,
> for my productions to zero ...[5]

The loss of confidence, plus the accompanying financial motive –
always crucial for James, who had to live by the proceeds of what
he wrote – also comes out strongly in a later letter to Stevenson, in
1891:

> simplifying and chastening necessity has laid its brutal hand on
> me and I have had to try to make somehow or other the money
> I don't make by literature. My books don't sell, and it looks as if
> my plays might. Therefore I am going with a brazen front to
> write half a dozen.[6]

James was accurate about his books. *The Tragic Muse*, in volume
form, sold dismally – one edition of 500 and one reprint of 2000 in
England, and only one printing of 1000 in America (the actual
number of those left unsold not being recorded). And though *The
Princess Casamassima* had sold much better – a total printing of 7750
– it still, like *The Bostonians*, left its author humiliatingly in debt to
the publisher for the advance on royalties. Most significant of all
was the quick disappearance from print of all three such major
novels – compared, say, with Hardy's *The Woodlanders*, published
in 1887, which was reprinted some nineteen times in its author's
lifetime. But his motives in turning to the theatre, and giving up the
novel, were far more mixed than either of those very different ex-
planations to Stevenson would suggest. And the complexity of these

years of crisis and recovery is beyond what even the complexity and heated style of 'The Middle Years' managed to express.

Certainly something quite profound and potentially threatening was at work in James's literary career from just before 1890 until almost the end of the decade; something, indeed, classically *fin-de-siècle*. It is as though many of the innate contradictions in his nature, and in his modes of writing, simply came to a head on the completion of *The Tragic Muse*, one of his longest, most ambitious, and in terms of his reading public most unsuccessful works. It is clear that all his life James (again like his own 'poor Dencombe') enjoyed a high opinion of his own achievment, and at the same time was subject to frequent collapses into total self-doubt: his moods ranging from the wittily (never solemnly) megalomanic to the almost cringingly defeatist (what his brother William once noted as the 'at bottom very powerless-feeling Harry'). It can be surmised – complexly – that he gave up the novel and tried to turn himself into a dramatist partly in desperation, partly from pique, partly under financial pressure, partly out of overweening confidence in his capacity to take the theatrical world by storm, partly out of a lifelong and almost childlike love of the glamour of the theatre, and partly out of a refined artistic apprehension of the qualities of the genre – especially the qualities of concision, expressive gesture, and high colour that he had always sought to achieve in his fiction. Again, as a further part of the complexity of his five 'dramatic' years, it is difficult to separate two contradictory things: the degree to which a psychological (and also financial) crisis forced James into the theatre, and the degree to which his experiment in playwriting actually brought about the worst of the crisis, with the traumatic failure of *Guy Domville* in 1895. Without the apparent failure of his novels of the 1880s, he would probably not have thrown himself, with such mostly disastrous consequences, into the venture of playwriting. But without the failure of that particular venture he would probably not have been forced then into the very different (though still theatre-influenced) experiments in new fictional modes between 1896 and 1900. James was not only someone who could write dazzlingly and tragically about human failure – 'the solidarity . . . of all human weakness', as he wrote of Turgenev in 1874 – but one who was able to transform his own failures, and his own weaknesses, into actual artistic strengths. It is this which makes his critical decade of the 1890s appear so touching and so vivid to us. Only a very great writer could make so drastic a mistake about the nature of his own

genius as virtually to abandon his proper genre for five years, then
out of the effect of that mistake – the newly humiliating, crushing
effect – find new, successful ways of releasing into fiction the new
sensibility that failure itself had stimulated in him. It is as though
Dencombe, in 'The Middle Years', instead of dying, had after all
painfully worked through to his 'splendid last manner', which contained within it, redeemed and energised by an intelligent art, something of the deathliness, the defeat, the self-indulgent swooning
and high manner of the previous crisis.

When his play *Guy Domville* failed in January 1895 James's crisis
was not over – if anything, it was then compounded. But the terms
of it were quite changed. He had failed in the theatre – into which
he had ventured because he had thought he had failed in the novel.
But the novels he then turned to in order to escape from that experience – *The Spoils of Poynton*, *What Maisie Knew*, *The Awkward Age*,
and *The Sacred Fount* – had as it were passed through the experience
of theatre, and are touched significantly by the technique and by
the peculiar histrionic sensibility of drama. And in turn the new
strangeness, both stylistic and emotional, which these novels released provided a new tension in their author's literary career, in
that their highly demanding style, their elliptical manner, their
strangely side-on, and not full-face, relationship to ordinary life
certainly announced a 'last manner' hardly calculated to reverse the
unpopularity that had partly brought on the crisis in the first place.
The second half of this critical decade, from 1896 to 1900, is fascinating in that under the stimulus of varying crisis and sometimes
failed experimentation James began to make totally new external
forms to express aspects of personal feeling and fantasy that had
been only intermittently visible in his earlier writing – for example
in that very strange early novel (his first in fact) *Watch and Ward*
(1871), or above all in some of the short stories and novellas like
'The Author of Beltraffio' (1884), 'Georgina's Reasons' (1884), or
'The Aspern Papers' (1888), which in their turn prefigured the even
stranger, 'last manner' tales of the early 1890s like 'The Pupil' (1891),
'The Altar of the Dead', 'Owen Wingrave', and 'The Figure in the
Carpet' (all in 1894). In some ways the case might remind us of the
concept – and practice – of imaginative *conversion* that was so prominent, and so self-conscious, in James's early mental life, both in his
upbringing and in his first ventures into fiction. By the mid-1890s,
James seems to have been in the throes of a not-totally-conscious
attempt to *convert* into newly articulate forms, through experiments

of genre and style, certain aspects of his old Romantic sensibility, his old narcissism, his old internal anxieties and dreams of power. By imaginative transformation, via crisis, he would seek to turn personal weaknesses or indulgences into hard-edged artistic strengths. And by releasing the full, dangerous energies of his self-awareness, an awareness that combined cool analysis with fevered fantasy, moral intelligence with dandiacal perversity, he would also succeed in converting some of the basic traits of *fin-de-siècle* decadence into the sustaining principles of Modernism.

It should be emphasised, however, that James's sudden plunge into the world of the drama, about 1890, was on the face of it not a plunge into his repressed psyche, or into art for art's sake, but the very opposite. In general terms, he had always loved the public glitter of the theatre – as well as admired some of its generic advantages (its concision and directness, in particular). As a child he had adored theatricals in every form, and in his London life – as we have seen with regard to *The Tragic Muse* – he had become familiar with actors and actresses, and all the mystique (so unlike the solitary unappreciatedness of the dedicated novelist) of the dressing-room, the wings, the stage-door, the cigarette-smoking Miriam Rooths, the raffish banter and gossip. Fanny Kemble, niece of Mrs Siddons and herself a histrionic *grande dame* of life as well as of the stage, had been one of his most established friends and fellow-theatre-goers since the 1870s; and in Elizabeth Robins, who became the leading lady in his own play, *The American*, in 1891, and was the greatest Ibsen actress of her time, he made one of the most fascinating women-friends of his later life. As early as 1882, while in America, James had had his first major flirtation with playwriting, adapting 'Daisy Miller' (with a happy ending!) for the stage, but having it turned down unceremoniously by stage-managers in Boston, New York, then in London (the best he could do was to have it published in a stage version). And then in December 1888, while he was in Paris, having first sent off the early instalments of *The Tragic Muse* to the *Atlantic* and noted down a backstage visit to the actress Julia Bartet at the Théâtre Français as material to be used in the novel, he apparently received a proposal from the London stage-manager Edward Compton (father of Compton Mackenzie) that brought everything to the boil. By May 1889 he was preparing the ground by a long public-sounding explanation – aimed at himself – in his notebooks, which catches well his perpetually mixed

reactions to the stage, almost emblematically introduced by the opening word 'interrupt', and varying from the theatre as having been
a 'long cherished dream' in its own right to the 'time, leisure, independence for "real literature"' that a merely theatrical success would
buy for him:

> I interrupt some other work this moist still Sunday morning to
> make a few notes on the subject of the play I have engaged to
> write for Edward Compton. I needn't go over the little history of
> this engagement and the reasons – they are familiar enough –
> which led me to respond to the proposal coming to me from him
> while I was in Paris last December. I had practically given up my
> old, valued, long cherished dream of doing something for the
> stage, for fame's sake, and art's, and fortune's: overcome by the
> vulgarity, the brutality, the baseness of the condition of the
> English-speaking theatre today. But after an interval, a long one,
> the vision has revived, on a new and a very much humbler basis,
> and especially under the lash of necessity. Of art or fame *il est
> maintenant fort peu question*: I simply *must* try, and try seriously,
> to produce half a dozen – a dozen, five dozen – plays for the sake
> of my pocket, my material future. Of how little money the novel
> makes for me I needn't discourse here. The theatre has sought me
> out – in the person of the good, the yet unseen, Compton . . . To
> accept the circumstances, in their extreme humility, and do the
> best I can *in* them: this is the moral of my present situation . . . If
> I succeed a little I can easily – I think – succeed more; I can make
> my own conditions more as I go on . . . And if there is money in
> it that will greatly help: for all the profit that may come to me in
> this way will mean real freedom for one's general artistic life: it
> all hangs together (time, leisure, independence for 'real litera-
> ture', and, in addition, a great deal of experience of *tout un côté
> de la vie*). . . . One should *use* such things – grind them to powder.[7]

By February 1890 James had sent off the second act of the play
that Compton had commissioned: an adaptation of *The American*
(with an advance of £250). And with a whirl of contradictory effusions in his letters and Notebooks – now apologising high-tonedly
for the crassness of his task, now throbbing with excitement at the
formal challenge of his new genre, now vituperative over enforced
compromises, cuttings, and rewritings, now incandescent with confidence at the imminence of fame and riches – James found himself

well and truly drawn into the practical realities of rehearsals, problems over attempted American accents, a problematic costume for Christopher Newman with too-large buttons. He also found himself in Southport, Lancashire. For this, rather than the West End (or the Théâtre Français) was where fame and riches had to begin. And here, on 3 January 1891, on 'a wet winter night in a windy Lancashire town', the budding dramatist had indeed his first great moment. Southport was loud and enthusiastic, Compton gratified and flattered, and the acutely nervous James ('in my little "cubby" beside the curtain in the right wing, where I stuck all the evening, save to dash out and embrace every one in the entractes') in a kind of apotheosis of glee. Next morning, from the Prince of Wales Hotel, James sent two very different but equally vivid accounts to his sister Alice. One was a superlatively congested, complacent telegram:

Unqualified triumphant magnificent success universal congratulations great ovation for author great future for play Comptons radiant and his acting admirable writing Henry

(perhaps excitement betrayed the sender into the one strictly unnecessary 'and'). The other account was in a wonderfully fresh and direct letter written half an hour later:

It was really *beautiful* . . . The attention, the interest, the outbursts of applause and appreciation hushed quickly for fear of losing (especially with the very bad acoustic properties of the house) what was to follow, the final plaudits, and recalls (I mean after each act) and the big universal outbreak at the end for 'author, *author*, AUTHOR!' in duly *delayed* response to which, with the whole company grinning delight and sympathy (behind the curtain) I was led before by Compton to receive the first 'ovation', but not I trust the last, of my life.[8]

Yet exactly four years later, almost to the day, on 5 January 1895, the whole thing was in ruins. Southport's ovation had turned into London's boos, and James's experiment with the theatre, to all intents and purposes, was at an end. The failure of *Guy Domville* in 1895 – or, rather, its failure to be a real success, for after the boos of the first night it had a perfectly decent run of a month – was the culmination of other failures and frustrations in the same genre during the four intervening years. *The American*, transferred to

London and much revised and recast, attracted attention, especially
after the Prince of Wales paid a visit, and James once again had the
pleasure of responding to cries of 'author, author!' after the first
night (he also had sandwiches delivered by hamper from De Vere
Gardens to the cast during rehearsals). But the critical reception
was lukewarm, and the play closed after seventy performances,
leaving James far from the glory he had envisioned – and even
further away from the £20 000 in a year he had estimated desirefully
as Henry Arthur Jones's possible proceeds from *The Dancing Girl*,
then running at the Haymarket. Two other plays were quickly
written by James, offered to managements and actresses, criticised,
revised 'as effectually and bloodily as the most barbarous dramatic
butchers could desire', hawked around, one even put into rehearsal,
then ignominiously shelved. Other theatrical projects remained at
the stage of scenarios, until in 1893 – year of 'The Middle Years' –
having admired Pinero's *The Second Mrs Tanqueray*, and Mrs Patrick
Campbell in it, he began to write *Guy Domville* for George Alexander, actor-manager of the St. James's. The play was written by the
end of the year, and royalties – hardly munificent, at £7 a performance – negotiated with difficulty. James worked hard, though protestingly, on the required revisions late in 1894 – one of the worst
years in his life, in other respects – and by the turn of the year was
euphorically (yet also anguishedly) ready to stake his theatrical
ambitions on what we can now see to be such a flimsy historical
romance-melodrama as *Guy Domville*. The story of the first night
has been told many times – with special vividness and knowledge
by Leon Edel in his biography and in his Introduction to the 1960
reprint of the play.[9] There may or may not have been theatrical
politics at work behind the interjections and cat-calls from the balcony that began to grow as the play proceeded, George Alexander
being a manager who had created not a few enemies. But undoubtedly the acting was mannered and weak – and the play itself equally
so. Typical of James's inability to write theatrical dialogue is this
fragment of a would-be climactic exchange near the end of the play
(complete with James's ponderously uneasy stage directions):

GUY. I'm the last, my lord, of the Domvilles! [*Then anticipating*
DEVENISH's *reply and speaking on his quick gesture of impatient
despair.*] You've been so good as to take a zealous interest in
my future – and in that of my family: for which I owe you,
and now ask you to accept, all *thanks*. But I beg you, still more

solemnly, to let that prodigious zeal rest, from this moment, for ever! I listened to your accents for a day – I followed you where you led me. I looked at life as you showed it, and then I turned away my face. That's why I stand here again; for [*with intensely controlled emotion*] there are other things – there are partings. [*Then very gently to* MRS PEVEREL.] Will my conveyance have come back?

MRS PEVEREL. [*Listening an instant, and as if subjugated by his returning sanctity.*] I think I hear it now.

GUY. Then I start this moment for Bristol. [*Sadly, kindly smiling.*] Father Murray has had the patience. I go with him to France, to take up my work in the Church! if the Church will *take* again an erring son!

MRS. PEVEREL. She'll take him.[10]

What one is left with most clearly is the impression of a fine and sensitive writer in a desperately wrong place: a place of crisis, and indeed, for him, of nadir. It was also a place, for that one night, strangely central in English literary history, with James – hopelessly incongruous – exposed in it. It is extraordinary how many names, careers, and lines of influence all converged on that slightly farcical first night in the St. James's Theatre. The shadow of Ibsen, for one, was somewhere in the background. It can be argued (as by Leon Edel) that a few direct traces of Ibsen's influence can be detected in James's writing of the play, and James had certainly moved towards enthusiasm, after initial dislike, for Ibsen, whose plays had arrived in London in the early 1890s amid controversy and avantgarde excitement. One of the male actors in *Guy Domville* had recently acted Solness – along with James's friend (and leading lady of *The American*), Elizabeth Robins – in *The Master Builder*. Just before *Guy Domville* went into rehearsal, James, with time on his hands, was reading *Little Eyolf* with admiration. And prominent among the critics in the St. James's Theatre on 5 January was William Archer – he had made the journey to Southport four years before, and enthused over *The American* – who was a major critical force in the establishment of Ibsen's reputation in England, as well as his translator. And Archer, putting the great Ibsen momentarily to one side, next day wrote a very positive review of *Guy Domville*.

Not far off in the background, too, was Oscar Wilde. Rather than face the ordeal of watching his own play in the St. James's, James bizarrely chose to go to the Haymarket, close by, to see Wilde's *An Ideal Husband*, which was taking London by storm. He always despised Wilde's wit and flamboyance, and found it ominous that the same London public who were even then judging *his* play a few hundred yards away could be so delighted by Wilde's 'infantine' drollery. In some ways it was to be Wilde's decade – both of high artistic success and of shattering scandal (his sensational trial and imprisonment for homosexuality came only three months later, in April 1895). And by a further supreme irony the play hastily chosen by George Alexander to fill the gap in his programme left by the failure and withdrawal of *Guy Domville* was to be Wilde's masterpiece, *The Importance of Being Earnest* (until the scandal forced it, too, to be withdrawn). So that if the majestic presence of Ibsen brooded at one side over the inception and the staging of James's play, the rising star of Wilde succeeded it – leaving its mortified author precisely nowhere as a nineteenth-century dramatist.

If James was at the centre, in the place of humiliation, it was not simply that two other much greater dramatists were present, judgingly, in spirit. Also present in the audience, with the task of reviewing the play for their respective newspapers (apart from William Archer), were no less than George Bernard Shaw, for the *Saturday Review*, H. G. Wells, for the *Pall Mall Gazette*, and Arnold Bennett, for *Woman*: that is, three of the most outstanding literary figures of the Edwardian era, now close at hand. Shaw was already a successful novelist, essayist, and music-critic, an influential Ibsenite and a beginning dramatist (*Man and Superman* was to establish his stature in 1903). And he now wrote a very favourable review, comparing James's writing to Mozart's music, and (remarkably, for a Socialist pamphleteer) upholding 'the cultivated majority' in the stalls against 'the handful of rowdies in the balcony' at the first night. Wells, less favourably inclined to *Guy Domville* in his review, was just about to publish *The Time Machine*, to be quickly followed by a stream of acclaimed books, from *The Invisible Man* (1897) to *Kipps* (1905) and *Mr Polly* (1910). And Bennett, cursory and generally critical in his notice of James's play, was still a short-story writer, but would publish his first novel, *A Man from the North*, in 1898, and achieve enormous success (and riches) with *The Old Wives' Tale* in 1908 and *Clayhanger* in 1910. The irony of it all is clear – clearer now, of course, than in 1895. James would never have anything like the popular triumph of any of these three, and popular triumph was what he had planned and hoped for with *Guy Domville*. So that just as his dramatic experiment came abruptly to its end there were other signs – three symbolic presences in the audience, as it were – that the literary tide in the years ahead would still be running strongly against him even as a novelist.

In the first days of this middle year of the century's last decade, then, in the presence (and in the shadow) of so many other literary lives at their own turning-points, with the artistic establishment of late-Victorian England in the audience – Lord Leighton, Burne-Jones, G. F. Watts, John Singer Sargent, George Du Maurier, Edmund Gosse, Mrs Humphry Ward, and many others – James, having entered innocently by the stage-door of the St. James's, was led, perhaps maliciously, by George Alexander to the front of the stage to face the loud reactions of his public – from whose booing the crushed and appalled author quickly fled, according to one of the actors, 'green with dismay'. James, having signed himself to his brother William a few hours before the performance as 'your plucky, but, all the same, lonely and terrified Henry', wrote again to William four days later:

In three words the delicate, picturesque, extremely human and extremely artistic little play, was taken profanely by a brutal and ill-disposed gallery which had shown signs of malice prepense from the first and which, held in hand till the end, kicked up an infernal row at the fall of the curtain. There followed an abominable quarter of an hour during which all the forces of civilization in the house waged a battle of the most gallant, prolonged and sustained applause with the hoots and jeers and catcalls of the roughs, whose *roars* (like those of a cage of beasts at some infernal 'zoo') were only exacerbated (as it were!) by the conflict. It was a cheering scene, as you may imagine, for a nervous, sensitive, exhausted author to face – and you must spare my going over again the horrid hour, or those of disappointment and depression that have followed it; from which last, however, I am rapidly and resolutely, thank God, emerging. . . . The thing fills me with horror for the abysmal vulgarity and brutality of the theatre and its regular public (I mean as represented by most of the Newspaper people – a really squalid crew) . . . Don't worry about me: I'm a Rock.[11]

'Rock' was certainly an exaggeration meant for home consumption, and there seems to have been something close to a breakdown on James's part – strongly countered, however, by his usual ability to put on a bold show before others, and often, in his Notebooks, before himself. He actually – indeed, Rock-like – went back to sit incognito in the St. James's balcony on the very next night, when things went much better. And within a few weeks he was accepting a commission from Ellen Terry to write her a one-act play (which he did, during 1895 – though she never produced it). But his letters and Notebooks are filled with angry and near-final denunciations of the stage and its demeaning requirements – 'You *can't*, after all make a sow's ear out of a silk purse – which is what I have been too heroically trying'. Very soon – on 22 January – he wrote to Howells that he was 'bursting with ideas and subjects: though the act of composition is, with me, more and more slow, painful and difficult. I shall never again write a *long* novel; but I hope to write six immortal short ones – and some tales of the same quality'. And by the beginning of September he was explaining to Horace Scudder, the new editor of the *Atlantic*, that his promised tale, 'The House Beautiful', 'absolutely declines to be contained in 15 000 words': that is, that it was in the process of developing into his first full-length novel for six years, *The Spoils of Poynton*.[12]

James's period of crisis and experiment, it should be said again, was extremely complex – no Jamesian crisis could ever be simple. And the writing in quick succession of *The Spoils of Poynton* and *What Maisie Knew* in 1895–6 can be seen not only as a striking riposte to the temporary delusions of playwriting, and not only as a partial adaptation of some theatrical devices into the language of prose fiction, but also as a new exploration of a style and sensibility that during James's theatrical years were already beginning to emerge in his tales of the period. To one side of the obvious trauma of the St. James's Theatre, the short runs, the unperformed pieces, there was another less obvious trauma, some unresolved tension of imaginative feeling, being played out in, for example, 'The Pupil', 'Owen Wingrave', and 'The Altar of the Dead'. It is not simply that such tales of the early 1890s can be related to the state of James's own psyche at the time – their fascination with victimisation, for example, and with the fatally private sensibility being betrayed by an external, uncomprehending world – but that their writing runs through a new, and at times unsteady, gamut of different tones and stylistic gestures. 'The Pupil' – James wrote it in the late summer of 1890, between a holiday trip to Italy and *The American*, Southport-bound, starting rehearsals – embraces high tragedy, sophisticated farce, an almost Dickensian quality of caricature, direct tenderness of feeling, muffled outrage, astringent perception, and more than a touch of high camp. The eleven-year-old pupil in question is old-fashioned, precocious, with 'elderly shoulders', a mockingly poly-glot intelligence, and a fatefully weak heart – and is presented to us within the increasingly characteristic loopings and postponements of James's hyperconscious style:

> Morgan Moreen was, somehow, sickly without being delicate, and that he looked intelligent (it is true Pemberton wouldn't have enjoyed his being stupid), only added to the suggestion that, as with his big mouth and big ears he really couldn't be called pretty, he might be unpleasant.

The rest of the Moreen family, penurious adventurers and unsuc-cessful social confidence-tricksters, are figures of almost slapstick fun (though the slapstick is elegant, and the underlying squalor always made clear):

> What [Mr Moreen's manner] emphatically did confide was that he was a man of the world. Ulick, the firstborn, was in visible training for the same profession – under the disadvantage as yet, however, of a buttonhole only feebly floral and a moustache with no pretensions to type. The girls had hair and figures and man-ners and small fat feet, but had never been out alone.[13]

Significant, perhaps, is the narrator's note at one point that Pemberton's memory of the Moreen affair in later life took on a 'phantasmagoric' quality, almost too 'inconsequent for anything but dreamland'. This is the strangeness of the story, and that of other stories of the period: that its combination of self-conscious drollery, exaggeration of gesture and image, delicate verbosity, and vivid emotional crisis (as little Morgan draws closer and closer to his uneasy new tutor, and his disintegrating family prepare to abandon him) bulges in the direction of the fantastic, even the Gothic, yet keeps drawing back into contemporary *comédie de moeurs* and realistic psychological tragedy. The quality of feeling (always crucial in these tales) focused on Morgan is inordinate ('effusively', 'extravagant'), and perhaps not clearly expressed or fully understood within the narrative itself:

> [the Moreens] were wonderfully amiable and ecstatic about Morgan. It was a genuine tenderness, an artless admiration, equally strong in each. They even praised his beauty, which was small, and were rather afraid of him, as if they recognized that he was of a finer clay. They called him a little angel and a little prodigy and pitied his want of health effusively. Pemberton feared at first that their extravagance would make him hate the boy, but before this happened he had become extravagant himself.[14]

In the end, the betrayal of little Morgan – by Pemberton, who hesitates for a fatal moment when the indigent family finally hand their weak-hearted little prodigy over to him for good – is handled with a peculiar cursoriness by James. It is either extremely delicate, subtle, and understated – or else it is done with too stylised, too neurotically flamboyant a gesture. Morgan, white-faced and stricken, stammers and puts one hand to his side; Pemberton feels fear; then, caught up in his hypocritical mother's ardent embrace, the pupil's 'darling little heart' breaks, and Pemberton and the Moreens are left together quivering and exposed in the aspic of James's closing ironies. However one sees the ending, it is all an amazing performance and an unforgettably sardonic and emotionally suggestive little drama – perhaps more essentially theatrical in some ways (ways of sensibility if not of stagecraft) than James's plays themselves. But the weird mixture of modes is quite unique and Jamesian, not as yet quite fully achieved; and in a passage like the following shows a typically demanding transition (in one extended sentence) from the dramatic to the analytic, from gesture to abstraction, and from one high style (the slightly operatic dialogue) to another (the narrator's 'thinking', clause by clause by clause);

> 'Take me away – take me away', Morgan went on, smiling to Pemberton from his white face.
> 'Where shall I take you, and how – oh, *how*, my boy?' the young man stammered, thinking of the rude way in which his friends in London held that, for his convenience, and without a pledge of instantaneous return, he had thrown them over; of the just resentment with which they would already have called in a successor, and of the little help as regarded finding fresh

employment that resided for him in the flatness of his having failed to pass his pupil.[15]

Other tales of the early 1890s may be less complicated in their range than 'The Pupil'; but in 'Owen Wingrave', for example, written in 1892 for the *Graphic*, there is a tension between the clever, clear-eyed worldliness of most of the writing up to near the end and the climax itself, which seems distorted by some felt necessity in James's profounder imagining of the situation. In that climax we have a haunted country-house, portraits on the walls of ominously disapproving and infanticidal ancestors, a shriek in the night, and the unnatural death (from a ghostly ancestral encounter) of the noble, proudly independent, and handsome Owen, all of which imposes a Gothic and quite Hawthornean luridness. Owen, the reluctant heir to an obsessively military tradition which intends him for Sandhurst and for Napoleonic glory, is located perfectly by James in a restrictive web of English conventions, of slangy, contemporary language, English upper-middle-class matriarchy and patriarchy, and of felt family pressure – that very 'mill of the conventional' in which Isabel Archer was trapped. But the slightly ambiguous evocations of military exploits (James, we know, had a surprisingly heated interest in Napoleon, despite much disapproval), and the typically sudden switch from the world of Baker Street and Kensington Gardens to the 'uncanny' Paramore, its 'strange voices' that seem to mutter at Owen, its face (of his aunt) peering through 'the ancient blur' and 'thick dim panes' of the centuries-old windows – all this is to foist 'The Turn of the Screw' on to *Portrait of a Lady*. The last sentences catch the deeply Jamesian swell into hyperbole only just redeemed from melodrama by an underlying warmth of personal involvement, lyrical grief, and indignation, and, on the other hand, by a carefully, coolly-imaged tableau that contains sentiment but checks sentimentality:

At a turn of one of the passages [Spencer Coyle, Owen's tutor] came upon the white figure of a girl in a swoon on a bench, and in the vividness of the revelation he read as he went that Kate Julian, stricken in her pride too late with a chill or compunction for what she had mockingly done, had, after coming to release the victim of her derision, reeled away, overwhelmed, from the catastrophe that was her work – the catastrophe that the next moment he found himself aghast at on the threshold of an open

door. Owen Wingrave, dressed as he had last seen him, lay dead
on the spot on which his ancestor had been found. He looked like
a young soldier on a battle-field.[16]

The power (unsteady though it might be) of 'Owen Wingrave'
lies in that abrupt transition from witty social realism to operatic
catastrophe and despair; but 'The Altar of the Dead' is one perfect,
seamless weave of transcendent morbidity from first to last. It was
written in the autumn of 1894, for James a year of many deaths and
much desolation. And, rather like 'The Pupil' *vis-à-vis The American*,
it was written in the pause before rehearsals of a play, *Guy Domville*,
that he hoped would lift his fortunes out of the slough. Significantly, perhaps, he was unable to place it with any periodical – as
he wrote later, 'it had vainly been "hawked about", knocking, in
the world of magazines, at half a dozen editorial doors impenetrably closed to it'[17] – and he first published it in his collection, *Terminations*, in 1895. Its orotund style, untouched in this case by farce,
wit, or social realism, its fevered mingling of obsessive, bereaved
tenderness, self-cherishing isolation, jealousy, a baffled bitterness,
paranoia, and a compensating private religious ecstasy, all mark it
as one of the strangest effusions of James's sensibility: a sensibility
that with hindsight can be detected retrospectively in traces throughout even his early books, but that seems particularly to characterise
these critical, experimental, and theatre-ridden years of the 1890s.
Stransom, wedded in a lifelong passion 'of being bereft' to the sanc-
tified memory of a dead fiancée, has created a secret ritual of ob-
servance and of candles, heaped up perpetually in a suburban
London church to all his 'Dead', that has become 'an immense
escape from the actual'. James's end-of-sentence cadences take on
a ritualistic, incantatory rhythm in themselves: 'feast of memory',
'a sovereign presence', 'ample resources of the soul', 'temples of the
spirit', 'the liberal heart', 'the whiteness of death'. The ordinary
world – the world of second marriages, straightforward sexuality,
short memories, secular compromises – moves Stransom to moral
and physical revulsion. And this revulsion in turn fuels his ecstatic,
though exhausted, submersion in the private world of eternal fidelity,
and is endorsed by James's own half-intoxicated submission to his
protagonist's lonely, self-delighting, world-renouncing fantasies:

He thought, for a long time, of how the closed eyes of dead
women could still live – how they could open again, in a quiet

lamplit room, long after they had looked their last. They had looks that remained, as great poets had quoted lines.[18]

These ideas – and even the language – are strongly reminiscent of Poe (in this case, of Poe's 'Ligeia'), and seem to represent a late, profuse flowering of that High Romantic strain in James's American literary past allied to something rather closer at hand, though itself also a Romantic offshoot, the sensibility of the so-called Decadence and of the *fin-de-siècle*. There is even at times a completely inadvertent note of Oscar Wilde (but disconcertingly without Wilde's humour):

> There were hours at which he almost caught himself wishing that certain of his friends would now die, that he might establish with them in this manner a connection more charming than, as it happened, it was possible to enjoy with them in life.[19]

The symbolism of light – the 'blaze of candles', a 'sea of light', a 'mountain of fire', that becomes 'a mystery of radiance' – expands the tale and converts decadence into a prose poetry of considerable power and wide half-meanings: 'He had at any rate quitted the great grey suburb and come nearer to the warm centre'; 'These plunges were into depths quieter than the deep sea caves'; 'that dark defile of our earthly descent in which someone dies every day'; 'He wandered in the fields of light; he passed, among the tall tapers, from tier to tier, from fire to fire, from name to name, from the white intensity of one clear emblem, of one saved soul, to another'. James causes life to break into Stransom's half-narcissistic trance – but only in the form of another intrusive worshipper at the same altar, a black-robed anonymous lady, kneeling before the same candles, *his* candles, but – sacrilegiously – in memory of Stransom's one great unforgiven enemy in life, whom she had loved and whom she now, another obsessive lover of the dead, must continue to commemorate. The complication, including the hint of a possible relationship between the two worshippers, a repressive aunt, and the mounting challenge to Stransom's generosity, has a stagey quality; but the language and the claustrophobic, incense-laden atmosphere of the tale can just about cope with such artifice, and convert it into the highly stylised gestures of some richly-robed masque of mourning, accusation, momentary intimacy, and the power of love turned perversely away from life towards death. The lady was betrayed by Stransom's old enemy, but worships him the more in death for his betrayal of her in life, in an exaltation of self-sacrifice. Rather like Stransom's half-wish to have his friends die, so that he can be closer to them in imagination, it is a case of Death the great converter, Death the climactically transfiguring style and last manner, fuelled by abnegation, high principle, and withdrawal. It is the ultimate – indeed, fatally ultimate – aestheticising of life into its opposite. The two, Stransom and the lady, torture one another refinedly (again, like a Poe tale), he by refusing to place the one candle for his dead enemy that will satisfy her, she by abandoning, like a fast unto death, the church, the altar, and Stransom's company. All that is left wanting is the final completion and 'symmetry' of the candles – 'Symmetry was harmony, and the idea of harmony began to haunt him'. In a closing vision of his own dead lover, whose face now reproves him for his ungenerosity, he encounters the lady once again – at which crisis, with his head heavy on her shoulder, his own death-throes usher in the harmony and the crowning candle – the candle for *him* – that will enforce the final symmetry of art. The whole thing is a wonderful farrago and a twilight – even a celtic twilight – performance. Art itself, and even love, has become synonymous with death: 'the idea of harmony'. As with 'The Middle Years', the world of *Death in Venice* is not far away. And Stransom's weary swoon into death could well have been acted out, if not quite to the music and gestures of *Tristan und Isolde* then at the very least to a soundtrack from Mahler.

James belonged to his time – to his various times and his various places – even while he fantasised about supersensitive souls who tried to renounce or were crushed by their time and their world, and even while in so many of his tales about artists of this period, such as 'The Lesson of the Master' (1888), 'The Death of the Lion' (1894), 'The Coxon Fund' (1894), 'The Next Time' (1895), and 'The Figure in the Carpet' (1896), he portrayed, with much wit and rather less decadence, the ambiguous failure of artists to fit in with their philistine society. It is interesting to note that three of these artist tales, 'The Death of the Lion', 'The Coxon Fund', and 'The Next Time', were published in the *Yellow Book* (a periodical about which he nevertheless had more than a few reservations: 'I hate too much the horrid aspect and company of the whole publication'[20]). This was the most famous organ of 'Decadence' in England, and in particular associated with figures like Wilde, Aubrey Beardsley,

Arthur Symons, and the poets of the Rhymers' Club – many of whose attitudes of lyrical world-weariness and dandyish, quasi-religious self-cultivation might be recognized in Stransom languishing before his candle-piled altar of the dead. And while one need only compare anything by James with Wilde's *The Picture of Dorian Gray* (1890), in some ways the most prominently representative work of the English Decadent movement, to see how distinctly un-Decadent James could be, how much less juvenile and gimcrack, how much more solid a writer in every way, there are nevertheless certain ways in which James, in the 1890s, touched the nerve (the rather strained nerve) of his decadent decade. The broadly humane, realist, world-centered novels of the 1880s – *The Portrait of a Lady*, *The Bostonians*, *The Princess Casamassima*, *The Tragic Muse* – seem light years away from 'The Altar of the Dead'. The newly-intense preoccupation in his writing with illness, exclusion, and death is his highly modified equivalent of the *fin-de-siècle*'s post-Baudelairean obsession with a dissolving corruption, criminality, and highly-coloured *diablerie*. The rather precious satire in his stories against commercialism, journalism, restrictive conventionality, and materialism, combined with his fervid high regard for artistic integrity and formal principles, echoes some of the more showy aestheticism and *épater-le-bourgeois* gesturings of Wilde and his followers, and (more restrainedly and intelligently) of Walter Pater before them. And his only half-controlled switches of tone in the direction of a quasi-religious intensity, accompanied by a fulsome rhetoric of image and swelling adjective, point to the way in which Decadence, at its best, itself tended towards the more serious transformations and experiments of the Symbolist movement. Decadence and Symbolism come from the same Romantic stock, are virtually contemporary with each other, and – apart from the question of long-lasting achievement and influence – overlap intimately. Arthur Symons's *The Symbolist Movement in Literature* (Yeats was probably a collaborator in the writing of it) did not appear till 1899, when it brought the writing of Baudelaire, Verlaine, Rimbaud, and Mallarmé closer to the English literary scene (and much influenced T. S. Eliot soon afterwards). But Yeats himself, in an essay of 1898, 'The Autumn of the Body', looked back on the earlier years of the decade in terms that suggest the essential oneness of Decadence and Symbolism – and did so in his own quasi-Symbolist rhetoric. Yeats's language here catches the slightly narcotic transcendentalism and the spiritual turning away from the everyday world that had begun to infiltrate James's fiction of the period and to twist James's old wit, observation, and ethical grasp into strange new forms and 'essences':

> ... quite suddenly I lost the desire of describing outward things, and found that I took little pleasure in a book unless it was spiritual and unemphatic. I did not then understand that the change was from beyond my own mind, but I understand now that writers are struggling all over Europe, though not often with a philosophic understanding of their struggle, against that picturesque and declamatory way of writing, against that 'externality' which a time of scientific and political thought has brought into literature.

Yeats eulogises Villiers de l'Isle Adam and Maeterlinck (seminal Symbolist dramatists of the period) for setting before us 'faint souls, naked and pathetic shadows already half vapour and sighing to one another upon the border of the last abyss', and goes on:

> I see indeed, in the arts of every country those faint lights and faint colours and faint outlines and faint energies which many call 'the decadence', and which I, because I believe that the arts lie dreaming of things to come, prefer to call the autumn of the body ... we are beginning to be interested in many things which positive science, the interpreter of exterior law, has always denied: communion of mind with mind in thought and without words, foreknowledge in dreams and in visions, and the coming among us of the dead, and of much else. We are, it may be, at a crowning crisis of the world ...
> ... The arts are, I believe, about to take upon their shoulders the burdens that have fallen from the shoulders of priests, and to lead us back upon our journey by filling our thoughts with the essences of things, and not with things.[21]

The question of James's relation to what Yeats here sees as the revolutionary, even apocalyptic new spirit of the 1890s is one that will have to be returned to in looking at his larger fictions of the second half of the decade. Yeats casts his own net dangerously wide when he draws together Mallarmé, Robert Bridges, Rossetti, Wagner, Blake, Aubrey Beardsley, Whistler, Verlaine, and, not least, himself (for example, in 'Symbolism in Painting', of the same year, 1898). And there is much about James that would sit very uneasily, even protestingly, in such company. He detested and despised Wilde, found Beardsley's work 'extraordinarily base', showed no knowledge of Verlaine or Mallarmé in his criticism (he wrote one embarrassingly dismissive early essay on Baudelaire), loathed Huysman's *À Rebours* (the most influential 'Decadent' French novel of its times, in 1884), was bored by Wagner and shocked by his acolytes, and had once dismissed Whistler's painting as 'the self-complacency of technicality'. His own very pronounced stylistic movement towards 'the essences of things', his increasing use of symbolism, his refined morbidity, his interest in dreams (mild compared with Yeats's), in ghosts, illness, and the past, his visionary heightening in language and imagery – all this 'autumn of the body' in the new stage of his writing life is too individual in expression, too idiosyncratic, to belong quite to any school. But it is also far too marked and powerful, and far too different from his writing of the 1880s, not to be seen as belonging in part to its immediate historical period – even to Yeats's highly poeticised vision of that period as 'the crisis of the world'.

James's awakened interest in death was also simply biographical as well as visionary – and belonged to his 'age' in a different sense of the word. Like Stransom, in his fifties he 'had entered that dark defile of our earthly descent in which someone dies every day', and in his spacious fourth-floor flat at 34 De Vere Gardens, Kensington, in the midst of London life and bustle, he had no choice but to set up his own ever-growing altar of the dead. His Aunt Kate, his mother's sister and a dominant figure in his early family life, died in 1889; his old friend and patron, James Russell Lowell, in September 1891; tragically, three months later, his new young friend, adviser, and warm admirer, the publisher's agent Wolcott Balestier (whose sister James then had the task of giving away in marriage to Rudyard Kipling – 'a queer office for *me* to perform'). Then in March 1892 came the death of his long-suffering sister, Alice, painfully talented and neurotic, whose bond with him had always been close and difficult (he watched, and recorded, her death in harrowing detail: 'They were infinitely pathetic and, to me, most unspeakable hours. They would have been intolerable if it had not been so evident that all the hideous burden of suffering consciousness was utterly gone. As it is, they were the most appealing and pitiful thing I ever saw'[22]). Theodore Child, his long-standing friend and editor, died later in 1892, and his old theatre-going intimate, Mrs Kemble, in January 1893. In January 1894 Constance Fenimore

Woolson killed herself in Venice, a deeply traumatic and guilt-arous-
ing death for James, who – as Leon Edel has investigated at length
– was probably more involved in her affections, and more responsible for encouraging them over the years, than he had ever clearly
acknowledged to himself. 1894 was one of his most difficult years
– a year of depression and intermittent illness (influenza and gout),
when even his spring-and-summer escape to Italy (one of the last
in his life) turned into a hideously disillusioning encounter with the
effects of modern tourism (his phrase a year later in the Notebooks
was, 'the Americans looming up – dim, vast, portentous – in their
millions – like gathering waves – the barbarians of the Roman
Empire'[23]). Though he unexpectedly found Rome 'delightfully empty
and still', the shadow of Miss Woolson's death was always present
(he had to help her family arrange to dispose of her complicated
effects, still in Venice); and he was soon writing to William from
Venice: 'I am demoralized and my spirit broken by the most disastrous three months' attempt I have *ever* made to come "abroad"
for privacy and quiet. These three months have been simply hell'.
And at the end of that black year news came from the Pacific of the
death of his much-loved Robert Louis Stevenson – 'It is too miser-
able for cold words – it's an absolute desolation. It makes me cold
and sick', he wrote to Edmund Gosse on 17 December. And again
to Gosse, two days after Christmas: 'The ghost of poor R. L. S.
waves its great dusky wings between me and all occupations'.[24]
These 'occupations', as the rest of the letter makes clear, were the
final rehearsals of *Guy Domville*. Another death – the death of all his
hopes and efforts as a dramatist – was in the offing.

The failure of *Guy Domville* in January 1895, and James's strong-
willed recovery from the trauma of it, meant the end of an experiment, the end of a crisis – yet also, in certain ways, the continuation
of both. His psychological recovery – the farewell to the stage and
the hailing of the old muse of fiction – was a little too announced,
too rhetorical, to be completely convincing. Less than three weeks
after the fiasco in the St. James's Theatre he wrote a bold clarion-
call into his Notebooks that collapses at the end into strangely
portentous mutterings:

> I take up my own old pen again – the pen of all my old unfor-
> gettable efforts and sacred struggles. To myself – today – I need
> say no more. Large and full and high the future still opens. It is
> now indeed that I may do the work of my life. And I will. x x x x x I

have only to *face* my problems. x x x x x But all that is of the in-effable – too deep and pure for any utterance. Shrouded in sacred silence let it rest. x x x x x[25]

He threw himself with a newly intense preoccupation into the careful planning, as well as the hopefully concise execution, of his next novels – *The Spoils of Poynton* was soon on the stocks – seeing in such formal concentration the best way of absorbing the technical lessons of his theatrical experiment, and of coping with the unhappiness of its failure. The following highly-charged entry in the Notebooks is of 14 February, five weeks after *Guy Domville*:

Has a *part* of all this wasted passion and squandered time (of the last 5 years) been simply the precious lesson, taught me in that roundabout and devious, that cruelly expensive, way, *of the singular value for a narrative plan too* of the (I don't know *what* adequately to call it) divine principle of the Scenario? If that *has* been one side of the whole unspeakable, the whole tragic experience, I almost bless the pangs and the pains and the miseries of it. IF there has lurked in the central core of it this exquisite truth – I almost hold my breath with suspense as I try to formulate it; so much, so *much*, hangs radiantly there as depending on it – this exquisite truth that what I call the divine principle in question is a key that, working in the same *general* way fits the complicated chambers of *both* the dramatic and the narrative lock: IF, I say, I have crept round through long apparent barrenness, through suffering and sadness intolerable, to that rare perception – why my infinite little loss is converted into an almost infinite little again. The long figuring out, the patient, passionate little *cahier*, becomes the *mot de l'énigme*, the thing to live by.[26]

Right through that long, rather hysterical entry runs the fear that the scenario and the dramatic *cahier* may not prove as magical as he desires – and certainly the newly-elaborate planning-out of tales and novels in his Notebooks seems to have more to do with his own desperate need to feel he has gained something from his theatrical years than with any profound resemblance to the form of drama in the actual novels produced – except here and there. The need for 'economy, economy' echoes quite stridently through these new scenarios, along with the exhortation 'dramatize, dramatize!' Yet almost inevitably the finished novel was at least twice as long as projected (*The Sacred Fount* grew from 7000 to 70 000 words!), the newly theatrical effectiveness (and staginess) of dialogue was accompanied by an increasingly untheatrical complexity and abstractness of narrative commentary, and the 'scenic' construction was often outweighed by the burgeoning metaphors and the analytic extravagance. He later identified his technique and 'law of successive Aspects' (as in *The Awkward Age*) with 'the blest operation of my Dramatic principle'[27] – but it might be wondered if his use of variable point of view in narration, alternating 'centres' of narrative focus, and the juxtaposing of complementary and even contradictory nuances of interpretation which this 'law' seems to refer to are not fundamentally at variance with the far less multivalent medium of drama. James's later method, a method of ambiguity and of endlessly proliferating qualifications and interrelations, is a complex amalgam of devices, some of them tightly controlled and many of them completely instinctual and subjective. And his *belief* that this method was like that of a play seems itself more of a psychological gambit than an objective principle – though perfectly justified by what it made possible, in that pragmatic way. He focuses on significantly highlighted entrances and exits – but he had done that brilliantly as long ago as *The Europeans*. He can (in a post-theatre image) zoom in on a single focalising detail, like the half-eaten biscuit significantly knocked to the floor after a heated scene between Fleda and Owen and ominously observed there by Mrs Brigstock in Chapter 15 of *Spoils*; or there is the strange giggling slap aimed at Sir Claude by Mrs Wix in Chapter 24 of *Maisie*. But we have had that already in Madame Merle finding a crack in her teacup in *Portrait*, or Eugenia bending to pick a daisy in *The Europeans*, or Olive Chancellor's glittering green eyes in *The Bostonians*, and a hundred other instances of the theatrical gesture or the pointed detail. And though James can develop a new form of dialogue, by which his characters knowingly bandy word for word, even a portentous 'Oh' for a minutely differing 'Oh', and read oceanic depths into one another's slangy superficialities or elegant ellipses, like thought-readers – this, too, however new in James's writing, is hardly of the essence of theatre, though it may have begun with the example of theatrical *badinage* in his mind. At most what has happened in terms of his creative method is a complete transmutation of the craft of theatre into something that still reveals important traces of the original but above all stands out for its idiosyncracy and newness, and for its suitability to no other genre than the Jamesian

novel. Drama has been passed through the alembic of James's basically discursive, poetic, and narrative mind, has been absorbed
into, yet has also catalysed, many of his old fictional devices, and
has participated in the general and fundamental re-making of his
expressive medium that so characterises the turmoil of his mental
life in the 1890s.

The Spoils of Poynton and *What Maisie Knew* – which he was writing, for a time simultaneously, between the summer of 1895 and the
end of 1896, the former being serialised in the *Atlantic Monthly* from
April to October 1896, and the latter in the Chicago *Chap Book* from
January to August 1897 and the London *New Review* from February
to September – are the first major and successful experiments in
James's re-making of his material and style. With the equally experimental *The Awkward Age* (1898–9) and *The Sacred Fount* (1901) –
though experimental in very different modes – James fought (and
played) his way finally out of the flux of the 1890s and attained the
personal composure and eventually the achieved stylistic manner
which made the writing of his last three great novels possible
between 1900 and 1904. All four just mentioned are essentially
variations (distinct variations) on the great Jamesian theme of the
heightened individual sensibility and consciousness seeking to irra-
diate, or to survive, or aesthetically to apprehend the contemporary
world in all its vital crassness and its seductive mendacity. In *The
Spoils of Poynton* Fleda Vetch's hyperbolic moral delicacy and aesthetic good taste are defeated by the irrepressible philistine vigour
of the Brigstocks, by her lover Owen Gereth's innate lack of will,
and not least by her own dangerously unworldly inability to compromise. In *What Maisie Knew* Maisie's pre-adolescent insights, forced
on her by the crude self-seeking of the adults who hem her in and
use her, are too subtle, too spiritual in their lambency for the grasp
of the worldling, Sir Claude, to whose good they are mostly directed, and probably too unalleviated by maturity or by experience
for her own worldly good either. In *The Awkward Age*, the elegantly
eloquent worldlings in Mrs Brookenham's charmed circle are given
full play by an only part-satiric James, but eighteen-year-old Nanda,
compromised by their *louche* freedoms, is nevertheless shown as
their slightly denatured victim, if not accomplice, and the elderly
Mr Longdon who 'rescues' her is the embodiment in their midst of
an alienated and rather absurd code of moral values. And in *The
Sacred Fount*, finally, James wrote his weirdest novel, a fantastic,
self-indulgent parody both for and against the obsessively searching,

abstracting mind of the artist, when forced by contemporary mores
– and by consciousness itself – into intellectualised form-spinning,
invention, and prurience.

If these four works are to be seen as filling out James's writing
life in the critical five years that followed the equally critical five
years of hesitation and playwriting (he began *The Spoils of Poynton*
in the summer of 1895 and finished *The Sacred Fount* in his new
home in Rye in the summer of 1900), what they have carried over
from the drama seems to be more significantly a quality of artificial,
stylised behaviour in the characters than anything more specifically
of stage technique. With the possible exception of *Spoils*, they are
hardly concise, sharp, or fast-moving. They use selected vivid scenes,
but no more sharply or with any more cumulative, serial energy –
the true drama's knock-on effect – than in other novels. Even *The
Awkward Age*, the most ostentatiously drama-like in format of the
four, in that it consists of long set-pieces of dialogue, plus commentary, in various fixed drawing-room settings, is far less visual than
aural, and indeed far more interlinear – more cerebral and suggestive – than memorably verbal or gestural. But stylisation (whether
from the theatre or not) of action, convention, description, and even
of situation is of the essence of James's new manner. Each novel in
bare synopsis sounds more like an imaginative conceit, a dehuman-
ised freak of fancifulness (if not of the merely mechanical). A poor
but tasteful young woman (Fleda Vetch in *Spoils*) fatefully and over-
delicately refuses to encourage her rich patroness' son (who is in
love with her, and she with him) in his wish to break his loveless
engagement to another (appalling) woman, especially when her
widowed patroness, in order to preserve her collection of fine 'things'
from falling by marriage into the clutches of the philistine fiancée,
adds her own inducements for Fleda to undermine the engagement
and marry both son and 'things'. The philistine fiancée holds on to
the engagement. Fleda, self-sacrificially, loses everything. The noble
house, with all its spoils, burns down. Or take the unpromising
sound of *What Maisie Knew*: a little girl, exchanged regularly and
recriminatingly between estranged mother and father, sees various
liaisons develop luridly in both households, is used by her father's
second wife and her mother's second husband (whom the little girl
adores) as a cover-up for their own affair, fails to impose some kind
of transformingly 'innocent' structure on all their to-ings and fro-
ings, and retires from the scene (by now Boulogne) in distress with
her disapproving but imperceptive governess. The same *reductio ad*

absurdum could be applied to Nanda Brookenham's prolonged 'awkwardness' (of age and of presence) among the titterings and the *double entendres* and the blasé allusions (and elisions) of her mother's smart Buckingham Crescent 'set', where her unchosen exposure has compromised her marriageability, even among the 'set'; and equally to the anonymous narrator's feverish attempts, in *The Scared Fount*, to discover exactly from which jaded woman (which 'sacred fount') at a country-house week-end a hitherto banal male guest could be drawing, intimately and vampire-like, such startlingly visible attributes of new cleverness and personal power.

Such summaries sound grotesque – rather than just theatrical. But the actual rendering of each novel, while it importantly retains much of that grotesque quality, enriches it radically with wit, with indirect and direct feeling, with mimetic suggestion, and with the shock – as in the 'conceit' of a seventeenth-century metaphysical poem – of extravagant conjunctions of tone and association producing new off-key patterns of meaning. The way James portrays philistinism in *The Spoils of Poynton*, for example, is as much surreal as comic, and by its extravagance translates philistinism – the cutting edge of the unspiritual world – into a new zone of absurdist menace and bad dream. This, for example, of Waterbath, the House Ugly of the Brigstocks, whose daughter Mona will cling on to Fleda Vetch's weak-willed Owen:

> The worst horror was the acres of varnish, something advertised and smelly, with which everything was smeared: it was Fleda Vetch's conviction that the application of it, by their own hands and hilariously shoving each other, was the amusement of the Brigstocks on rainy days.[28]

As in Dickens, the great English master of the grotesque, people become identified by bizarrely isolated details of their appearance. Mona has, and indeed is, the hard toes of her own patent-leather boots – and has a voice like 'the squeeze of a doll's stomach'. Owen, weak-willed but attractive, is all flashing white teeth and great height, with fifteen rifles and forty whips in his study, and has a male impatience that shines 'in his idle eyes as the dining-hour shines in club-windows'. Fleda's whole stance in the imbroglio is hyperbolic, her basic motive being as stylised as these other mere details of appearance. Owen, despite her love for him, must be left alone by her to try, hopelessly, to fumble his own way out of his engagement to Mona, all for the sake of honour, love, and goodness – Fleda all the while knowing the worldly pressures that the unloving Mona will exert on him to maintain the engagement. 'This imagination of Fleda's was a faculty that easily embraced all the heights and depths and extremities of things; that made a single mouthful of any tragic or desperate necessity.'[29] In his Preface James compares the tussle for ownership of the Spoils between Owen's mother and Mona Brigstock to the Trojan War; and this note of overstatement (however qualified by humour) seethes through the whole novel, converting its merely contemporary vulgarity and pettiness of subject matter, its storm-in-a-Sèvres-teacup, into an action as near-mythic, as tautly passionate, and as coolly controlled as a French seventeenth-century neoclassic drama (perhaps after all it is an explosive combination, at a deep level of thought and feeling, of Racine, Congreve, Wilde, and Ibsen that more convincingly marks the dramatic inheritance of such a late-James work than any particular stage technique).

What Maisie Knew, too, is explosively artificial: explosive in terms of the feelings (outrage, pathos, yearning, protective tenderness, self-abnegation, desire, fear) that fight up through and against its restraining forms of high-camp farce and social satire. It is full of distortion and mannerism; its characters frequently jerk like puppets on a wire; its tone veers from the burlesque to the high tragic; and it evokes both a sense of dream and a sense of the real world, often in bewildering – and fascinating – alternation. When the child and her stepfather melodramatically encounter her mother, compromisingly with a new lover, in Kensington Gardens, 'Maisie received in petrification the full force of her mother's huge painted eyes – they were like Japanese lanterns swung under festive arches'; and the perversion of maternal love is imaged – metallically – when Maisie is histrionically grappled by her furious mother to her breast, 'where, amid a wilderness of trinkets, she felt as if she had suddenly been thrust, with a smash of glass, into a jeweller's shopfront'.[30] Characters pant, roar with laughter, toy with a *tartine*, thwack their trouser-leg with a walking stick, throb with joy, bundle one another into hansom cabs, make strident and false-toned appeals for sympathy or help, one hand on bosom, or utter loud cries of renunciation or denunciation, framed by the door of a significant hotel bedroom. Here for example, is a low-keyed, intimate breakfast exchange in Boulogne between the glamorous Sir Claude and the tremulous Maisie concerning her elderly governess, Mrs Wix, who has resisted his lover, Mrs Beale's, attempts to talk her into conniving at their liaison:

'Ah then,' he promptly exclaimed, '[Mrs Wix] *has* tried to affect you! I don't love *her*, don't you see? I do her perfect justice,' he pursued, 'but I mean I don't love her as I do you, and I'm sure you wouldn't seriously expect it. She's not my daughter – come, old chap! She's not even my mother, though I dare say it would have been better for me if she had been. I'll do for her what I'd do for my mother, but I won't do more.' His real excitement broke out in a need to explain and justify himself, though he kept trying to correct and conceal it with laughs and mouthfuls and other vain familiarities. Suddenly he broke off, wiping his moustache with sharp pulls and coming back to Mrs Beale. 'Did she try to talk *you* over?'

'No – to me she said very little. Very little indeed,' Maisie continued.

Sir Claude seemed struck with this. 'She was only sweet to Mrs Wix?'

'As sweet as sugar!' cried Maisie.[31]

The same technique of caricature, of elegant deformation of appearance, talk, and motivation remains consistent through both other novels, *The Awkward Age* and *The Sacred Fount*, which are simultaneously masque-like, hyperrefined, timeless, courtly, yet also slangy, cigarette-smoking, train-catching, and (for James) amusingly streetwise. There was always a tendency to use a certain comic shorthand of characterisation – above all in minor figures – in James's early work (Mr Brand in *The Europeans*, for example, or Henrietta Stackpole in *Portrait of a Lady*), and also here and there in his more naturalistic writing of the 1880s (Selah Tarrant and Miss Birdseye in *The Bostonians*, Gabriel Nash or Mr Carteret in *The Tragic Muse*). And motivation like that behind Isabel's final return to Osmond in *Portrait*, or Claire de Cintré's passivity beneath family pressure in *The American*, or Hyacinth's sensitive drift towards suicide in *The Princess Casamassima* always had about them a trace of something extreme and not-quite-of-this-world. But that previously restrained tendency towards the special, the over-aesthetic, the spiritual has now become a dominating and suddenly confident mode of operating for James. The characters of *The Awkward Age* are as hyperbolic in their queer, unappealing, subtle knowingness, their leisured yet tense life of pure style, their drooping eyes and murmurous

whimsicalities and rococo innuendos, as figures in some Arthurian
legend rewritten by Wycherley. Chosen virtually at random, for
example, out of the hardly-quotable seamless weave of slow, preg-
nant talk and tableau-like postures is this drawing-room conversation between the Italianised Duchess and the old-fashioned outsider,
Mr Longdon, about Mrs Brookenham's reaction to the possibility of
Mr Longdon 'adopting' her daughter Nanda in order to 'save' her
from such pervasive worldliness:

'She sees – through your generosity – Nanda's life, more or less,
at the worst, arranged for, and that's just what gives her a good
conscience.'
If Mr Longdon breathed rather hard it seemed to show at least
that he followed. 'What does she want of a good conscience?'
From under her high tiara an instant she almost looked down
at him. 'Ah, you do hate her!'
He coloured, but held his ground. 'Don't you tell me yourself
she's to be feared?'
'Yes, and watched. But – if possible – with amusement.'
'Amusement?' Mr Longdon faintly gasped.
'Look at her now', his friend went on with an indication that
was indeed easy to embrace. Separated from them by the width
of the room, Mrs Brook was, though placed in profile, fully presented; the satisfaction with which she had lately sunk upon a
light gilt chair marked itself as superficial and was moreover
visibly not confirmed by the fact that Vanderbank's high-perched
head, arrested before her in a general survey of opportunity, gave
her eyes in conversation too prayerful a flight. Their companions
were dispersed, some in the other room, and for the occupants of
the Duchess's sofa they made, as a couple in communion, a picture, framed and detached, vaguely reduplicated in the high polish
of the French floor, 'She *is* tremendously pretty.' The Duchess
appeared to drop this as a plea for indulgence and to be impelled
in fact by her interlocutor's silence to carry it further. 'I've never
at all thought, you know, that Nanda touches her.'
Mr Longdon demurred. 'Do you mean for beauty?'
His friend, for his simplicity, discriminated. 'Ah, they've neither of them "beauty". That's not a word to make free with. But
the mother has grace.'
'And the daughter hasn't?'
'Not a line.'[32]

Of course this is an appallingly dangerous mode of writing. In all four of these late-1890s novels James is often on the brink of losing all touch with normality, and of disappearing into the vortex of his own self-regarding jocosity and preciosity. There has never been a more razor-edged performance – as between success or failure, a radical witty newness or a merely heady eccentricity – in the *oeuvre* of any major novelist in English, before or since. Part of the excitement of reading these works is this very suspense as to whether James's so-personal experimentation in style will at any moment collapse into the bizarre and the rejectable, or, against the odds, forge a persuasive and utterly new mode of imaginative prose. And what on the whole makes for its success is one particular feature of that style more than any of the others: that is, the special and very Jamesian combination of feeling and metaphor.

The Sacred Fount is the most lacking in emotional depth and variety of the four, but even its cerebral sportiveness and self-flaunting *grotesquerie* throw up some extraordinary moments of feeling which come close to transforming the whole action, and almost turn into a momentary drama of tragic loss, self-delusion, and power-seeking what has otherwise remained a highly-inventive but garish doodling on the theme of the artist-as-voyeur. Feeling comes through extravagant language, as the first-person narrator – himself suffused by apparently neurotic self-doubt and terror of inadequacy – stumbles on a failure in someone else that both mirrors and infinitely surpasses his own: the unhappiness of the beautiful, drifting May Server, whom he suspects of being the now-discarded 'sacred fount' of passion for the undeserving Gilbert Long:

> She went through the form of expression, but what told me everything was the way the form of expression broke down. Her lovely grimace, the light of the previous hours, was as blurred as a bit of brushwork in water-colour spoiled by the upsetting of the artist's glass. She fixed me with it as she had fixed during the day forty persons, but it fluttered like a bird with a broken wing. She looked about and above, down each of our dusky avenues and up at our gilded tree-tops and our painted sky, where, at the moment, the passage of a flight of rooks made a clamour. She appeared to wish to produce some explanation of her solitude, but I was quickly enough sure that she would never find a presentable one.[33]

And as a consummation to the delicately, poetically evoked pathos of May Server's situation in that passage there is, in quite a different register of metaphor, the narrator's sense of her misery, in imagery that encapsulates James's capacity in these late books to force the grotesque one step further into a new, slightly surreal, zone of nevertheless intensest feeling:

> I saw as I had never seen before what consuming passion can make of the marked mortal on whom, with fixed beak and claws, it has settled as on a prey. She reminded me of a sponge wrung dry and with fine pores agape. Voided and scraped of everything, her shell was merely crushable.[34]

In *The Spoils of Poynton*, too, what one finds is a transformation through the sudden infusion of emotion and startlingly expressive imagery. The conceit-like brittleness of the initial conception is turned into a rich, though still highly stylised, fable concerning repressed feeling and the dangers of spiritual extremism. After various cartoon-like encounters and some high-farcical exaggeration – 'the fine open mouth (it showed such perfect teeth) with which poor Owen's slow cerebration gaped' – we are suddenly transported, by the same ostentatious use of figures of speech, into a quite different world of private passion, that of Fleda, locked in her false position, for the engaged Owen:

> Their protected error (for she indulged a fancy that it was hers too) was like some dangerous, lovely living thing that she had caught and could keep – keep vivid and helpless in the cage of her own passion and look at and talk to all day long. She had got it well locked up there by the time that from an upper window, she saw Mrs Gereth again in the garden.[35]

When feeling at last breaks through the carapace of Fleda's restraint, the sense of released sexual tension provides an unforgettable example of how James's highly mannered language, and the highly mannered gestures of his characters, can nevertheless become vehicles for overpowering lyrical expression – down to the breathtaking reversal, the fully tragic *frisson*, of the last line:

> The words had broken from her in a sudden loud cry, and what next happened was that the very sound of her pain upset her.

She heard her own true note; she turned short away from him; in a moment she had burst into sobs; in another his arms were round her; the next she had let herself go so far that even Mrs Gereth might have seen it. He clasped her, and she gave herself – she poured out her tears on his breast; something prisoned and pent throbbed and gushed; something deep and sweet surged up – something that came from far within and far off, that had begun with the sight of him in his indifference and had never had rest since then. The surrender was short, but the relief was long: she felt his lips upon her face and his arms tightened with his full divination. What she did, what she *had* done, she scarcely knew: she only was aware, as she broke from him again, of what had taken place in his own quick breast. What had taken place was that, with the click of a spring, he saw. He had cleared the high wall at a bound; they were together without a veil. She had not a shred of a secret left; it was as if a whirlwind had come and gone, laying low the great false front that she had built up stone by stone. The strangest thing of all was the momentary sense of desolation.[36]

What Maisie Knew is equally transformed by sudden transposition of mood and language: in this case, at the exact point where the scene of the novel switches from England to Boulogne, where James's warming sense of place (and the fresh imagery of place) makes possible the narrative's swerve from *risqué* sexual romp into full psychological expressiveness, moral subtlety, and near-tragedy. A missed train to Paris, which Maisie has urged Sir Claude to take with her (a kind of proferred dubious escape from his compromised imbroglio with Mrs Beale), becomes a mysterious dream-image of fear and urgency for both of them. And the book's increasing tendency towards the transcendent and the symbolic – though actual symbols are very sparingly handled – becomes focused on the significant gilt figure of the Madonna on the church on the ramparts of old Boulogne, and on Maisie's last, spiritual appeal to the weak-willed, only-too-worldly Sir Claude:

'I'll stay out till the boat has gone [Maisie tells him]. I'll go up to the old rampart.'
'The old rampart?'
'I'll sit on that old bench where you see the gold Virgin.'
'The gold Virgin?' he vaguely echoed. But it brought his eyes

back to her as if after an instant he could see the place and the thing she named – could see her sitting there alone. 'While I break with Mrs Beale?'

'While you break with Mrs Beale.'

He gave a long deep smothered sigh.[37]

'Symbol' can mean something precise – a gold statue, an animal in a cage – but it can also involve a blurring of edges, an outward emanation of suggested meaning without circumference or possible paraphrase. It is in this latter sense that these four novels, written between 1895 and 1900, allow us to see James's new manner as allied to the Symbolism that Yeats hailed in 1898, with reference to Mallarmé, Maeterlinck, Beardsley, and Whistler:

> frail and tremulous bodies unfitted for the labour of life, and landscape where subtle rhythms of colour and of form have overcome the clear outline of things as we see them in the labour of life . . . poetry will henceforth be a poetry of essences.[38]

If James gave us 'the labour of life' in his realist novels of the 1880s – however touched even then by a certain 'poetry' of transformative forms and language – what we certainly have in his writing of the 1890s, both the short stories and the four novels, is a movement towards 'essences'. His humour has become more angular and eccentric than before, both in its farcical extrusions (Mrs Wix the austere, the elderly, suddenly giving Sir Claude, whom she glamorises, 'a great giggling, insinuating, naughty slap') and in its elegant *badinage* – as that between all the characters in *The Awkward Age*, where even humour becomes a very special stylising and heightening medium. The balletic word-play between Mrs Brookenham and the blasé, hyperaware Vanderbank (her Mirabell-like favourite, whom Nanda also hopelessly loves) becomes at one with those overall 'rhythms of colour and form' that 'overcome the clear outline of things', in Yeats's phrase:

> 'Deprived of the sweet resource of the Hovel [her country-house]', Mrs Brook continued, 'we shall each, from about the tenth on, forage somehow or other for ourselves. Mitchy perhaps', she added, 'will insist on taking us to Baireuth.'
>
> 'That will be the form, you mean, of his own forage?'
>
> Mrs Brook just hesitated. 'Unless you should prefer to take it as the form of yours?'

Vanderbank appeared for a moment obligingly enough to turn this over, but with the effect of perceiving an objection. 'Oh, I'm afraid I shall have to grind straight through the month and that by the time I'm free every Ring at Baireuth will certainly have been rung'.[39]

And in a similar way, James's apparently un-Symbolist moral seriousness does not remain quite in its old form of the 1870s and 1880s but is transmuted into a new ambiguity, by which a spiritual idealism like Fleda Vetch's is shown to be both resplendent and as potentially destructive as its opposite; the prying narrator of *The Sacred Fount* seems both a heartless monster and a heroically committed free intelligence; and the extreme moral scrupulousness of a Vanderbank can coexist (to the reader's baffled judgement) with something revealed as utterly hollow and heartless. James was always against over-clear or too-final moral judgement in his fiction; but that trait has now itself, like his humour, become alembicated into forming part of this strange new medium that makes his whole human landscape so 'tremulous', so intriguing, and so purely Jamesian: his own neo-Symbolist 'Autumn of the Body'.

The way James reacted to late Ibsen – 'the sturdy old symbolist', he calls him in his note on the published translation of *John Gabriel Borkman* in 1897 – not only suggests a parallel with his own new manner but confirms the way in which James was writing, with full alertness, in an era where the stylisations of symbolism had become one of the dominant notes of the literary and intellectual scene. Distinctly uneasy at first about Ibsen's provinciality and starkness, James nevertheless came to respond strongly (and fancifully) to the heightening of effect that such starkness allowed:

[Ibsen's figures] have no tone but their moral tone. They are highly animated abstractions, with the extraordinary, the brilliant property of becoming when represented at once more abstract and more living. If the spirit is a lamp within us, glowing through what the world and the flesh make of us as through a ground-glass shade, then such pictures as *Little Eyolf* and *John Gabriel* are each a *chassé-croisé* of lamps burning, as in tasteless parlours, with the flame practically exposed . . . The background . . . is the sunset over the ice. Well in the very front of the scene lunges with extraordinary length of arm the Ego against the Ego, and rocks in a rigour of passion the soul against the soul – a spectacle,

a movement, as definite as the relief of silhouettes in black paper
or of a train of Eskimo dogs on the snow.[40]

The strange quality of being 'at once more abstract and more living', the unrealistically direct display of inner spirituality, inner
evil, inner consciousness, with the extremist battle of ego against
ego, and the silhouette-sharp stylising of event and character – all
this is like a description of James's own experiments in fiction of the
1890s. The decadent-seeming morbidity and poetry of tales like 'The
Altar of the Dead', the glowing self-pity of 'The Middle Years', the
abrupt lunge into expressionist melodrama of 'Owen Wingrave' –
all this has passed into the later novels, and been given there a new
witty control and placed in a formally more inventive context: a
sharper silhouette against the snow. What was only too evidently
in the tales a projection of personal predicaments – the misunder-
stood artist, the older man encountering a younger disciple, the
attractions of death, isolation, and retreat – is now much more
projected, more seen around, more balanced and more fully expressed, by larger-scale variations of narrative rhythm and tone.
James, that is, learned once again to 'convert': to turn personal
weakness, personal crisis, into artistic strengths. Unsteady excursion into the Gothic and the supernatural – like 'Sir Edmund Orme'
(1892) and 'The Friends of the Friends' (1896) – are now succeeded
by 'The Turn of the Screw', in 1898, the most successfully sustained
of all James's intellectualised and teasing horror-stories. And perhaps above all, in terms of significance for the final phase of his
writing career, the whole crisis of isolation, of felt failure and world-
rejection that the playwriting years only exacerbated, and the short
stories expressed, took on a new note in works like *The Spoils of
Poynton* and *The Awkward Age*. Isolation and introspection had
thrown James more and more deeply into himself. But what he
had found there, at a great depth, was a kind of confidence in isolation and in the act of introspection – even the act, and style, of
abstraction. It seems to have been in the 1890s that James fully
experienced, perforce, the lonely act of consciousness as in itself
life-sustaining and, even more, as art-sustaining: including his so-
very-conscious awareness of the perils and corruptibility of pure
consciousness. What he calls 'abstraction' in Ibsen's characters is
one of the conditions – and one of the effects – of James's preter-
naturally aware, incandescently discriminating protagonists: his
Fleda Vetches and Maisies, the tragically self-defeating intensities

of the governess in 'The Turn of the Screw', the mandarin allocutions of Mrs Brook's *fin-de-siècle* courtiers, the manic hypothesis-spinning of the narrator in *The Sacred Fount*. And it came to be very close indeed to what Yeats celebrated, for his time, as 'a new poetry of essences'. This new focus on the forms of consciousness at the expense of direct contact with all the everyday actions and trappings of the world (Yeats's 'labour of life') is by 1900 well on the way to becoming the subject-matter in itself of James's fiction – and one of the keys to the onset of Modernism.

James and his consciousness confronted the arrival of the new century from a new home. Not least among the personal stresses of this decade of crisis and experiment had been his growing disenchantment with his London life – and even, after his unhappy visit to a tourist-infected Italy in 1894, with the life of foreign travel. In a touching analogy with the ups-and-downs of his writing career during these years, and even with the plots of some of his stories and novels, James began to search for a centre. De Vere Gardens had become too metropolitan, too encumbered by visitors and by the social pressures that he had welcomed so voraciously fifteen or twenty years before. In the summer and autumn after *Guy Domville* he discovered for a while a compensatory idyll in which he could work, in Torquay – 'this deliciously vacant and admirably blue-sea'd and densely-verdured and lovely-viewed warm corner of England . . . I would give a great deal not to be going back to London for the Winter – I yearn to spend it in the so simplified country.'[41] And in the summer of 1896, while finishing off *The Spoils of Poynton* in a rented house in Sussex, he discovered nearby Rye: the small, picturesque town which for James, in his years of alienation, and as he explored in fiction the concept of alienation more thoroughly than ever before, offered at last a warm centre, a home, and – in the words of the title of one of his fantasy-tales of this very year – his 'Great Good Place'. By September 1897 – not long after he had fled to Bournemouth to escape the horrors of London during Queen Victoria's Diamond Jubilee – the very house he had admired in Rye became available on a long lease (at £70 a year, including external repairs). James's discovery of Lamb House, its fortuitous availability, first to let and two years later to buy (for £2000), his glowing delight at its early-Georgian intimacy, its wainscoting, its mellowed red brick, its sheltered, well-stocked garden, its mulberry tree, the garden-room where he was to dictate his novels, the cobbled street outside, the charm of Rye itself – all of this is one of the happiest events in James's life, and a wonderful culmination to his lifetime of wandering, of renting, of indecision, and of general impermanence:

> I like this place – I like my little old house and little old garden. It blows, today, it blew all last night – great guns; and I hear them magnificently boom in my old chimneys. But my little house stands firm and gives me most refreshing assurance of the thickness of its walls and the depth of its foundations. After so many years of London flats and other fearsome fragilities, I feel quite housed in a feudal fortress.[42]

Despite the new 'fortress', his sense of alienation was far too profound to disappear either from his mental life or, in particular, from the subject-matter of his fiction even after (having sub-let De Vere Gardens) he entered into his settled years at Rye as a grand old man of letters (and of bicycling, and of well-planned walks, and advice about herbaceous borders, and much local gossip, and even some loquacious, inattentive presence at local cricket matches and golf clubs). But there is a new piquancy in the fact of his so dramatising the rootlessness and supersophisticated artifice of contemporary London life, in *The Awkward Age*, from the arcadian garden-room at Lamb House in the summer of 1898 – and at the same time making stiff terms with *Harper's Weekly* for the serial rights ($3000) in order to pay for the expenses of decorating, furnishing, and removing to Arcadia.

James's escape was partly a gesture against all he had come to dislike in England's *fin-de-siècle*: the loud, ranting hypocrisy of the Oscar Wilde trial in 1895, the increasingly strident jingoism of an Imperial England on the verge of humiliating itself in South Africa (an imperialistic and expansionist America sickened him just as much during the Spanish–American War of 1898), and a literary scene where there was little public place for himself, and where the floor seemed to be held by the raucous talents of a Rudyard Kipling, the schoolboy bombast of W. E. Henley, or the romantic glitter of Anthony Hope's *The Prisoner of Zenda* and *Rupert of Hentzau* (1894 and 1898). Lamb House proved to be no hermitage for James. Though certainly he had no wide reading public, his prestige among many of the literati was assured and his place at their (and at other) dinner-tables still in demand. He had got out of London (typically, he could not quite abandon it, and worried constantly about the provincialising effect of life in Rye), but his old social life in many respects transferred itself – by train, by taxi, eventually by private car – to its new venue (his letters abound with ponderously elaborate instructions to visitors about train-times, connections, and road-turnings). Old friends had died, and had swollen his altar of the dead through the 1890s. But now he was making many new friends – young male friends especially, with several of whom (Hendrik Andersen and Jocelyn Persse in particular) he was to engage in suggestively warm, even gushing correspondence. He became used to electric light, the telephone, cars, even on occasion the cinema. He ceremonially shaved off his beard (after nearly forty years) in 1900, as a gesture against the prospect of white hair and age. And as significant for his literary life as anything, from 1897 he gave up writing his fiction by hand, and dictated to a hired typist – first, a taciturn Scot, William MacAlpine, then the self-effacing Mary Weld, and later the formidable Theodora Bosanquet, who was to write up her secretarial experiences. If the stylised world of consciousness can be seen as James's developing subject in fiction through the late 1890s, the practice of dictation can only have encouraged his mental taste and his growing linguistic manner of introspective involution, and of self-qualifying, self-mirroring, self-proliferating sentences. The style fitted the mind – but in many ways the act of dictation fitted both: the novel became for him a matter of personal voice and not just of written signs. The Garden-Room at Lamb House, as the local townspeople testified, echoed each morning to the rolling sound of James's voice – above the accompanying click-click of the early Remington – spinning out the increasingly magisterial shapes of his consciousness. The voice had juggled with 'essences' and 'abstraction' in its *fin-de-siècle*, even Symbolist way – even its proto-Postmodern word-based way. But the concept of voice, far more than the concept of words as signs, always involves personality, and is rooted in a life. It was an appropriate, and in most ways a triumphant end to such a decade of hesitation and crisis that James's creative imagination, his actual spoken words, and his own home should at last have become one and the same: the mind's voice filling out a loved room.

5

Master and Modernist

In 1900 Henry James, at fifty-six, had sixteen years left to live. In the first four of these years he wrote, in stunningly quick succession, his three most elaborate, most demanding, and, most critics would say, his greatest novels: *The Ambassadors*, *The Wings of the Dove*, and *The Golden Bowl*. Some of his richest short stories, like 'The Beast in the Jungle' and 'The Jolly Corner' also appeared between 1900 and 1909, and several of his most thought-out critical articles on the other novelists who had marked out his reading life, like Balzac, Flaubert, George Sand, and Zola. After a momentous ten-month visit to America in 1904–5, he wrote *The American Scene*, the most inimitably Jamesian of all travel books and one that critics of our own time have come increasingly to regard, for its self-reflexive focus on consciousness and style, as a major experimental work in James's *oeuvre*. And as a more-or-less intended climax to his career, between 1905 and 1907 he devised and saw through the press the 24-volume New York Edition of the novels and tales he most wished to be represented by, a work of infinitely painstaking revision, page by page, and one that also produced the series of Prefaces that are now seen as a milestone in the development of modern criticism. He was by now very much a literary celebrity among the *cognoscenti* – the 'Master' to a small but increasing band of younger male friends and (just as Turgenev had been to him, thirty years before) to admiring, aspiring fellow-writers like Conrad, Ford Madox Ford, Edith Wharton, and Hugh Walpole. And despite the eventual, very late tailing-off of his actual fictional output, and the tendency for the external image of the Master to confirm him in some of his portentous mannerisms and whimsicalities to the point of self-caricature, what remains extraordinary is the evidence of unflagging mental energy and intellectual, professional curiosity. The unfixed traveller through life – the 'passionate pilgrim' – that his upbringing had made of him half-a-century before was still ever-restless, ever-ironising, ever-analysing. He wrote a notable letter in March 1914 at the age of seventy, a kind of credo of his creative restlessness, to his old and by now lugubriously disillusioned friend Henry Adams

– five months before Europe collapsed into the Armageddon of the First World War – which deserves to be quoted in full as an epigraph to this final period of James's career, and in many ways as an epigraph to his whole writing life:

My dear Henry.

I have your melancholy outpouring of the 7th, and I know not how better to acknowledge it than by the full recognition of its unmitigated blackness. *Of course* we are lone survivors, of course the past that was our lives is at the bottom of an abyss – if the abyss *has* any bottom; of course too there's no use talking unless one particularly *wants* to. But the purpose, almost, of my printed divagations [his second volume of autobiography] was to show you that one *can*, strange to say, still want to – or at least can behave as if one did. Behold me therefore so behaving – and apparently capable of continuing to do so. I still find my consciousness interesting – under *cultivation* of the interest. Cultivate it *with* me, dear Henry – that's what I hoped to make you do; to cultivate yours for all that it has in common with mine. *Why* mine yields an interest I don't know that I can tell you, but I don't challenge or quarrel with it – I encourage it with a ghastly grin. You see I still, in presence of life (or of what you deny to be such), have reactions – as many as possible – and the book I sent you is a proof of them. It's, I suppose, because I am that queer monster the artist, an obstinate finality, an inexhaustible sensibility. Hence the reactions – appearances, memories, many things go on playing upon it with consequences that I note and 'enjoy' (grim word!) noting. It all takes doing – and I *do*. I believe I shall do yet again – it is still an act of life. But you perform them still yourself – and I don't know what keeps me from calling your letter a charming one! There we are, and it's a blessing that you understand – I admit indeed alone – Your all-faithful

Henry James[1]

Happily ensconced in the quasi-rusticity of Lamb House – but inundated by visitors, and with increasingly frequent excursions to his room in the Reform Club just off Piccadilly – James continued to cultivate his consciousness with an intensity and a boldness that marked him out not only as 'that queer monster the artist' but also

as a specifically modern master. 'Consciousness' is perhaps the key
to it all – especially, as James indicates in the letter to Adams, the
deliberate *cultivation* of consciousness. The three great novels are
elaborate testimonies to the fullest verbalisation of consciousness in
their method, and explore the living nature and paradoxes of consciousness as their themes. That is, they are *about* consciousness
and they *embody* consciousness in a complex fusion of content and
style that in itself establishes their originality and authority as novels written on the very threshold of the modernist period. And
more than that: they seem to express, though in the form of fiction,
a mode of thinking, a mode of utterance, that was also part of
James's social and personal life. The consciousness in question, for
all its loneliness, is never truly isolated or alienated. The three late
novels, however extreme in their mandarin involutions of language,
are nevertheless paradoxically imbued with the texture and stresses
of social living, of personal relationships and feelings, and of cultural and historical awareness. While in some places they may seem
premonitory of the extreme world of the private consciousness as
in Virginia Woolf's *The Waves*, or even – at a stretch – the zany, self-
enclosed word-spinning of a Kafka or a Beckett, their distinctness
lies in the way they *engage* consciousness, and show different con-
sciousnesses as being engaged, within a still-graspable, still-resistant,
and desirable world. And in this they mirror James's own engagement of consciousness within his particular English (and American)
world of the years after 1900, his own inalienable awareness of
complicated family and of demanding friends, of his own past and
(no less) of his future, and his desire always not just to be conscious
but to communicate.

James's life at Rye is the period of his life most prolific of anecdote: the period of the so-called Legend of the Master.[2] We have
many more eye-witness (and ear-witness) accounts of his habits
and peculiarities than at any other time (many of them, like Ford
Madox Ford's or even Edith Wharton's, not to be accepted without
qualification and some distrust). His letters, if anything, become
longer, more revealing, and increasingly flavoursome, and his zest
for correspondence keeps up with his ability to make new friends,
new correspondents, new disciples up to his last years. The letters
– often many pages in length, sometimes handwritten, sometimes
dictated to his typist ('I can address you only through an embroi-
dered veil of sound. The sound is that of the admirable and expensive machine that I have just purchased for the purpose of bridging

our silences'[3]) – are themselves full testimonials to James's obsession with the fullest articulation and play (in every sense) of consciousness. Their language is often exaggerated and precious, even
fantastic in its highly mannered syntax, but it is above all expressive and malleable, a mode of full responsiveness, whether of affection or reproof or of self-encouragement, and the perfect medium
for the novelist dedicated to life and to the consciousness that for
him *made* life. For example, in this perfectly typical (handwritten)
letter of November 1902, to his friend Morton Fullerton (expatri-
ated American journalist and playboy, lover of Edith Wharton –
among many others – and just possibly the original hint for Merton
Densher in *The Wings of the Dove*), James manages, as always when
at his best, to convey the sense of a *relationship*, of something still
flowing between his own mind and the image of another person,
and also, within that sensitive communicative act, the sense of himself as being of interest to himself:

My very dear Fullerton,

... your beautiful letter [apparently concerning *The Wings of
the Dove*, just published] deeply delights and moves me – being
the most beautiful, I really think, I ever received from *any* man:
pervaded as it is by an exquisite intelligence (ineffable luxury!) as
well as by the penetrating cordial of affection. Admirable, inspir-
ing, inflaming, the sympathy with which you read me. Well, I
deserve it too, I can say to *you*; for I do write from out of the deep
and dire complexity of that sentient 'machine' [presumably an
allusion to identity or selfhood] on which you put your unerring
finger and to be encased in which *is* to be, *à toute heure* and
forever, mortally isolated. But I am less so from your very naming of it to me – naming of your sense of it; which gives me the
chance to say to you 'Think of me so, *know* me so, always, and
you will think of me tenderly'. In short, for your lucid reflection
of, disengagement of a reponse to, the soul, as it were, of my *too*-
embodied book, I seize you gratefully fast, I hold you supremely
close. You absolutely add to my wish, and to my need, to lead
the life of – whatever I may call it! – my genius. And I *shall*, I feel,
somehow, while there's a rag left of me. Largely thanks to you.[4]

The style is one full of decorative playfulness as well as intelligence,
and frequently loses its best effect of communication by succumbing

to its never-too-distant narcissism – that greatest peril of any self-cultivating consciousness. When he replies to another letter of praise – this time to Max Beerbohm, in December 1908 – the whimsical self-regard and the syntactical delaying-tactics become self-parodying (playing, that is, straight into Max's hands as a supreme caricaturist). But even here there is still the fascinating effect of the writer *in* his words, the novelist only half off-duty, taking delight in the very act of word-spinning, and in varying, quite sensuously as well as intellectually, the dynamics of his sentences:

My dear Max Beerbohm,

I won't say in acknowledgement of your beautiful letter that it's exactly the sort of letter I like best to receive, because that would sound as if I had *data* for generalizing – which I haven't and therefore I can only go so far as to say that if it belonged to a class, or weren't a mere remarkable individual, I *should* rank it with the type supremely gratifying. On its mere lonely independent merits it appeals to me intimately and exquisitely, and I can only gather myself in and up, arching and presenting my not inconsiderable back – a back, as who should say, offered for any further stray scratching and patting of that delightful kind. I can bear wounds and fell smitings (so far as I have been ever honoured with such – and indeed life smites us on the whole enough, taking one thing with another) better than expressive gentleness of touch; so you must imagine me for a little while quite prostrate and overcome with the force of your good words. But I shall recover, when they have really sunk in – and then be not only the 'better', but the more nimble and artful and alert by what they will have done for me. You had, and you obeyed, a very generous and humane inspiration; it charms me to think – or rather so authentically to know, that my (I confess) ambitious Muse does work upon you; it really helps me to believe in her the more myself – by which I am really very gratefully yours

Henry James[5]

But finally, as an instance of how James's consciousness, in the art of letter-writing, could also be focused quite differently, quite tightly and unselfregardingly, on his correspondent, and could direct its baroque imagery and its mannerisms to the helpful evocation of a situation (as in a novel), here is part of a letter of October 1908 to Edith Wharton, in deep trouble with her marriage:

My very dear Friend.

... I am deeply distressed at the situation you describe and as to which my power to suggest or enlighten now quite miserably fails me. I move in darkness; I rack my brain; I gnash my teeth; I don't pretend to understand or to imagine. And yet incredibly to you doubtless – I am still moved to say 'Don't *conclude!*' Some light will *still* absolutely come to you – I believe – though I can't pretend to say what it conceivably may be. Anything is more credible – conceivable – than a mere inhuman *plan*. A great trouble, an infinite worry or a situation of the last anxiety or uncertainty are conceivable – though I don't see that such things, I admit, can explain *all*. Only sit tight yourself *and go through the movements of life*. That keeps up our connection with life – I mean of the immediate and apparent life; behind which, all the while, the deeper and darker and the unapparent, in which things *really* happen to us, learns, under that hygiene, to stay in its place. Let it get out of its place and it swamps the scene; besides which its place, God knows, is enough for it! Live it all through, every inch of it – out of it something valuable will come – but live it ever so quietly; and – *je maintiens mon dire* – waitingly! I have had but that one letter, of weeks ago – and there are *kinds* of news I can't ask for ...

Believe meanwhile and always in the aboundingly tender friendship – the understanding, the participation, the *princely* (though I say it who shouldn't) hospitality of spirit and soul of yours more than ever

Henry James[6]

Edith Wharton with her plentiful provision of motor-cars, houses in France, social gossip, and fellow-practitioner's discussion (from 1905, with *The House of Mirth*, she was a highly successful practitioner), was only one – though probably the most overwhelming one – of the throng of visitors who at times seemed to be laying siege to Lamb House. The throng included Ford Madox Hueffer (later Ford), Edmund Gosse, Wendell Holmes, H. G. Wells, George Gissing, Stephen Crane, Joseph Conrad (with 'wife, baby and trap and pony'), his favourite niece and nephew Peggy and Billy James, Bernard Shaw, Olivia Garnett, the passionately beloved Hendrik Andersen and Jocelyn Persse, Hugh Walpole, A. C. Benson, Sydney Waterlow, and E. M. Forster (once only: 'Your name's Moore', James said to Forster, kindly but not quite accurately). Few other novelists of any era can have attracted quite so much sustained visiting – such ringings at the doorbell, by arrangement or otherwise – from friends, acquaintances, family, and even hopeful strangers. James of course complained at the inroads on his writing time, and on his funds for housekeeping – which were still very dependent, year by year, on his writing: his typical annual earnings being about £1000 at this time (a peak of $9500 in 1905, a low of $997 in 1908), supplemented by income from American property that reverted to him after the death of Alice ranging from about $1500 to $3500 – but it is significant that on the whole he brought the incursions, as well as the no less frequent excursions, on himself. His warnings about the loneliness of the writer's position, and, more interestingly, about essential loneliness as being 'the deepest thing' about himself as a person, must always be seen against the fact that James sent out invitations as frequently and as fulsomely as he complained about being over-visited: the *need* to be visited, to be social, to talk and talk, being perhaps no contradiction of essential inner loneliness. At any rate, despite managing to keep reasonably sacrosanct his working period of 10 until 1.45, James's life at Rye (and out of Rye) was at least as completely imbued with conversation, anecdotes, and encounters as it had ever been – and therefore his consciousness as a novelist and critic as significantly steeped as ever in the sense of other people, their needs and entanglements, their follies and their affection, their marriages and affairs, their writing plans, their political involvements, their disasters and betrayals. He week-ended with the Astors at Cliveden, Lady Lovelace at Ockham, had tea with the Ranee of Sarawak, dined with Lord Curzon and the Humphry Wards, called on Lady Ottoline Morrell and Lady Gregory, admired the 'crushed strawberry glow' of Vanessa Bell sitting on his lawn (her sister Virginia, 'facially most fair', 'on a near hilltop, writes reviews for the *Times*'), boomed briefly at a youthful Ezra Pound, and was drawn into Margot Asquith's lunches (with her husband, the Prime Minister) where he shared one bad-tempered occasion with Winston Churchill.

One six-week period in 1909, when he was sixty-six, gives some idea of the sheer motion of James's life, and its unimaginable congestion of social contact, endless eating, and (elaborate) conversation. On 4 June he dined in London with Edith Wharton and Morton Fullerton, then spent three days near Windsor, until the 7th, with Howard Sturgis and others. On the 9th he lunched in company and went to the theatre in the evening; on the 10th had two afternoon visitors. From the 11th to the 14th he was in Cambridge at the invitation of a group of young admirers, where he met Geoffrey Keynes and John Maynard Keynes, Sydney Cockerell, Desmond MacCarthy, Francis Cornford, and – most memorably and infatuatingly of all – Rupert Brooke; attended a concert, visited a gallery, went punting, and – of course – talked. On the 15th he dined with Edith Wharton's sister-in-law, and on the 16th with Edith Wharton herself, at Lady St. Helier's. On the 17th he had tea with Mrs Humphry Ward and dined out in company at the Carlton Club; on the 18th lunch at the Ritz and two other calls; on the 19th an exhibition and then dinner and the theatre with friends; on the 20th to Howard Sturgis at Windsor; on the 21st lunch with Hugh Walpole and an evening call on a friend; on the 22nd dinner out; on the 23rd dinner with Edith Wharton; two calls on the 24th; to Windsor again on the 26th; lunch, out of London, with Mrs Humphry Ward on the 27th; a trip to Salisbury and Dorchester on the 28th; dinner at the St. James's with an editor on the 29th; lunch (at the Athenaeum) and dinner out with friends on the 30th. He left London (presumably a little jaded) for Rye on July 6th, but returned to London on the 9th (tea out, then the theatre), getting back to Rye on the 10th in time to welcome Jocelyn Persse for the week-end. Mrs Wharton and Fullerton (in the thick of their affair) followed on the 12th, to stay the night. On the 13th he had lunch in Eastbourne with Jonathan Sturges, stayed at Chichester, had lunch next day in Petworth, tea in Brighton, came home; then immediately motored on the 15th with the two lovers to Folkestone and Canterbury. 'I sneak back here more dead than alive', James understandably complained to Howard Sturgis on the 16th – but then on the 17th there was a garden-party, and Hugh Walpole arrived for a few days on the 19th. And all this by a man who often wrote whimsically and ruefully of living the life of a rustic hermit – but who more often had good cause, as here, to bewail the cost of cultivating, so socially, the interest of his creative consciousness.

James as Master and Modernist – the James of the three late, great novels, the ponderous, circumlocutory James of legend and anecdote, the James of Lamb House and the Reform Club and then, since he had managed to dispose of De Vere Gardens and needed a winter base in London, the James also from January 1913 of Carlyle Mansions, Cheyne Walk, in Chelsea – these various Jameses of the twentieth century had arrived at one definite style: one of the most unmistakeable styles of living, writing, and talking of any novelist in the language. The personal uncertainties and the strained experimentation in mode of the 1890s had given way to a comparative security and social rhythm in his private life and, equally, to a literary style of ineffable elaboration and (at best) subtlety that could never be confused for a moment – or for one many-claused sentence – with that of any of his contemporaries. The profoundly searching eyes – which so many of his visitors described with awe – and the great domed head perched slightly to one side in continually ironic appraisal bespoke an imaginative awareness of epic dimensions. To everyone who knew him the personality seemed totally in accord with, and even to necessitate, the burgeoning qualifiers, the extended cadences and postponements, the prolonged, rumbling search for the *mot juste*, of his conversation. There has rarely been a better example of the style being the man – and of the style being the essential outlook on the world, both social and personal. If James in the twentieth century – building, naturally, on all that went before in his career and in his psyche – is a writer, even *the* writer, of consciousness-in-action, then his love of personal and social relationships, his theory of the novel as being based precisely on interrelationships and aspects, his very sentences and metaphors, written or spoken, and the themes and devices of *The Ambassadors*, *The Wings of the Dove*, and *The Golden Bowl* are all as one in their enactment of that drama of consciousness and of the proliferating interrelationships that a full consciousness both perceives and creates. His conversation, so often parodied in his own day, was at its best the style of the novels transposed to the table and the drawing-room – as can be deduced from this fine description of his talk by A. C. Benson, littérateur, son of the Archbishop of Canterbury, and one of the most regular young *habitués* of Lamb House:

> The extreme and almost tantalizing charm of his talk lay not only in his quick transitions, his exquisite touches of humour and irony, the width and force of his sympathy, the range of his intelligence, but in the fact that the whole process of his thought, the qualifications, the resumptions, the interlineations, were laid bare. The beautiful sentences, so finished, so deliberate, shaped themselves

audibly upon the air. It was like being present at the actual construction of a little palace of thought, of improvised yet perfect
design. The manner was not difficult to imitate: the slow accu-
mulation of detail, the widening sweep, the interjection of grotesque and emphatic images, the studied exaggerations; but what
could not be copied was the firmness of the whole conception.
He never strayed loosely, as most voluble talkers do, from subject to subject. The *motif* was precisely enunciated, revised, elon-
gated, improved upon, enriched, but it was always, so to speak,
strictly contrapuntal. He dealt with the case and nothing but the
case; he completed it, dissected it, rounded it off. It was done
with much deliberation and even with both repetition and hesitation. But it was not only irresistibly beautiful, it was by far the
richest species of intellectual performance that I have ever been
privileged to hear.[7]

The fact that James relied so heavily on dictation to a typist from
1897 onwards is also crucial – and again something unique in the
history of the modern novel. The habit came to him by the accident
of a rheumatic wrist, but clearly no accident could have been better
designed to suit a mode of reflection already tending strongly in
the direction of the ruminative, the proliferative, the 'cultivation', in
short, of consciousness. James created his fiction, and earned his
living, no longer just by the pen but by the mouth and the ear,
instruments intimately close to the mind and its processes. If he
liked society around him – and also feared it and fled from it – so
the act of dictation must have served as a kind of benign concentration of 'social' living and communicating: a dialogue and an
externalised system of verbal 'relationships' reduced perfectly to
the one active participant – 'dictator' in both senses of the word.
James's three successive secretaries – William MacAlpine, then Mary
Weld in 1901, and from 1907 Theodora Bosanquet – were in their
way the perfect interlocutor: not quite silent, by the perpetual clicking of their machine and their occasional question, not quite invisible, by their felt presence and their differing personalities (including
the onus of accommodating them on his travels), but nevertheless
reduced (or expanded?) to being mirrors of the Master's acts of
expression and analysis: a humanised *tabula rasa*. According to Miss
Bosanquet, James preferred his typists to be 'without a mind', and
certainly not – as apparently had occasionally happened – to dare
suggest a word when he paused and rumbled in search of one. The

dour silence of his first typist, MacAlpine, was on the other hand almost excessive. One anecdote has it that James was disconcerted, as he dictated 'The Turn of the Screw', to notice not the slightest emotion from MacAlpine in reponse to any of that story's scenes of terror ('I would dictate some phrase that I thought was blood-curdling; he would quietly take this down, look up at me and in a dry voice say, "What next?"'[8]). Theodora Bosanquet's booklet, *Henry James at Work*, published in 1924, gives the fullest description: his spelling out aloud of any difficult word, explaining any obscure allusion, and giving every punctuation point except occasionally a full stop – all without losing the flow of his invention. He would plan parts of a novel by 'thinking aloud' to the typist in advance, to be recorded as a kind of scenario; and again during difficult patches in the actual composition. But the main act of composition was done from no directly available draft, though often after the reading and possible mental recasting of the previous day's dicta-tion. Miss Bosanquet gives this account of James at work – probably on his autobiographical volumes in 1911, but presumably giving an adequate enough image of James when he dictated the last part of *The Ambassadors* and the whole of *The Wings of the Dove* and *The Golden Bowl* to the neat and unflappable Mary Weld a decade earlier:

> Each morning, after reading over the pages written the day be-fore, he would settle down in a chair for an hour or so of con-scious effort. Then, lifted on a rising tide of inspiration, he would get up and pace up and down the room, sounding out the peri-ods in tones of resonant assurance. At such times he was beyond reach of irrelevant sounds or sights. Hosts of cats – a tribe he usually routed with shouts of execration – might wail ouside the window, phalanxes of motor-cars bearing dreaded visitors might hoot at the door. He heard nothing of them. The only thing that could arrest his progress was the escape of the word he wanted to use. When that had vanished he broke off the rhythmic pacing and made his way to a chimney-piece or book-case tall enough to support his elbows while he rested his head in his hands and audibly pursued the fugitive.[9]

Rich in his possession of a new style and a new-old voice, rich, even over-rich, in his friends and acquaintance, rich in his confident possession of Lamb House, rich in his freshly confident response to the challenge of a new century, James, by a recognisable quirk of human nature, chose to apply these novelties to the oldest theme in his literary repertoire – the American in Europe – in all three of the major novels by which he marked his final phase. It was as though in this way, by linking what was so new with what was so old – the new milieu of Conrad, Wells, and Shaw, even the coming milieu of Woolf, Forster, and Joyce, with his older world of Turgenev, Balzac, and Emerson – he instinctively chose to define the continuity and the rounding-off of his career. Lambert Strether in *The Ambassadors*, confronting the ambiguously glittering delights of Paris after his fifty-five years of New England probity, is in a clear line of descent from Rowland Mallett of *Roderick Hudson* and above all Christopher Newman of *The American*. And Europe, in the person of the successful, worldly artist Gloriani (who reappears from *Roderick Hudson*), and more importantly in the alluring figure of Madame de Vionnet (a profounder, more sensual Claire de Cintré, from *The American*), has the same old capacity to bedazzle then disillusion the naive idealism of the transatlantic pilgrim. In *The Wings of the Dove* and *The Golden Bowl* James's old theme of the American *ingénue* abroad – in this case Milly Theale and Maggie Verver, empowered by their millions and their looks – becomes a vehicle for all his passionate nostalgia for the image of Minny Temple, dead for thirty years, and brings together in a poetic unity his capacity to identify with such innocence and to lament its necessitated exposure to betrayal. But what is new in all three books is the participation of the reader in such dramas of reawakening and of loss through a deep immersion in the slowly unfolding, slowly implicating texture of each scene's inmost nuances, each mental impression, each extended metaphor's possibilities of suggestion, each uncoiling sentence's cadences of contradiction, ornament, and new knowledge. James's speaking and dictating style may have been the man; but for these late three novels their style is the fiction itself. Consciousness has become a full-scale adventure: often ruefully comic in the case of *The Ambassadors*, almost entirely sombre or tragic in the other two. And the Jamesian adventure, filtered through such style, has become a new singular fusion of American and Romantic, realist and fantasist, traditionalist and high modernist.

On the brink of his particular adventure, Lambert Strether is seated on a public chair in the Luxembourg Gardens, brooding Jamesianly over his life of humdrum restraint and widowerhood, his memories of the Paris of his youth, and over the recent experiences that the

opening hundred pages of the novel have made us share: anxiety
about his assigned New England duty to detach a young country-
man, Chad, from the fleshpots of Paris, anxiety about his relationship with the young man's widowed mother, the formidable Mrs
Newsome, anxiety mixed with pleasure at the reinitiation into the
selfish, aesthetic pleasures of Europe he has just sustained at the
hands of Maria Gostrey in England – that is, a whole tissue of
mental experience concerning relationships and motives, and above
all the relationship between the private, shy, observing self, on his
park chair, and the larger world of the past, of present Paris, and
of his own future:

> His greatest uneasiness seemed to peep at him out of the immin-
> ent impression that almost any acceptance of Paris might give
> one's authority away. It hung before him this morning, the vast
> bright Babylon, like some huge iridescent object, a jewel brilliant
> and hard, in which parts were not to be discriminated nor differ-
> ences comfortably marked. It twinkled and trembled and melted
> together, and what seemed all surface one moment seemed all
> depth the next. It was a place of which, unmistakeably, Chad was
> fond; wherefore if he, Strether, should like it too much, what on
> earth, with such a bond, would become of either of them? It all
> depended of course – which was a gleam of light – on how the
> 'too much' was measured; though indeed our friend fairly felt,
> while he prolonged the meditation I describe, that for himself
> even already a certain measure had been reached. It will have
> been sufficiently seen that he was not a man to neglect any good
> chance for reflexion. Was it at all possible for instance to like
> Paris enough without liking it too much? He luckily however
> hadn't promised Mrs Newsome not to like it at all. He was ready
> to recognize at this stage that such an engagement *would* have
> tied his hands. The Luxembourg Gardens were incontestably just
> so adorable at this hour by reason – in addition to their intrinsic
> charm – of his not having taken it. The only engagement he had
> taken, when he looked the thing in the face, was to do what he
> reasonably could.[10]

The writing brings together the external scene and the mental impressions of that scene, which are in turn totally blended with other
spreading internal impressions and reflections. Hard image and

abstract thought are in continual interplay: an 'uneasiness' is personified into something that 'seemed to peep', a measurement of 'too much' becomes 'a gleam of light', and an 'engagement' becomes something that 'tied the hands'. Paris is a Babylon and a jewel, the facets of which become ambiguous nuances of value, and surfaces become interchangeable with depths; and soon liking 'enough' becomes 'liking too much'. Strether's mind speculates on a possible unthinkable 'bond' with Chad. Negations flutter through the paragraph with the strange effect of being positives: 'parts' and 'differences' are refreshingly '*not* to be discriminated'; Strether is *not* someone *not* to reflect; it is lucky *not* to have promised *not* to like; and the Gardens are 'adorable' by reason of his *not* having so promised. We are *in* Strether's impressions and anxieties, yet simultaneously – as throughout the novel – we are *outside* him, surprisingly alongside a revealed narratorial 'I' in the process of describing him. 'Process', in fact, is what it all is: a revealed process of complicated thought and feeling, a process of external analysis *beside* the internal process, a revealed play of intelligence and personal charm, a process of plot, a moving bond, an incipient relationship, all of which creates the interest and dynamics of narrative. 'What on earth, with such a bond, would become of either of them?' becomes almost an epigraph, a novel's plot in self-conscious miniature.

Detachable from the 'process' to some degree, there stand out vivid scenes, as vivid as in James's realist or theatrical modes – Strether in the street seeing a male figure on Chad's alluringly lofty balcony who is interestingly not Chad himself; Strether urging Little Bilham in Gloriani's garden to 'live' all he can (here was the 'germ' of the novel's conception, an anecdote given to James about the middle-aged Howells in Paris, similarly bedazzled in Whistler's garden); Strether discovering Chad and Madame de Vionnet boating together in the French countryside, and flagrantly not in that high, chivalric 'bond' of innocence that he had naively and idealistically imagined for them; Strether, half-infatuated, visiting the soon-to-be-abandoned Madame de Vionnet in her apartments. And of course the themes and the perceived emotions of the novel, too, partly rise above their articulation-within-process, as the interpreting mind always requires: the yearning to make up for the lost chance in life, the imaginative deprivation – and farcicality – of being a provincial or a moral authoritarian, the pathos of the selfless woman in love with the unself-sacrificing young man, the question of whether such a woman is quite 'selfless' anyway, the quandary of the self-distrusting older man too old to re-make himself, the image of the world as one vast, adorable, totally untrustworthy Babylon. But to detach scene or idea from the living mesh of James's language is extremely difficult to do – more difficult, more disruptive, more *cancelling* of effect, than probably in any other English novel, including James's, up to this date (with the possible exception, incongruously, of *Tristram Shandy*). And the registered effect of *process* – a fiction-making process that pulls us in, yet also draws attention to all its devices and to its central motor of a nuance-capturing, image-making intelligence – remains the most vital characteristic of these three novels, and the one that is most revolutionary and modernist.

Momentarily extractable from *The Wings of the Dove*, similarly, is a tale, even a starkly melodramatic tale (as in earlier James), of two moneyless lovers, Merton Densher and Kate Croy, plotting elaborately that the rich, fatally-ill heiress, Milly Theale, might be enticed into falling in love with Densher, whom she will then plentifully endow before conveniently dying – but whose dormant spiritual sense she awakens by her own dove-like sacrificial quality, especially after she learns of the plot, leaving the two plotting lovers psychologically and morally too separated ever to marry on Densher's inheritance. And extractable, too, are the large-scale Jamesian patterns of a corrupt, attractive worldliness (Kate Croy's) set against an unworldly, or less worldly, inner light (Milly's); of male passivity and moral drifting (Densher's) set against a strong, decisive, female will (Kate's); and, not least, helpless American innocence (Milly's) learning, just a little and too late, the manipulative skills of a more fallen, more social and more mannered world (Lancaster Gate). But again, the uniqueness of the novel, and its startlingly modern inwardness and elliptical indirectness, are achieved in the texture and processes of its language – which fuses idea, mood, scene, psychological insight, a sense of society, and the poetry of imagery into the one Jamesian medium. Milly, beginning – like Strether – to respond excitedly to the new demands on her consciousness of a richer, more dangerous world around her in London, is dining, with her companion Susan Stringham, at her new friend's, Mrs Lowder's, where dinner-party trivia and realistic social nuances are transposed into felt mental events, and where abstractions ('excursions', 'being possible', 'appearances', 'phenomena', 'alternative', 'whatever it was', 'a success', 'idea of the thing') take on the near-tangibility of solid counters in a sensuous 'process', aided by the intermittent baroque figures of speech ('plashes of a low thick tide', 'a wave or two of her wings'):

> These were immense excursions for the spirit of a young person at Mrs Lowder's mere dinner-party; but what was so significant and so admonitory as the fact of their being possible? What could they have been but just a part, already, of the crowded consciousness? And it was just a part likewise that while plates were changed and dishes presented and periods in the banquet marked; while appearances insisted and phenomena multiplied and words reached her from here and there like plashes of a slow thick tide; while Mrs Lowder grew somehow more stout and more instituted and Susie, at her distance and in comparison, more thinly improvised and more different – different, that is, from every one and every thing: it was just a part that while this process went forward our young lady alighted, came back, taking up her destiny again as if she had been able by a wave or two of her wings to place herself briefly in sight of an alternative to it. Whatever it was it had showed in this brief interval as better than the alternative; and it now presented itself altogether in the image and in the place in which she had left it. The image was that of her being, as Lord Mark had declared, a success. This depended more or less of course on his idea of the thing – into which at present, however, she wouldn't go.[11]

Even in the small phrase, 'the crowded consciousness', we have a pointer to James's strange alchemy throughout the passage, and therefore throughout the novel – an alchemy of transposition, by which the abstract becomes physical, and the physical becomes abstract, and the old Jamesian principle of 'conversion' reaches its utmost point – perhaps its *ne plus ultra* – of development.

Consciousness is power – though not all of power. Milly gains new power over others, especially over the dangling Densher, by her heightened awareness of the human scene, and her new awareness of her own mortality. But her money is also a realistic source of her power over others (as well as of her vulnerability to *their* power of cupidity); and Kate Croy has a sexual power over Densher and a power of will that are not fully transposed into consciousness – money and sexuality always, in James, retaining a power that is partly outside of the mind and the mind's style. The dove, Milly, becomes more conscious; but the splendid bird of prey, Kate, remains

tensely gathered around her instincts – and therefore less available
by far to the reader in the novel's performance of consciousness. All
of James's old fascination with the phenomena of power – social,
sexual, financial, aesthetic – finds new utterance in the strange, elliptical power games that throb suggestively in the drawing-rooms,
the palazzi, the country-houses, the hansom-cabs of *The Wings of the
Dove* and *The Golden Bowl*. Olive Chancellor fixated on Verena, the
obsessed editor robbing and bribing his way towards the treasure-
trove of the Aspern papers, even Miriam Rooth pouring all her raw
energies into the art of the stage, and the cool violence and ambitions of a Paul Muniment or his fellow-anarchists, all of these power-
seekers and power-manipulators underlie the weirdly effective,
culminating imagery of Kate as a pacing panther, of Charlotte Stant
with her neck looped in a silver noose, all the oppressive inter-
changes of glances across a crowded room or St Mark's Square, a
gazed-at string of pearls, a game of cards in a room watched from
a terrace outside, something released from a cage, an image of a
head borne past on a pike, above all the sense of waiting, waiting,
for a storm to break, for an ivory pagoda seen in a dream to give
back a sound at your knock, a husband to come back late from a
dubious assignation. It is by Maggie Verver's cultivation of consciousness in *The Golden Bowl* that she comes finally to worldly
power and simultaneously to a kind of spiritual abasement: new
consciousness of her husband the Prince's infidelity with her friend
and stepmother, Charlotte Stant, consciousness of his desire nevertheless to be readmitted to her love without humiliation, consciousness of her father's possible knowledge of the affair that he will
never reveal, and consciousness of her own capacity at last to hold
all the strings, either to preserve or to rupture forever the flawed
golden bowl of their two-way, three-way, four-way marriage. Maggie
at last *knows*: her consciousness is crammed with the money-laden,
betrayal-laden, desire-laden awareness of the whole novel. 'Knowledge', like those abstract nouns in *The Ambassadors*, has become a
tangible weight in the complex relationship of the four and in their
carefully evasive conversations. Knowledge is something to be
negotiated wordlessly, wielded, used as a threat, as a promise, as
a bearer of passion, to be talked around, built into a new and
fluctuating, perhaps even damnable, bond between all of them.
'Fluctuation' is perhaps the essence of it, both in style and content
– certainly the essence of the theatrically tense and elliptical exchanges that flash between them. For example, Maggie here is at

last having it out with her husband over his pre-marital, and now adulterously continuing, affair with Charlotte, her old friend, whom Maggie has too cleverly married off, for mutual convenience, to her widowed father:

> The assurance of [the Prince's] speech, she could note, quite held up its head in him; his eyes met her own so for the declaration that it was as if something cold and momentarily unimaginable breathed upon her, from afar off, out of his strange consistency. She kept her direction still however under that. 'Oh the thing I've known best of all is that you've never wanted together to offend us. You've wanted quite intensely not to, and the precautions you've had to take for it have been for a long time one of the strongest of my impressions. That, I think,' she added, 'is the way I've best known.'
>
> ' "Known"?' he repeated after a moment.
>
> 'Known. Known that you were older friends, and so much more intimate ones, than I had any reason to suppose when we married. Known there were things that hadn't been told me – and that gave their meaning little by little to other things that were before me.'
>
> 'Would they have made a difference in the matter of our marriage', the Prince presently asked, 'if you had known them?'
>
> She took her time to think. 'I grant you not – in the matter of ours.' And then as he again fixed her with his hard yearning, which he couldn't keep down: 'The question is so much bigger than that. You see how much what I know makes of it for me.' That was what acted on him, this iteration of her knowledge, into the question of the validity of the various bearings of which he couldn't on the spot trust himself to pretend in any high way to go. What her claim, as she made it, represented for him – that he couldn't help betraying if only as a consequence of the effect of the word itself, her repeated distinct 'know, know', on his nerves. She was capable of being sorry for his nerves at a time when he should need them for dining out, pompously, rather responsibly, without his heart in it; yet she wasn't to let that prevent her using, with all economy, so precious a chance for supreme clearness. 'I didn't force this upon you, you must recollect, and it probably wouldn't have happened for you if you hadn't come in.'
>
> 'Ah', said the Prince, 'I was liable to come in, you know.'

'I didn't think you were this evening.'

'And why not?'

'Well', she answered, 'you have many liabilities – of different
sorts.' With which she recalled what she had said to Fanny
Assingham. 'And then you're so deep'.

It produced in his features, despite his control of them, one of
those quick plays of expression, the shade of a grimace, that testified as nothing else did to his race. 'It's you, cara, who are
deep.'[12]

It is striking how the act of analysis and the hyperintelligent discrimination of shades in these three characteristic extracts from the
three late masterpieces become imbued with theatrical gesture,
colourful imagery, and intuitive silences. The later style perpetually
fluctuates between and across categories – being to that degree the
ultimate development of the earlier Jamesian destabilization of the
categorical by irony (this being the very theme of 'Daisy Miller').
This, again, is at the heart of the style's modernity: it systematically
baffles our traditional notions of ordered discourse, and even of
literary genre, and provides a new revelation of the process-nature
of experience and of the capacity of a self-conscious literary mode
to capture it. The very early novels moved, in their own processes,
between the Romantic and the *comédie de moeurs*, the American and
the European, between Hawthorne and Jane Austen. The middle-
period novels, from *The Bostonians* to *The Tragic Muse*, crossed
boundaries, too, in their heavily-freighted naturalism that was always interspersed with the lyrical and the theatrical. And the experimental novels of the nineties oscillated between symbolic,
psychological, tragic, realist-comic, and fantasy modes – between
Maeterlinck, Ibsen, and Oscar Wilde – the end-product, however,
being purely Jamesian. The style of the major three novels of 1902–
4 is a far steadier and more confident medium. It moves at a daunt-
ingly slow pace, no imaginable nuance of event and situation being
left unturned. It takes a more prolonged pleasure in the sound of
its own voice, the rise and fall and displacement of its clauses, the
baroque metaphors for its more crepuscular insights, the sudden
bright shrewdnesses. But its inner vitality comes from its being
both new and old. It is a late style, and a successful late style, in so
far as it subsumes many features of the early styles, and builds its
self-regarding confidence, its poetic grasp of its human material,
on the medium of linguistic play, perpetual discrimination, and

fluidity that had determined James's individuality as a writer from the very beginning. But quite simply – or complexly, rather – it is more so: more linguistically adventurous (at times sportive), more concentratedly discriminating, more hyperscrupulously fluid and demanding: a style perfectly made, one might think, for its new century of revolutionary experimentalism, and one that in certain respects set a warning limit to modernism before modernism had properly begun.

When James completed *The Golden Bowl* in August, 1904, Conrad, at the height of his powers, had just published *Nostromo*; in the same month Joyce published the first story of *Dubliners*, and had written much of *Stephen Hero*; also in August, Forster published his first short story and was working on both *Where Angels Fear to Tread* and *A Room with a View* (and noting in his diary, 'Shall read a little "Wings of the Dove"'): and in that year, Virginia Woolf published her first review (for *The Guardian*). Gertrude Stein (having been a student of William James at Harvard) had published her first poem, on her discovery of Cézanne, and was writing *Three Lives* in Paris; and Ezra Pound, still a college student, was writing poems, toying with Provencal, and (or so he claimed later in life) already planning *The Cantos*. Proust, having written one novel, was about to begin the first version of *À la Recherche*; Einstein, in Bern, was about to publish his first revolutionary articles on physics (in 1905) and had already sketched out much of his Relativity Theory; and Picasso, just established in Paris, had left his Blue for his Rose period, and would soon meet Matisse at Gertrude Stein's. It would be artificial to attempt to 'place' the author of *The Golden Bowl* (who was also the author of *Roderick Hudson*, we must remember, published in 1874) among these modernists by any detailed comparison of theme and technique that ignored his individuality – or for that matter ignored the individuality and uniqueness of each of those other modern masters. A roll-call of great names remains merely a reductive roll-call, and is a great breeder of clichés. Nevertheless certain very general traits do seem to characterize the James of the late novels as a writer of his time, and of the three great decades of modernism to come.

In particular, the late style, for all its representational and mimetic grasp, is so inward in its direction, and so full of the effect of an investigative mentality at work, tunnelling fathoms deep beneath each slight social banality and elaborating the faintest tendrils of situations, that our sense of the everyday structure of life is fundamentally shaken. To follow James all the way into Strether's ramifying hesitations and revelations in Paris about how best to live – whether by the ruthless, aesthetic way of Gloriani, or by the Puritan way of Woollett, Massachusetts, or by the (perhaps) noble, sacrificial way of Madame de Vionnet, or by the way of his own maturing imagination that seems more and more to embrace the ideal, the real, and the self-defeating in one heroic (and mock-heroic) complexity – is to emerge with a somewhat dazed perception that the human personality is being as radically re-presented by James as by Freud, contemporaneously, in his quite other way, or as by Proust or Joyce or Woolf in their own fictions, their own many-layered languages. Kate's and Densher's passionate conspiracy and all the book's other figures-in-action, figures-in-language have, over the 500 pages of *The Wings of the Dove*, shaken to the roots our conception of many things: our conception of the practical will, our conception of Machiavellian daring, of sexual possessiveness, of corrupted courage, of moral passivity, of pushy vulgarity, of elegantly dishonest kindness, of manipulative innocence, of conniving loyalty, of desire, of fear, of death, of loneliness, of sense of kinship, of guilt, of worship, of power in many forms. So that at the end, after Milly's death in Venice has sent out its beatific yet destructive ripples of effect, the book's last words, Kate's self-betraying dismissal of her lover Densher, 'We shall never be again as we were', speak also for the astonished (and rather exhausted) reader.

It is of the essence of modernism not only to break the mould of the old and reveal the new – the Cubist face that combined profile and full-face, Schoenberg's twelve-tone scale, Joyce's encyclopaedic word-play and myth-play, Einstein's total re-drawing of time and space – but, in the realm of art at least, to startle its audience into feeling the full personal inwardness of that revelation and change: into perceiving that they, too, will never be again as they were. It was D. H. Lawrence, writing in 1914, who spoke boldly of having broken 'the old stable ego of the character' in his fiction, and of having penetrated to 'another ego, according to whose action the individual is unrecognizable'.[13] But (though James was unimpressed by *Sons and Lovers* when he reviewed it in 1914, a year after its publication, and embarrassingly placed Lawrence 'in the dusty rear' of Compton Mackenzie and Gilbert Cannan[14]) the modernist breakdown of the old conception that character, fictional and real-life, was an entity rather than a flow, an integral unit rather than a crossing-point of relationships, is clearly prefigured in James. It is prefigured in the dissolving-yet-restructuring evocations of Maggie Verver's slow-dawning awareness of a complex surrounding situation that both affects her and is simultaneously made different by her perception of it; of Strether discovering or inventing by his private consciousness certain images of the world and of other people that break down the fixed categories of objective and subjective, and reveal his self as an unresolvable drama of impressions, dreams, hard certitudes, vital delusions, and contradictions. Above all, what seems so modernly to constitute the self in late James – to mark the beginning of the break-down of the old unitary 'ego' of character – is an energy of response to the equally hypothesized selfhood of others with whom that self is in relationship. For example, near the end of *The Ambassadors*, Strether, possibly by now half in love with Madame de Vionnet despite her and Chad's recent 'lie' to him about the innocence of their relationship, bids her farewell, knowing she is being abandoned by Chad as he, Strether, had been required to bring about from the beginning, but which he now compassionates in a total switch of direction and in fluidly imaginative sympathy. For both Strether and Madame de Vionnet, change and even untruth of a kind have been of the essence of their relationship and, indeed, of their identities:

What was truly wonderful was her way of differing so from time to time without detriment to her simplicity. Caprices, he was sure she felt, were before anything else bad manners, and that judgement in her was by itself a thing making more for safety of intercourse than anything that in his various own past intercourses he had had to reckon on. If therefore her presence was now quite other than the one she had shown him the night before, there was nothing of violence in the change – it was all harmony and reason. It gave him a mild deep person, whereas he had had on the occasion to which their interview was a direct reference a person committed to movement and surface and abounding in them; but she was in either character more remarkable for nothing than for her bridging of intervals, and this now fell in with what he understood he was to leave to her. The only thing was that, if he was to leave it all to her, why exactly had she sent for him? He had had, vaguely, in advance, his explanation, his view of the probability of her wishing to set something right, to deal in some way with the fraud so lately practised on his presumed credulity. Would she attempt to carry it further or would she blot it out?

Would she throw over it some more or less happy colour; or would she do nothing about it at all? He perceived soon enough at least that, however reasonable she might be, she wasn't vulgarly confused, and it herewith pressed upon him that their eminent 'lie', Chad's and hers, was simply after all such an inevitable tribute to good taste as he couldn't have wished them not to render. Away from them, during his vigil, he had seemed to wince at the amount of comedy involved; whereas in his present posture he could only ask himself how he should enjoy any attempt from her to take the comedy back. He shouldn't enjoy it at all; but, once more and yet once more, he could trust her. That is he could trust her to make deception right. As she presented things the ugliness – goodness knew why – went out of them; none the less too that she could present them, with an art of her own, by not so much as touching them. She let the matter, at all events, lie where it was – where the previous twenty-four hours had placed it; appearing merely to circle about it respectfully, tenderly, almost piously, while she took up another question.[15]

There is something balletic about these analyses of how one full consciousness (in James's phrase in his letter to Henry Adams) *cultivates* the interest of its own acuity, its responses, towards the movements of another's consciousness, another's shape-changing, ambiguously gesturing personality – 'what he understood he was to leave to her', 'his present posture', 'an art of her own', 'appearing merely to circle about it'. And this partial aestheticisation of consciousness (only partial because the consciousness is still *of* a human predicament, a worldly individual's pain and embarrassment) again points backwards, to James's 'decadent' manner of the 1890s, and forwards, to the protractedly internal 'stream of consciousness' technique of Dorothy Richardson in *Pointed Roofs*, in 1915, to Virginia Woolf's and William Faulkner's more lyrical and extreme shapings of the play of consciousness, and to the equally aestheticised self-probings and formalised loopings of Proust. It is the aestheticisation of nevertheless realistic psychological experience that takes James's late fiction into an unsteady zone somewhere between dream-fantasy and hard realism: that cross-over zone, full of shifting lights and stylistic metamorphosis, so characteristic of much modern writing – from Mann's *Magic Mountain* to Lawrence's *Women in Love*. What began with the unsteadily mingled *fin-de-siècle* preciosity yet pragmatic clarity of *The Spoils of*

Poynton and *What Maisie Knew* led, through the new grave assur-
ance of the last three novels, towards the same revelatory shuttlings
of dream and reality in Joyce's *Portrait of the Artist as a Young Man*,
in Woolf's *To the Lighthouse*, and, in its way, in the hallucinatory
mosaic-effect of Eliot's 'The Waste Land'. Aestheticisation, conscious
symbolism, theatrical preciosity and melodrama, all become a medium for the acutest psychological tension and social awareness –
as, for example, in the tension and temptation within Maggie Verver
when, knowing everything at last, knowing she can destroy by a
word the relationships that sustain them all, she watches at night
through the windows of the terrace at Fawns her father, her husband, her father's wife Charlotte (who is her husband's lover), and
Fanny Assingham, her confidante, all playing cards by candlelight
inside. The scene is as unforgettably real in its lurid, angst-heavy
exaggeration as Eliot's 'A Game of Chess' in 'The Waste Land'
or as Razumov's long charade of duplicity in the grounds of the
Chateau Borel in Conrad's *Under Western Eyes*:

The hour was moonless and starless and the air heavy and still
– which was why, in her evening dress, she need fear no chill and
could get away, in the outer darkness, from that provocation of
opportunity which had assaulted her, within on her sofa, as a
beast might have leaped at her throat.

... [Her companions] might have been – really charming as
they showed in the beautiful room, and Charlotte certainly, as
always, magnificently handsome and supremely distinguished –
they might have been figures rehearsing some play of which she
herself was the author ... She walked to the end and far out of
the light; she returned and saw the others still where she had left
them; she passed round the house and looked into the drawing-
room ... Spacious and splendid, like a stage again awaiting a
drama, it was a scene she might people, by the press of her spring,
either with serenities and dignities and decencies, or with terrors
and shames and ruins, things as ugly as those formless fragments
of her golden bowl she was trying so hard to pick up.

... She saw at all events why horror itself had almost failed
her; the horror that, foreshadowed in advance, would by her
thought have made everything that was unaccustomed in her cry
out with pain; the horror of finding evil seated all its ease where
she had only dreamed of good ... like some bad-faced stranger

surprised in one of the thick-carpeted corridors of a house of quiet on a Sunday afternoon . . .[16]

Alienation, self-distrust, the fear of 'the skull beneath the skin', the lurking presence of betrayal, failure in communication, the sense of a culture in malaise and without shareable values – in large thematic terms these dark principles of the imaginative world of Conrad and Eliot (of *Heart of Darkness* and 'The Hollow Men'), of Pound's 'Mauberley' and Faulkner's *The Sound and the Fury*, of Yeats's 'The Second Coming' and Kafka's *The Trial*, can certainly be seen to loom up somewhere behind the slow introspective stations made by Maggie as she walks on her terrace, and equally behind the feline pacings of Kate Croy and the half-paralysed hesitations of Densher. And almost as an iconic representation of these modernist shadows in James's world there is the figure of John Marcher, in 'The Beast in the Jungle' (written in 1902, the same year as *The Wings of the Dove*), waiting obsessively for the one redeemingly significant, climactic event of his life to come to him, only to discover at the last, Prufrock-like, after his years of solipsistic waiting, that what is intended to happen to him, as his doom, is precisely nothing – and that 'nothing' is to be the culmination and central meaning of his life.

But on the whole, despite these traits, late James is no Kafka, no Beckett – and his John Marcher is more a memorably vivid case to be studied, recognised, and feared than a clearly representative figure of James's world-view. There is certainly an increasing sense in his fiction – from *The Spoils of Poynton* onwards – of the enforced isolation of the sensitive, the intelligent, the spiritual in the midst of a turn-of-the-century ambience of rampant philistinism, or arrogant money-consciousness, or degenerate, will-less drifting. Millie Theale's social patroness in England, Mrs Lowder, who is also Kate Croy's aunt, presides over a Lancaster Gate coterie that clearly figures James's sardonic sense of a society in irreversible decline:

. . . [Lord Mark] was working Lancaster Gate for all it was worth: just as it was, no doubt, working *him*, and just as the working and the worked were in London, as one might explain, the parties to every relation.

Kate did explain, for her listening friend; every one who had anything to give – it was true they were the fewest – made the sharpest possible bargain for it, got at least its value in return. The strangest thing furthermore was that this might be in cases a happy understanding. The worker in one connexion was the worked in another; it was as broad as it was long – with the wheels of the system, as might be seen, wonderfully oiled.[17]

There is a conveyed hollowness to the sophisticated banter and persiflage of Little Bilham and the *demi-mondaine* Miss Barrace in *The Ambassadors*, and even to the intense yet duplicitous murmurings of a Madame de Vionnet – and certainly to the buying-and-selling, spouse-exchanging, reality-avoiding world of Portland Place, Eaton Square, and Cadogan Square in *The Golden Bowl*. And as brilliant – and as modernist – a novel as Ford Madox Ford's *The Good Soldier*, in 1915, was to be a distinctly Jamesian product, in technique as well as in disillusioned insight, of this same *Weltschmerz*. But in the end a distinctive note of the late novels is one of a refusal to despair. Once again, it is the very note of the 1914 letter to Henry Adams – James's response, in advance, as it were, to the 'melancholy outpouring' of the modern movement. Despite his own very real intimations of malaise and of chaos, James remained confirmed, with a certain grim joy, in the meaningfulness of his own creative act of comprehension and of presentation. It is not simply his belief in the importance of art. In that, he was completely at one with the modern movement, many of whom took him as their mentor and criterion as regards any novelist's necesary belief in the high calling of his profession. As regards theory and artistic self-esteem James was to become one of the figureheads of modernism. But in his hailing – in the letter to Adams – of the art of the novelist as being simultaneously an act of the self-cultivated consciousness and an 'act of life', James was also taking his stand on the humanism of a previous generation, and resisting – albeit unconsciously – the stronger drift of modernism in the direction of the arcane, the ultimate rejection of the given and the everyday: Conrad's incipient nihilism, in which irony eats irony; Woolf's internalisation of consciousness to the degree of alienation; Joyce's meteoric disappearance into the galaxies of the word, in *Finnegans Wake*; Eliot's bleakly transcendent withdrawal into the higher reaches of Christianity; Lawrence's eventually self-baffling cult of the impersonal and the absolute. Kate Croy and Merton Densher will never be again as they were; but Kate is indestructible, and in her unscrupulous way is on the side of life. Densher's withdrawal into *his* higher and faintly morbid reaches, where the image of Milly the Dove resides, is shown to be far from exemplary. Strether has probably had his revelation of the sensuous, sexual, aesthetic world too late, but his retreat back to Woollett, Massachusetts, in no ways denies the power and reality of the Parisian Babylon – *our* promised Babylon – that he leaves behind. And Maggie Verver, having seen her golden bowl smashed, is at the end remaking it – with a loss of personal innocence and security, and a loss to her, through their exile, of Charlotte and her father, but nevertheless through newly acquired worldly will and by stratagem and intelligence rather than by any Dove-like apotheosis: almost uniquely in James's canon, *The Golden Bowl* ends, however ambiguously, in a real embrace.

So that in the end it perhaps remains James's emphasis on consciousness – the hyperbolic consciousness of his characters, the equally hyperbolic consciousness his style enacts – that most clearly identifies him as a master and a modern in those opening years of the century. The most strongly influential currents in intellectual life for the imaginative artist were still the ideas of Darwin and Nietzsche from the previous century, plus Bergson's more contemporary rethinking of the relations between mind and the material world, with particular reference to the concepts of memory and time; and more far-reaching revolutions in thought were just taking place in the first decade of the century in the early work of Freud and of Einstein. But by one of the more pleasing ironies of intellectual history Henry James's modernity as a novelist of the human consciousness comes closest in some ways to the ideas of his own brother, William James, who has come more and more to be seen as one of the key figures in the history of modern philosophy and also of modern psychology. The personal relation between the two brothers is one of the vexed questions of Jamesian biography. Leon Edel, in particular, deduced a hypothetical profound rivalry between the two brothers that is one of the governing notions of his 'psychobiography' of James, and has caused much commentary and some scepticism; and very differing views of the relationship have been given, for example, by F. O. Matthiessen in *The James Family* (1947) and more recently by R. W. B. Lewis in *The Jameses: a Family Narrative* (1991). Clearly, the relation was not a straightforward one, and there seem to be too many instances – detailed by Edel – of each brother avoiding the other's presence, or immediately beginning to suffer from headaches, chest-pains, or bowel symptoms whenever a meeting occurred or was in prospect. But the question of a parallelism in their respective work – one a novelist, the other an academic philosopher and psychologist – is of more relevance at the moment, and is less clouded by the dangers of supposition or tendentious neo-Freudian detective work. In no convincing way can Henry be seen as having been influenced in his fiction by his brother's writings, the most relevant of which were all published after the fiction was almost complete. The early *Principles of Psychology*, in 1890, certainly introduced one of William's most famous and influential ideas of consciousness as something that 'does not appear to itself chopped up in bits . . . It is nothing jointed; it flows . . . let us call it the stream of thought, of consciousness, or of subjective life';[18] and from this was directly derived the later literary-critical concept of 'stream of consciousness' as a technique of the Joycean and Woolfian modern novel. But there is far more evidence of Henry having read and enjoyed his brother's later, more philosophical works, especially *The Varieties of Religious Experience* (1903), *Pragmatism* (1907), and *The Meaning of Truth* (1909). Of *Pragmatism*, Henry wrote enthusiastically to his brother about 'the spell itself (of interest and enthralment) that the book cast upon me; I simply sank down, under it, into such depths of submission and assimilation . . . I was lost in the wonder of the extent to which all my life I have . . . unconsciously pragmatised.'[19] William was unable to return the compliment as regards Henry's novels, which he commented on – often highly critically, though with some honest fraternal effort at comprehension – all through Henry's writing career, to the latter's deep discomfort ('I'm always sorry when I hear of your reading anything of mine, and always hope you won't – you seem to me so constitutionally unable to 'enjoy' it, and so condemned to look at it from a point of view remotely alien to mine in writing it . . . And yet I can read *you* with rapture . . .').[20] Henry's whimsical claim in 1907 that he had 'unconsciously pragmatised' all his life points us in a more profitable direction than seeking out direct influences. By genetic similarity, or by force of upbringing, or by mutual responsiveness to the *Zeitgeist*, or even just by simple coincidence, they were in their different ways and their different chosen genres essentially ploughing the same furrow. William himself gave *Pragmatism* the modest subtitle of 'A New Name for Some Old Ways of Thinking', and many of his ideas were indeed latent in common experience as well as in some late nineteenth-century idealist philosophy: for example, his emphasis on pluralism and on

experience as a perpetual flow of relationships; on all intellectual
concepts being purely transitional rather than final, and being themselves within and not outside the flow of experience they try to
organise; on the subject simultaneously constituting his surrounding world and being constituted by that world; on the subjectifying
and demystifying of ethics; and on the basic need to overthrow the
old Cartesian division between spirit and matter, mind and body.
Much of this can be detected even earlier, in Goethe's attempts to
conflate subjective and objective in the one *Anschauung*, or in some
parts of James's native Emersonian tradition, or in his father's
attacks on 'moralism', and for that matter in the novels of many
writers before Henry James who had to some extent themselves
always 'unconsciously pragmatised'. Nevertheless, William James,
however dependent like any great thinker on the spirit of his times
and the ideas of his predecessors, was revolutionary in the compre-
hensiveness, clarity, and force with which he propounded a view of
human experience that so matched – and no doubt in certain ways
so fomented – the modernist tendency in art towards the multifac-
eted and the open-ended, its belief in the constitutive powers of
consciousness, in reality being fluid and truth provisional, in the
complex interplay of subjective and objective process as the basis
not just of cognition but of aesthetic form, and in the fatal inadequacy of abstract categorising. There is one statement by Henry in
his essay of 1884, 'The Art of Fiction', which bears a dramatic resemblance to what his brother was then only in the first stages of
formulating:

Experience is never limited, and it is never complete; it is an
immense sensibility, a kind of huge spider-web of the finest silken
threads suspended in the chamber of consciousness, and catching
every air-borne particle in its tissue. It is the very atmosphere of
the mind; and when the mind is imaginative – much more when
it happens to be that of a man of genius – it takes to itself the
faintest hints of life, it converts the very pulses of the air into
revelations . . . The power to guess the unseen from the seen, to
trace the implication of things, to judge the whole piece by the
pattern, the condition of feeling life in general so completely that
you are well on your way to knowing any particular corner of it
– this cluster of gifts may almost be said to constitute experience,
and they occur in country and in town, and in the most differing
stages of education. If experience consists of impressions, it may

be said that impressions are experience, just as (have we not seen it?) they are the very air we breathe.[21]

Twenty-three years later William was deploying a figure of speech, just in the manner of Henry, in order to propose – and greatly to expand – a similar fundamental notion of experience:

We are like fishes swimming in the sea of sense, bounded above by the superior element, but unable to breathe it pure or penetrate it. We get our oxygen from it, however, we touch it incessantly, now in this part, now in that, and every time we touch it, we turn back into the water with our course re-determined and re-energized. The abstract ideas of which the air consists are indispensable for life, but irrespirable by themselves, as it were, and only active in their re-directing function. All similes are halting, but this one rather takes my fancy. It shows how something, not sufficient for life in itself, may nevertheless be an effective determinant of life elsewhere.[22]

Henry James became one of the moving spirits of modernism by his development in fiction of a consciousness-permeated style that seeks to represent the felt complexity and interconnectedness of the real world – *his* real world – in a directly parallel way to the speculations of his brother. And William James, as one of the breakers of Cartesian dualism, as a notable precursor of Phenomenology, and as the promulgator in vivid, characterful prose of a view of reality as 'the through-and-through union of adjacent minima of experience, . . . the confluence of every passing moment of concretely felt experience with its immediately next neighbors',[23] can seem now, looking back, to have been the Henry James (how the idea would have enraged him!) of modern philosophy.

Apart from their comments on one another's work, and apart from the many suggestive analogies between them as creative thinkers in the van of the new century's intellectual changes – apart from the fruitful ways in which one could transpose William's 'stream of thought' to the modernist theory of fiction, or demonstrate the 'pragmatism' and 'radical empiricism' of Strether's impressions of Paris – there remains one tiny biographical fact of some piquancy that might finally dramatise the strange overlapping of the two Jameses. The incident might well have been made to serve as the germ for one of Henry's own tales – perhaps a rather schematic and ironic

one about two contending yet strongly conjoined brothers. In April
1901 William James, his wife, and daughter descended heavily on
Lamb House, returning from a winter trip to Rome, at the very time
that Mary Weld arrived in Rye to become James's new typist. *The
Ambassadors* was waiting to be completed; *The Wings of the Dove*
was already contracted and under way. But fiction, for once, had to
give way to philosophy in Lamb House, and Miss Weld was taken
over immediately by William to type out his forthcoming Gifford
Lectures (in Edinburgh) on *The Varieties of Religious Experience*, one
of his major works. Strether's fictional 'stream of thought' literally
had to wait until another more philosophic account of 'stream of
thought' had been propounded, in the same Garden Room, to the
same typewriter, by the novelist's elder brother. Henry's reactions,
pragmatic or otherwise, are not recorded. And within a few weeks
of philosophy's departure, back to the Continent, Miss Weld (and
Henry) had finished *The Ambassadors*, and gone straight on with
urgency to *The Wings of the Dove* – as though to seize, for literature,
what was left of the flow of experience and the 'confluence of every
passing moment'.

Two major literary achievements remained to James after the completion of *The Golden Bowl* in 1904. These were *The American Scene*,
published in 1907, the record of his return to America in 1904–5
after an absence of twenty-one years; and the publication of the
New York Edition of (most of) his fiction, between 1907 and 1909.
The Ambassadors, *The Wings of the Dove*, and *The Golden Bowl* had
been written with scarcely a break in four years – the former, though
written first, was published second, by Methuen and by Harper in
1903, after being serialised in that year in the *North American Review*; *The Wings of the Dove* was published by Constable and by
Scribner's in 1902; and *The Golden Bowl* by Scribner's in 1904 and
Methuen in 1905. There had also been articles and a number of
tales; and in 1903 a long-commissioned and dutifully-written biography of William Wetmore Story, an expatriate Bostonian sculptor
living in Rome whom James had slightly known (and not much
admired). For once reasonably flush with ready money from so
much concentrated activity (though, as a typical example, *The
Ambassadors* sold only about 3000 copies in England and about the
same in America, before suffering the familiar fate of being
remaindered in both countries and going out of print by 1909),
James at the age of sixty-one succumbed to an unexpected nostalgia

for America. He prudently contracted in advance to publish his travel impressions and even – for the first time in his life – to give public lectures there for large fees; then let out Lamb House for £5 a week (to include caring for Max the dachshund – 'the best and gentlest and most reasonable and well-mannered as well as most beautiful, small animal of his kind to be easily come across'[24]); and despite the earnest dissuasions of William, on 30 August 1904 found himself deposited on the chaotic quayside of Hoboken, New Jersey.

The hectic ten-month visit to the United States – which took him from New Hampshire to Florida to Chicago to San Francisco to Seattle to Maine, saw him lunch at the White House with Theodore Roosevelt, dine with dozens of old friends and new hosts and hostesses, address (not quite audibly) large but select gatherings on 'The Lesson of Balzac' at $250 a turn, with occasional reductions available, and become exhausted by endless hotels and Pullmans – in no way changed James's life or mentality. Anecdotally and narratively it makes for a vivid and varied episode: James lionised and interviewed, James bored, amused, revolted, overwhelmed, deafened, afflicted by toothache, frozen, overheated, nostalgically charmed, moved to tears – and it has been told well by Leon Edel, and told very differently by James himself. Its main significance in terms of his literary career is that it – of course – strongly confirmed him in the correctness of his choice of expatriation so many years before, and above all that it produced *The American Scene*. And *The American Scene*, where the late style, applied to such an unconstraining subject-matter, runs wild and free, can be seen in certain ways as of a piece with the three late novels, with the revisions and Prefaces to the New York Edition of 1907–9, and with the very late autobiographical pieces of 1913 and 1914. It all comes back, as before, to the central question of consciousness and its style. In *The American Scene* the central observer – 'the restless analyst' is James's whimsical self-decription – can almost be seen as an exaggerated version of Strether, responding vividly – and with a vivid self-consciousness of the fluctuating details of his own reponses – to a culture and place that challenge his sense of his own identity, his middle-aged present, and his unexorcised past. But without Strether's self-distrust and growing temptations, without 'real' other characters and other lives, and with James's own more self-confident wringing-out of nuances and subtle personal judgements at every pass, the single 'fine central intelligence' that in terms of the novel was an organising core has now become the circumference, and indeed the whole sphere in all its dimensions, as well as the centre. The result is an amazing amalgam of preposterousness and genius: the late style at its most self-delighting, self-parodying, world-inventing, and, in passages of brilliance, its most poetically insightful. The Preface to *The American Scene*, like his later letter to Henry Adams, contains one of James's boldest justifications of the deliberately 'cultivated sense of aspects' as his principle of subjective creativity:

> I would take my stand on my gathered impressions, since it was all for them, for them only, that I returned; I would in fact go to the stake for them – which is a sign of the value that I both in particular and in general attach to them and that I have endeavoured to preserve for them in this transcription. My cultivated sense of aspects and prospects affected me absolutely as an enrichment of my subject, and I was prepared to abide by the law of that sense – the appearance that it would react promptly in some presences only to remain imperturbably inert in others.[25]

One extract must suffice to give some sense of the wildly exaggerated yet minutely nuanced writing in which James seems – just as in parts of *The Golden Bowl*, for example – to be writing more than anything else about the displayed and proliferating act of consciousness itself, almost – though never quite – independently of the externally *given* object of that consciousness. 'Never quite' is an important qualification. *The American Scene* escalates the late style to the very brink of a totally self-generating solipsism; but only to the brink. As dizzyingly as in *The Golden Bowl* and *The Wings of the Dove*, we watch a hyperawareness watching itself, flexing its own clauses and conceits, a mirror held up to a mirror. And then, in dramatic switches of allusion or metaphor, the mirror is suddenly and momentarily re-filled by images of something external, outside the vaporousness of a purely verbal consciousness: Maggie Verver as a young wife living in Portland Place, Densher as a sexual young journalist with a living to earn, the 'restless analyst' of *The American Scene* giving us the names of streets and the qualities of a changing, 'melting-pot' civilisation (as here, in 'New York and the Hudson: A Spring Impression'):

> It was a concomitant, always, of the down-town hour that it could be felt as *most* playing into the surrendered consciousness

and making the sharpest impression; yet, since the up-town hour was apt, in its turn, to claim the same distinction, I could only let each of them take its way with me as it would. The oddity was that they seemed not at all to speak of different things – by so quick a process does any one aspect, in the United States, in general, I was to note, connect itself with the rest; so little does any link in the huge looseness of New York, in especial, appear to come as a whole, or as final, out of the fusion. The fusion, as of elements in solution in a vast hot pot, is always going on, and one stage of the process is as typical or as vivid as another. Whatever I might be looking at, or be struck with, the object or the phase was an item in the pressing conditions of the place, and as such had more in common with its sister items than it had in difference from them. It mattered little, moreover, whether this might be a proof that New York, among cities, most deeply languishes and palpitates, or vibrates and flourishes (whichever way one may put it) under the breath of her conditions, or whether, simply, this habit of finding a little of *all* my impressions reflected in any one of them testified to the enjoyment of a real relation with the subject. I like indeed to think of my relation to New York as, in that manner, almost inexpressibly intimate, and as hence making, for daily sensation, a keyboard as continuous, and as free from hard transitions, as if swept by the fingers of a master-pianist. You cannot, surely, say more for your sense of the underlying unity of an occasion than that the taste of each dish in the banquet recalls the taste of most of the others; which is what I mean by the 'continuity', not to say the affinity, on the island of Manhattan, between the fish and the sweets, between the soup and the game. The whole feast affects one as eaten – that is the point – with the general queer sauce of New York; a preparation as freely diffused, somehow, on the East side as on the West, in the quarter of Grand Street as in the quarter of Murray Hill. No fact, I hasten to add, would appear to make the place more amenable to delineations of the order that may be spoken of as hanging together.[26]

James so glorying in his 'gathered impressions', or, rather, in his impressions of the relations that he could envisage existing among his impressions; this epic-sized, pyrotechnical culmination of a brooder's and a wordsmith's (and a Pragmatist's) own 'sense of aspects and prospects'; all floats us straight into the self-revisions and self-investigatings of his work on the New York Edition that immediately began on his departure from the city of his birth, after which the edition was to be named, in July 1905. He had agreed with Scribner's on the plan of a definitive edition of his writings while he was still in America, and characteristically began revising *Roderick Hudson* on shipboard: as always, a veritable Anthony Trollope for getting on at once with the next title. The act of revision, into which he was plunged for four laborious years, going pen-in-hand, typist at the ready, over a paste-up of old sheets of varying earlier editions of most of his novels and tales (but with many significant and some adventitious omissions among them), was another *American Scene*: James, with mingled disapproval and enthusiasm, revisiting himself in a kind of verbal self-haunting and self-exorcism. Like his reliance on dictation for primary writing, this is another unique feature of his career, and one that has had even more significance for the dominant literary metatheorists of the last twenty years than for fellow-practitioners of the novel then or now. Poststructuralism, with its central tenet of the never-finite text and of all literary texts being essentially an ongoing commentary on the processes of their own production, has seized on the image of James so assiduously deconstructing James between 1905 and 1909, and has turned him into an icon (even a trademark) of textual indeterminacy. The tendency in the late James style, as in *The American Scene*, to be a mirror held up to a mirror, enhanced by the urge in preparing the New York Edition to layer a style upon a style, not only anticipated the solipsistic verbal whirlpooling of late Joyce and then of much postmodernist fiction (Thomas Pynchon and Donald Barthelme, for example), it also leapfrogged fifty years in its anticipatory hints of the post-midcentury intellectual world (or anti-world) of Roland Barthes and Jacques Derrida.

Not that James was a Derrida, only that his mandarin applications of consciousness provided some choice material for the Derridan deconstruction of the text – a heavy enough load to make James bear, as one small part of his variable legacy to the twentieth century. More immediately pertinent to the shape of his career was that the self-consciousness of the New York Edition was a final testimony to his sense of his own achievement as a novelist – the revisions being carried out more as an effort to perfect what he saw as rough or inadequate in his earlier works than to negate them. The slight touch of megalomania about the project – it may have been an attempt to emulate the complete *Comédie Humaine* of his

own *chèr maître* of so many years before, Balzac ('the father of us all'
he called him in 'The Lesson of Balzac')[27] – certainly confirms an
inner core of self-esteem in his nature that persisted through so
many humiliations and personal self-doubts, and that fuelled in
compensation the confident hypertrophy of his language from *The
Ambassadors* to *The American Scene*. To write out of a full consciousness, and in a style that so enlarged the boundaries of consciousness, virtually required a supportive core of self-esteem – and also,
of course, a belief in the intrinsic importance of fiction. For this, too,
is what links the conception and the execution of the New York
Edition to what had gone before, and especially to his creative mode
in fiction after the crisis of the 1890s. Getting his novels *together*
(most of them, at any rate, plus two-thirds of his tales, thematically
arranged), and, by detailed revision, getting them *right*, down to
the last chosen word and down to the last discrimination by his
most up-to-date artistic awareness, was to testify publicly to the
supreme value of internal relationships, of form, of 'aspects', and of
his own 'fine central intelligence'. Like one of his own later protagonists, he was trying in revision to catch the passing flow of
experience in the formed 'edition' of the mind.

The actual revisions themselves – heavy for the early novels,
naturally lighter for his recent work – will always divide readers as
to their being preferable or not to the earlier versions. They add
much subtlety and some poetry, and they take away much directness and freshness. Here are two small examples from 'Daisy Miller'.
The first is an addition to a simple exchange between Daisy and
Winterbourne about Mrs Miller that seems to add little to the text
except an unnecessary pomposity (which James unconvincingly
passes off as Winterbourne's). In 1878 James wrote:

> 'She's gone somewhere after Randolph; she wants to try to get
> him to go to bed. He doesn't like to go to bed.'
> 'Let us hope she will persuade him', observed Winterbourne.

Thirty years later he revised this to read:

> 'She's gone somewhere after Randolph; she wants to try to get
> him to go to bed. He doesn't like to go to bed.'
> The soft impartiality of her *constatations*, as Winterbourne would
> have termed them, was a thing by itself – exquisite little fatalist
> as they seemed to make her. 'Let us hope she'll persuade him', he
> encouragingly said.[28]

On the other hand, an addition to the account of Winterbourne's final 'illumination' about Daisy in the Colosseum considerably en-riches, among other things, the symbolic play of moral black-and-white, shadow and moonlight, secrecy and exposure in that climactic scene:

> She was a young lady whom a gentleman need no longer be at pains to respect

is replaced by:

> She was a young lady about the *shades* of whose perversity a foolish puzzled gentleman need no longer trouble his head or his heart. That once questionable quantity *had* no shades – it was a mere black little blot.[29]

The eighteen Prefaces for the edition that James dictated to Theodora Bosanquet between 1906 and 1908 – well over 100 000 words in total – are in many ways more remarkable than the revi-sions themselves. As leisurely meditations on the craft of fiction in general and in unprecedented technical detail, and as recollections of the conception and writing of the novels and tales in question, they are a summation of James's lifelong activity as a critic and a further monument to the typical Jamesian interplay of critical con-sciousness within (or in this case, around) a created text. James's career as an important critic and theorist in fact can be seen as covering a longer span than his career as a novelist – from reviews of Whitman in 1865 and of Dickens, George Eliot, and Trollope in 1866 down to his survey of Conrad, Lawrence, Wells, Bennett, Galsworthy and other contemporaries in 'The New Novel' in 1914, two years before his death. And his achievement as a critic was at least as original as his achievement in fiction – in some ways more original, as there is virtually nothing in English before James that is in the slightest way anticipative of the concentrated intelligence, the developing consistency of judgement and elaboration of principles for judgement, and the focus on formal coherence and technique which he brought to bear in his innumerable reviews and articles over those fifty years. His criticism could also be said to have been more directly influential on others than his fiction. The novels, and the late style, can hardly be imitated creatively – only parodically. But his ideas on, say, the relation between personal experience and artistic invention, between 'morality' in fiction and the personality of the fiction-writer, between the selectivity and shaping of form and the necessity to feel the pressures of the real, between the compositional and the referential, between time in life and time in literature, between the dramatic and the panoramic, between scene and discourse, plot and character, setting and tone, between the concentrative effect of one or several focusing characters on one hand and the shapeless fluidity and self-exposure of free narration or omniscient narration or first-person narration on the other, above all the obsessions with preparation, shapeliness, omission, connection of parts, and 'a handsome wholeness of effect' – and equally with the high importance and dignity of the craft of fiction – all of this has proved enormously assimilable by subsequent generations of critics, novelists, and readers, and for all the idiosyncrasy of its manner his criticism was to dominate novel-theory for the next half-century. All of which is to give some credence to the seemingly hyperbolic suggestion that James not only wrote the first modern novels in English but in his criticism invented the very idea, and the whole theoretical basis, of modern fiction.

In the above inadequate list of ideas that run through all his criticism the ubiquity of 'relationships' of every kind is significant. The essential wholeness of James's thinking in the last decades of his writing life – as novelist, as unconscious 'Pragmatist', as 'restless analyst' of the American scene – is again brought home by the centrality of the concept of 'relationship' in his overall theory of form. And the Prefaces, over which he laboured in a conscious attempt to extract the essence of his long career of craftsmanship, are at times prose-poems – analytic, discursive, self-indulgent, witty prose-poems – on the fluctuating web of aspects that comprises 'form' and 'effect'. 'Appreciation' is the heart of reading, for James, but it equally defines the perceiving act of consciousness, both of novelist and of created characters, that holds everything together and thereby creates 'value' – the only 'value' that counts for him (in a favourite French phrase) being that of *faire valoir*, to be *made to count*, to tell, to achieve intensity of effect. He writes, with infectious self-congratulation, about his use of Maisie in *What Maisie Knew* as a centre, not necessarily so intelligent or so mature, but a centre of indirect 'knowing' nevertheless, and therefore a central source of proliferating perspectives, aspects, and 'connexions':

She is not only the extraordinary 'ironic centre' I have already noted; she has the wonderful importance of shedding a light far beyond any reach of her comprehension; of lending to poorer persons and things, by the mere fact of their being involved with her and by the special scale she creates for them, a precious element of dignity. I lose myself, truly, in appreciation of my theme on noting what she does by her 'freshness' for appearances in themselves vulgar and empty enough. They become, as she deals with them, the stuff of poetry and tragedy and art; she has simply to wonder, as I say, about them, and they begin to have meanings, aspects, solidities, connexions – connexions with the 'universal'! – that they could scarce have hoped for.[30]

And again, on *Roderick Hudson*, he writes, with a newly gleeful involvement of his own, on the central need for a 'drama' of consciouness that will create a 'relation to everything involved':

> The centre of interest throughout 'Roderick' is in Rowland Mallet's consciousness, and the drama is the very drama of that consciousness – which I had of course to make sufficiently acute in order to enable it, like a set and lighted scene, to hold the play . . . The beautiful little problem was to keep it connected, connected intimately, with the general human exposure, and thereby bedimmed and befooled and bewildered, anxious, restless, fallible, and yet to endow it with such intelligence that the appearances reflected in it, and constituting together there the situation and the 'story', should become by that fact intelligible . . . This whole was to be the sum of what 'happened' to him, or in other words his total adventure; but as what happened to him was above all to feel certain things happening to others . . . so the beauty of the constructional game was to preserve in everything its especial value for *him*.[31]

Finally, and rather differently, in the Preface to 'Daisy Miller' he eloquently extends the idea of interrelationship to comprehend that of innate stress and tension: the *necessary* relationship of conflict that persists between formal economy and mimetic expansiveness, between constricting shape and the natural, usable energies of his material-in-the-world, between the 'surface iridescent' and 'what throbs' beneath – that is, a concept of form and of creativity radically founded in kinetic and dialectic:

> Any real art of representation is, I make out, a controlled and guarded acceptance, in fact a perfect economic mastery, of that

conflict: the general sense of the expansive, the explosive principle in one's material thoroughly noted, adroitly allowed to flush
and colour and animate the disputed value, but with its other
appetites and treacheries, its characteristic space-hunger and space-
cunning, kept down. The fair flower of this artful compromise is
to my sense the secret of 'foreshortening' – the particular economic device for which one must have a name and which has in
its single blessedness and its determined pitch, I think, a higher
price than twenty other clustered loosenesses; and just because
full-fed statement, just because the picture of as many of the
conditions as possible made and kept proportionate, just because
the surface iridescent, even in the short piece, by what is beneath
it and what throbs and gleams through, are things all conducive
to the only compactness that has a charm, to the only spareness
that has a force, to the only simplicity that has a grace – those, in
each order, that produce the *rich* effect.[32]

The two-way source of art's 'rich effect' – its reliance for 'force'
always on dialectic and interplay, on form and the resistances against
form, on one value gleaming up constantly through the surface of
an opposed value – is the basis of criticism itself for James, and not
just of the art of fiction. The critical style of the Prefaces, only slightly
more restrained than that of *The American Scene* in its circuitousness, its unbuttoned, golden-tongued, ruminative stroking and
prowling, completely and exemplarily enacts the dialectic of the
critical act itself: what James finely described in his article, 'The
Science of Criticism', in 1891, as the requirement for the critic to:

> lend himself, to project himself and steep himself, to feel and feel
> till he understands, and to understand so well that he can say, to
> have perception at the pitch of passion and expression as em-
> bracing as the air, to be infinitely curious and incorrigibly pa-
> tient, and yet plastic and inflammable and determinable, stooping
> to conquer and serving to direct.[33]

The dialectic of criticism, as described here, is to combine personal
'projection' and impersonal 'steeping', active 'conquering' and passive 'stooping', and coming to 'direct' only by 'serving'. This is the
same dialectic of giving and taking, creating and perceiving, that
makes for the 'rich effect' in literary form itself, as just described in
the Preface to 'Daisy Miller'. And it is essentially the same interplay

that comprises any fully experienced, relational 'truth' in experience, as William James was to argue in *A Pluralistic Universe* and
The Meaning of Truth, in 1909. 'The Lesson of Balzac', the lecture
with which James travelled across America in 1904–5 (then published in the *Atlantic Monthly* in 1905), is a complete exemplification
of this Jamesian critical method of a consciousness that perambulates,
sniffs, feels, analyses, fantasises, by verbal indirection and wit and
extravagant metaphor, all around the central enigma, or nugget, of
what it must have felt like to *be* Balzac. The 'restless analyst', or
James-the-critic, tries in various Protean guises and figures of speech
to 'steep' himself in the otherness of the Balzacian enigma, and by
imaginatively 'serving' it therefore to 'direct' and clarify it, thus
putting the essential two-way dialectic of impression and expression to an illuminatingly 'rich effect'. Again, no English critic (not
even Coleridge) had ever before written so multifacetedly, or provided so full a justification of his critical theory in practice: those
two for James, theory and practice, being so mutually implicated as
to be virtually indistinguishable.

James was no longer writing much fiction – two fine short stories,
'The Jolly Corner' in 1908 and 'The Bench of Desolation' in 1910,
and a number of others of his old quality; and some continuing
work, off and on, on two novels he never completed, *The Sense of
the Past* and (at the very end) *The Ivory Tower*. But the energy and
the type of mental engagement displayed in *The American Scene*, the
revisions and above all the Prefaces for the New York Edition, kept
him in a full state of creative dialectic with the world. His notebooks – themselves encyclopaedic records, like the Prefaces, of
his mind in *process*, of his critical method turned broodingly,
propagatingly upon himself and on each seed, hint, and groping
towards the fiction he was about to write – continue to contain try-
outs and touching self-exhortations. For example, this, during his
last visit to America in 1910–11:

> Can I catch hold – if it be in the least worth the effort? – of a
> very small fantasy that came to me the other month in New
> York? . . I mean the little idea about the good little picture in the
> bad sale, the small true and authentic old thing that the 'hero' of
> the sale recognizes in a sham collection . . . x x x x x But I break
> down – letting the thing for the moment go.[34]

And even more movingly, this, the authentic *cri de coeur* of James the artist, in his sixty-seventh year, quarrying, slightly hysterically but with a startling force of will, into the dwindling reaches of his inventive faculty:

January 4th, 1910. . . . I must now take up projected tasks – this long time *entrevus* and brooded over – with the firmest possible hand. I needn't expatiate on this – on the sharp consciousness of this hour of the dimly-dawning New Year, I mean; I simply invoke and appeal to all the powers and forces and divinities to whom I've ever been loyal and who haven't failed me yet – after all: never, never yet! Infinitely interesting – and yet somehow with a beautiful sharp poignancy in it that makes it strange and rather exquisitely formidable, as with an unspeakable deep agitation, the whole artistic question that comes up for me in the train of this idea of a new short serial for the Harpers, of the *donnée* for a situation that I began here the other day to fumble out. I mean I come back, I come back yet again and again, to my only seeing it in the dramatic way . . . I all throbbingly and yearningly and passionately, oh, *mon bon*, come back to this way that is clearly the only one in which I can do anything now, and that will open out to me more and more and that has overwhelming reasons pleading all beautifully in its breast. What really happens is that the closer I get to the problem of the application of it in any particular case, the more I get *into* that application, so the more doubts and torments fall away from me, the more I know where I am, the more everything spreads and shines and draws me on and I'm justified of my logic and my passion.[35]

The social dialectic remained as hectic as ever. The 'rich, rushing, ravening Whartons', as he called Edith and her husband, whipped him off for an extensive motoring tour of France in 1907, from Paris to the Pyrenees and back up the Rhône Valley, to which he added a trip to Rome, Naples, Florence, and Venice – his last sight of Italy (James pretended to miss Lamb House: 'which appears to me from here so russet and so humble and so modest and so British and so pervaded by boiled mutton and turnips'[36]). Still prepared to dress the part of the modified dandy (Miss Bosanquet noted with surprise on her first meeting him in 1907 that he wore a black coat over green trousers with a blue and yellow waistcoat), though by now ponderously heavy in body, gait, and voice; less shy and more confident than ever before in his life (though still vulnerable); majestically bald, full-lipped, with a flickering smile, head cocked slightly to one side, and devastatingly piercing-eyed ('He might very well have been a merciful Caesar or a benevolent Napoleon' – again according to Miss Bosanquet[37]), James had by now lived his way fully into the public role and legend of the Master. On the private level, there was still a passionate correspondence with the no-longer-youthful Hendrik Andersen and with the Anglo–Irish dandy Jocelyn Persse (Lady Gregory's nephew), and a perpetually warm, intimate friendship with Hugh Walpole. Letters and engagements – despite his 'essential loneliness' – continued to proliferate. He even boldly took up his old love-affair with the theatre, egged on by the actor-manager Forbes-Robertson, having *The High Bid* (a new version of the one-acter he wrote for Ellen Terry in 1895) briefly performed, without disaster, in Edinburgh in 1908, and for five matinée performances in London in 1909. He engaged – dialectically and energetically – in an exchange of drastically opposed points of view on the didactic versus the aesthetic duty of art with Bernard Shaw, arising out of *The Saloon*, an unperformed one-act dramatisation of 'Owen Wingrave' in 1909. Then *The Outcry* was written in the same year, for Granville-Barker and J. M. Barrie, but after various production difficulties was abandoned – perhaps fortunately – without being performed.

A far greater trial of his energy, and above all of his psychological self-confidence and of that 'inexhaustible sensibility' of which he was still to boast to Henry Adams in 1914, was the decisive failure of the New York Edition, and a (partly associated) serious depression that laid him low through much of 1910. The great Balzacian gesture of the Edition, which was to have crowned his career and had cost him years of labour, received hardly any reviews and brought royalties in the first two years of its publication of about $800 from Scribner's and probably no more than the one recorded payment of £84.17.0d from Macmillan in England. James's bitterness was intense. Afflicted by heart-symptoms (ambiguously diagnosed), gout, exhaustion, and frank, tearful melancholia, James was in a state of intermittent collapse, with periods of medical and family care, between January and July 1910. 'My *nervous* condition – trepidation, agitation, general dreadfulness – has been deplorable', he wrote to Jocelyn Persse in April, 'and it is now the thing that is primarily the matter with me – producing inability to *feed* adequately – and being in turn aggravated by it. In short things have been dismally bad.'[38] And again, to Edmund Gosse, two months later, from Bad Nauheim, where he had gone to convalesce, along with William, who was even more seriously ill himself:

> black depression – the blackest of darkness and the cruellest melancholia are my chronic enemy and curse . . . My fight is hard, believe me – but, with an immense patience, I expect to come out, the very devil as the bristling dragon of such a condition of nerves is.[39]

Come out – and come out writing – is what he did. In August 1910 he sailed to America with William and William's wife, Alice, William clearly by now not far from death with chronic heart disease. When William died at the end of that month, in his New Hampshire summer home, with Henry by his side, the novelist found himself drawn by fresh grief into what seems to have been for him a thera-peutic immersion in old associations and memories of family and childhood (the youngest brother, Robertson, had died earlier that year, leaving Henry now as the only survivor). He spent a whole year in America, very quietly, in New York or in William's home in Cambridge or on the Massachusetts coast, seeing a few old friends like Howells, or the irrepressible and ubiquitous Edith Wharton on a visit home, or a few new acquaintances like Somerset Maugham; reading proofs, transforming *The Outcry* from a play to a short novel (or a sort of novel: still too theatrical and too thin), and plan-ning out what was to be the fullest testimony of this final revisiting of the past, his *A Small Boy and Others* (published in 1913), *Notes of a Son and Brother* (1914), and *The Middle Years* (unfinished, and published posthumously in 1917). The attempt to write a family history, mostly as a tribute to William, quickly developed into a magisterially egotistic, yet warmly generous, re-creation of his own early life in America, in all its dense web of cousins and grand-parents and friends and pet dogs and theatre-goings and the tastes of fruit and sweets and trips abroad, and elaborated in the richly Proustian, golden meanderings of his latest – though not most com-plex – late style. The two complete volumes and the last fragmen-tary one – which ends mid-sentence after James's encounters with George Eliot and with Tennyson in 1878 – are the final full demon-stration in James's prose of his 'inexhaustible sensibility' that marked him, in his own words, as 'that queer monster the artist', and graphi-cally confirmed that his exercise of that sensibility was 'an act of life'. Far less alembicated and shot through by intellection than *The American Scene*, what is so astonishing about these autobiographical volumes is the way James's memory of the past – and his verbal style of the present, dictated in Rye and, increasingly, in Chelsea, to Miss Bosanquet – could still so grasp and convey the details of sense-perception and of long-gone social occasions, light-heartedly, slightly absurdly, but with profound feeling. James's reminiscences – 'loose ends ... of my tapestry' though he called them – are held together by a warm narrative tone and by an imaginative re-possession for which 'love' is hardly too strong a term (self-love being only one of its facets), and which reminds us of one of his own splendid perceptions that went to the very heart of Balzac's creativity, in 'The Lesson of Balzac': 'It was by loving [his characters] – as the terms of his subject and the nuggets of his mine – that he knew them; it was not by knowing them that he loved.'[40] James's unflagging love of his world, and his delight in his *consciousness* of that love and of that world, play over each recovered 'nugget' of memory, however distant and however small – like the memory of sea-bathing on Staten Island:

> there comes back to me another [impression], considerably more infantile than that of 1854, so infantile indeed that I wonder at its having stuck – that of a place called the Pavilion, which must have been an hotel sheltering us for July and August, and the form of which to childish retrospect, unprejudiced by later experience, was that of a great Greek temple shining over blue waters in the splendour of a white colonnade and a great yellow pediment. The elegant image remained, though imprinted in a child so small as to be easily portable by a stout nurse, I remember, and not less easily duckable; I gasp again, and was long to gasp, with the sense of salt immersion received at her strong hands. Wonderful altogether in fact, I find as I write, the quantity, the intensity of picture recoverable from even the blankest and tenderest state of the little canvas.[41]

His opening account of his intentions in autobiography, more abstract than such 'nuggets' of seabathing experience, is like that of the 'germs' of his novels in the Prefaces, similar even to his expressed theory of form in fiction, and – being in the past tense, and dictated so near the end of his life – is as suggestive and moving as Prospero's farewell to his art:

To recover anything like the full treasure of scattered, wasted circumstance was at the same time to live over the spent experience itself, so deep and rich and rare, with whatever sadder and sorer intensities, even with whatever poorer and thinner passages, after the manner of every one's experience; and the effect of this in turn was to find discrimination among the parts of my subject again and again difficult – so inseparably and beautifully they seemed to hang together and the comprehensive case to decline mutilation or refuse to be treated otherwise than handsomely. This meant that aspects began to multiply and images to swarm, so far at least as they showed, to appreciation, as true terms and happy values; and that I might positively and exceedingly rejoice in my relation to most of them, using it for all that, as the phrase is, it should be worth. To knock at the door of the past was in a word to see it open to me quite wide – to see the world within begin to 'compose' with a grace of its own round the primary figure, see it people itself vividly and insistently. Such then is the circle of my commemoration and so much these free and copious notes a labour of love and loyalty.[42]

The multiplication of 'images' and 'aspects' of a richly lived 'experience', the joy in seeing his own 'relation' to them and 'discrimination' among them and 'appreciation' of them, and the overmastering urge to see the world 'compose' and 'hang together' into 'grace' and 'values' – these characteristic phrases that Theodora Bosanquet took down, probably in the autumn of 1911, go a long way towards summing up the literary life of Henry James as it came towards its close. The private 'relation' and 'consciousness' remained dramatic and publically committed ('an act of life') to the very end. There was a final public lecture of great intelligence and *éclat*, 'The Novel in *The Ring and the Book*' on the hundredth anniversary of Browning's birth, in May 1912, and an honorary degree from Oxford in the following month; a presentation and a commission of a portrait by Sargent from three hundred of his friends to mark his seventieth birthday in 1913, with public tributes and newspaper editorials. Then, in the one month, March, 1914, there was the long essay 'The New Novel' (originally 'The Younger Generation') that magisterially (and far from objectively) surveyed the contemporary state of his craft in England; the publication of *Notes of a Son and Brother*; and the heroic, challenging letter to Henry Adams celebrating the cultivation of his own consciousness and the 'obstinate finality' of being an artist. Without much effort, and with dignified intelligence, he crushed H. G. Wells in an exchange of letters in 1915 for Wells's vituperative criticisms and parody of James's style in *Boon*, giving at the same time one of his most eloquent defences of literature as an art and an end in itself (and not, as for Wells, a means to other ends). He worked for a while – almost as fluently as of old – on *The Ivory Tower*, intricately planned and about one-third finished, and which was centred around some of his longest-lasting, most deeply felt themes: those of unabashed power and money, crudity against refinement and taste, innocence, sexuality, and, as part of it all, America. When *The Ivory Tower* proved too much for him, he even returned intermittently to *The Sense of the Past*, unfinished since it was begun in 1900 (he was reading it through, ready for another attempt, the night before his stroke, in December 1915).

The writing career that began in the shadow of Sherman's bloody march through Georgia near the end of the American Civil War ended in a burst of outrage, despair, affection, pity, and newly-focused patriotism over what James accurately recognised as the apocalypse of the First World War (a 'Niagara', he called it, 'a nightmare from which there is no waking', 'huge convulsions', 'strange fissures in the most familiar soil'). This was virtually his final, and prophetic, cultivation of consciousness, and his ultimate change of 'relation' to the world he lived in – especially, now, the England he had lived in for forty years. He could feel the eerie trance of the ironically sunlit days of August 1914:

> The country and the season here are of a beauty of peace, and loveliness of light, and summer grace, that make it inconceivable that just across the Channel, blue as *paint* today, the fields of France and Belgium are being, or about to be, given up to unthinkable massacre and misery.[43]

Like Whitman in the Civil War, he now channelled much of the former passion of his art into visiting military wounded, writing them letters, entertaining them, sending food and cigarettes, and caring for Belgian refugees in London; he wrote essays on these experiences, and others directed emotionally at the war effort; he responded freshly to the deaths of acquaintances and of the sons of friends and acquaintances at the front; he commemorated Rupert Brooke, as a victim of war, in the last piece he ever wrote; and threw himself into the work of Chairman of the American Ambulance

Corps, publicising and fund-raising. James's commitment to the real sufferings of real people in a world he understood and belonged to had never in his life been more clearly – at times almost too unrestrainedly – displayed. The war appalled him, touched him, and – characteristically – energised him ('the unspeakable adventure of being alive in these days'). In July 1915 he took the symbolic step of becoming a British citizen (Asquith, the Prime Minister, was one of his four sponsors). Then on 2 December, in his apartments in Cheyne Walk – a week or two after his last stay in Lamb House – James suffered the first of two strokes that partly paralysed him and destroyed much, though not all, of his capacity for clear thought. Ramblingly, on his deathbed, soothed by the sound of the typewriter, he continued to dictate to Miss Bosanquet, sometimes incoherent notes for a new novel, or imagining at times he was Napoleon, or in Edinburgh, or in Rome with William, or visiting Thomas Carlyle with his father; at times lucidly hovering over an elusive *mot juste* as he had always done. In that New Year's Honours List, he was given the Order of Merit, the highest award possible for a man of letters ('what curious manifestations such occasions call forth', he remarked, in bed, about his congratulatory telegrams). Almost immobile by late January, he lay watching the river-traffic from his Chelsea window and, as his sister-in-law recorded, moved his hand on the counterpane as though writing. On 28 February 1916, at the end of many days of confusion and suffering, he died. After a funeral service in Chelsea Old Church and cremation at Golders Green, in the land of his adoption, James's ashes were taken across the Atlantic to the family plot in Cambridge, in the land of his birth – thereby completing the circuit of his passionate pilgrimage.

In his writing career of fifty-two years Henry James wrote twenty-two novels, well over a hundred novellas and tales (later collected in twelve volumes), four volumes of collected criticism and at least eighty uncollected or posthumously collected literary essays or reviews, over thirty articles on drama and the same number on painting, a volume of art criticism, his eighteen Prefaces, five travel books, nine plays, two biographies, two volumes of autobiography, and his Notebooks. At the outset of that career he had met Thackeray and Dickens, who were born in 1811 and 1812; and before the end he had met and impressed himself on E. M. Forster and Ezra Pound, who died in 1970 and 1972. He had written as an American and a romantic, as an English Victorian and a realist, as a symbolist, an

avant-garde experimentalist, a modernist – and more often than not
as a master. It had always been an affair of the exercised and rami-
fied consciousness with him – of 'relations' and 'aspects', of scruples
and elided passions, of 'appreciation' and form, and of words, words,
words, pushed to the very brink. It was a mode that courted dan-
ger, as with all innovators. His style became self-generating, swollen, outlandish. But the kinetic of his shape-making mind was
essentially not single and inwards, but dialectical and self-testing,
and based on stress and opposition. He could almost have been
gesturing in the direction of his own work when he wrote in 1904
of a novel of Gabriele D'Annunzio:

> The book is a singularly rich exhibition of an inward state, the
> state of private poetic intercourse with things, the kind of current
> that in a given personal experience flows to and fro between the
> imagination and the world. It represents the aesthetic conscious-
> ness, proud of its conquests and discoveries, and yet trying, after
> all, as with the vexed sense of a want, to look through other
> windows and eyes.[44]

'Poetic intercourse with things', 'current', 'experience', 'flows', 'con-
quests and discoveries', 'vexed sense of a want', 'other windows
and eyes'. James's mental life – his literary life – had lain in that
very current, that Wordsworthian, even Coleridgean to-and-fro of
mind and world. And his art, in its movement between humane
familiarity and radical strangeness, was the pleased vexation of a
consciousness always seeking to become more than itself.

Notes

Chapter 1

1. For the dates of James's novels, I give here and throughout the dates of their first, that is, usually serial, publication. Of the major novels, only *The Sacred Fount, The Wings of the Dove,* and *The Golden Bowl* did not first appear in periodical form. Book publication usually occurred near or soon after the end of the serial run.
2. Henry James Senior, *Society the Redeemed Form of Man* (1879), quoted in R. W. B. Lewis, *The Jameses, A Family Narrative* (London: Deutsch, 1991) p. 51.
3. *A Small Boy and Others* (1913), reprinted in Henry James, *Autobiography,* edited F. W. Dupee (Princeton: Princeton University Press, 1983) pp. 196–7.
4. *Notes of a Son and Brother* (1914), repr. in *Autobiography,* p. 362; and *A Small Boy and Others,* p. 123.
5. *A Small Boy and Others,* p. 106.
6. 'On Henry James' (1918), reprinted in *The Question of Henry James,* ed. F. W. Dupee (New York: Holt & Co., 1945) p. 110.
7. *A Small Boy and Others,* pp. 32–3.
8. *Henry James. Letters,* vol, I. ed. Leon Edel (London: Macmillan, 1974) pp. 226–7.
9. *Notes of a Son and Brother* (1914), reprinted in *Autobiography,* p. 415.
10. *Henry James. Letters,* vol. I, p. 83; p. 80.
11. Letter of Howells, December 1866, in Mildred Howells (ed.), *The Life in Letters of W. D. Howells,* vol. I (Garden City, N.Y.: Doubleday, 1928) p. 116.
12. *Letters of Henry James,* vol. II, ed. Percy Lubbock (London: Macmillan, 1920) pp. 229–30.
13. *Henry James. Letters,* vol. I, p. 264.
14. *The Complete Notebooks of Henry James,* ed. Leon Edel and Lyall H. Powers (London: Oxford University Press, 1987) p. 239.
15. *Henry James. Letters,* vol. I, pp. 93–4; 116–17; 152; and (on Swinburne) *The Middle Years* (1917), reprinted in *Autobiography,* pp. 569–70.
16. Quoted by Oscar Cargill, *The Novels of Henry James* (New York: Macmillan, 1961) p. 14.
17. *Henry James. Letters,* vol. I, p. 252.
18. Ibid., p. 258.
19. Ibid., p. 246; p. 274.
20. Reprinted in *Portraits of Places* (London: Macmillan, 1883) p. 336.
21. Ibid., pp. 328–9.

Chapter 2

1. *The Art of the Novel. Critical Prefaces by Henry James*, edited R. P. Blackmur (New York: Scribner's, 1934) pp. 32–3.
2. See above, p. 28.
3. *Roderick Hudson* (1875), chap. 23 (Harmondsworth: Penguin Books, 1986) pp. 348–9.
4. 'Emerson' (1887), reprinted in *Henry James. Literary Criticism* (New York: Library of America, 1984), vol. I, pp. 268–9.
5. 'Ivan Turgénieff' (1874), reprinted in *Henry James. Literary Criticism* (New York: Library of America, 1984), vol. II, pp. 968–99.
6. Ibid., p. 998.
7. 'The Impressionists' (1876), reprinted in *The Painter's Eye. Notes and Essays on the Pictorial Arts by Henry James*, ed. John L. Sweeney (Madison: University of Wisconsin Press, 1956; repr. 1989) p. 115.
8. *Henry James. Letters*, vol. II, ed. Leon Edel (London: Macmillan, 1978) p. 243.
9. Ibid., p. 274.
10. *Hawthorne*, reprinted in *Henry James. Literary Criticism*, vol. I, pp. 351–2.

Chapter 3

1. *Henry James. Letters*, vol. II, p. 337.
2. Recorded by Simon Nowell-Smith, *The Legend of the Master* (London: Constable, 1947) p. 75.
3. *The Middle Years* (1917), in *Autobiography*, pp. 182–4.
4. 'The Life of George Eliot' (1885), reprinted in *Henry James. Literary Criticism*, vol. I, p. 1002.
    All ten articles and reviews – one on *Felix Holt*, one on the novels in general, three on the poems, one on *Middlemarch*, two on *Daniel Deronda*, one on the tales, and one on the *Life* – are reprinted in this volume, pp. 907–1010.
5. Ibid., pp. 959–60; and 965.
6. Ibid., p. 992.
7. *The Portrait of a Lady* (1880–1), chap. 1 (Harmondsworth: Penguin Books, 1964) p. 5; pp. 6–7.
8. For example, concerning Trollope, in 'The Art of Fiction' (1884), reprinted in *Henry James. Literary Criticism*, vol. I, p. 46.
9. At the end of 'Near Perigord'.
10. Reprinted in *The Art of the Novel*, pp. 42–3.
11. Chap. 4, ed. cit., pp. 35–6.
12. Chap. 7, ed. cit., p. 68.
13. Chap. 42, ed. cit., pp. 431–2.
14. *Henry James. Letters*, vol, II, p. 105.
15. *The Art of the Novel*, pp. 40–1.
16. *The Complete Notebooks of Henry James*, pp. 229–30; p. 214.
17. Ibid., p. 20.
18. *The Bostonians* (1885–6), chap. 26 (Harmondsworth: Penguin Books, 1966) p. 215.

19. Ibid., chap. 20, p. 146.
20. Letter of March 1885, in *Henry James. Letters*, vol. III, ed. Leon Edel (London: Macmillan, 1980) p. 73.
21. Ibid., p. 146.
22. *The Liberal Imagination* (1950), (Harmondsworth: Penguin Books, 1970) pp. 69–101.
23. Preface, in *The Art of the Novel*, p. 60.
24. Op. cit., p. 95.
25. *Henry James. Letters*, vol. III, p. 28.
26. W. W. Stowe, *Balzac, James, and the Realistic Novel* (Princeton: Princeton University Press, 1983) p. 8.
27. *The Bostonians*, ed. cit., p. 160.
28. *The Princess Casamassima* (1885–6), chap. 5 (Harmondsworth: Penguin Books, 1987) p. 106.
29. *Henry James. Letters*, vol. III, p. 58.
30. 'The Art of Fiction' (1884), reprinted in *Henry James. Literary Criticism*, vol. I, pp. 53–8.
31. 'A Humble Remonstrance' (1884), reprinted in *Henry James and Robert Louis Stevenson*, edited Janet Adam Smith (London: Hart-Davis, 1948) pp. 91–2.
32. *Henry James. Letters*, vol. III, p. 58.
33. *Henry James and Robert Louis Stevenson*, p. 106.
34. 'The Art of Fiction' (1884), ed. cit., p. 44.
35. *Westminster Review*, vol. 9 n.s. (1856), p. 626.
36. *Autobiography* (1883), chap. 8 (London: Oxford University Press, World's Classics, 1953) p. 125.
37. Review in the *Spectator*, vol. 38 (1865) pp. 1438–9; 'The Art of Fiction', ed. cit., p. 53.
38. vol. 5 n.s., pp. 196–7.
39. *Westminster Review*, vol. 44 n.s. (1873) p. 254; *British Quarterly Review*, Volume 69 (1879) pp. 413–4.
40. *Athenaeum*, (1885) (i), pp. 339–40.
41. 'The Profitable Reading of Fiction', *Forum* (New York), vol. 5 (1888) pp. 63–5.
42. *Cornhill Magazine*, vol. 17 (1868) p. 54 and pp. 294–8; *Once A Week*, vol. 3 n.s. (1869) pp. 123–5.
43. *British Quarterly Review*, vol. 71 (1880) pp. 234–6; *Pall Mall Gazette*, vol. 42 (1885) p. 5; *Academy*, vol. 12 (1877) p. 33.
44. *Academy*, vol. 22 (1882) p. 377; *Quarterly Review*, vol. 155 (1883) pp. 213–20.
45. Preface to *Piping Hot! (Pot-Bouille)* (1885) p. xiv.
46. vol. 4 (1890) pp. 194–5.
47. *Fortnightly Review*, vol. 42 n.s. (1887) pp. 410–17; *Contemporary Review*, vol. 51 (1887) pp. 172–80; vol. 52 (1887) pp. 683–93; vol. 57 (1890) pp. 479–88.
48. 'The Aspern Papers' (1888), chap. 9, *The Aspern Papers and The Turn of the Screw* (Harmondsworth: Penguin Books, 1986) p. 140.
49. *The Art of the Novel*, pp. 85–7.
50. *The Tragic Muse* (1889–90), chap. 9 (Harmondsworth: Penguin Books, 1978) p. 121.

51. Ibid., chap. 16, pp. 196–7.
52. *The Complete Notebooks of Henry James*, p. 28.
53. These are all reprinted in *Henry James. The Scenic Art. Notes on Acting and the Drama, 1872–1901*, ed. Allan Wade (1948), (New York: Hill and Wang, 1957) pp. 133–242.
   For a helpful survey of James and the theatre in this context, see D. J. Gordon and John Stokes, 'The Reference of *The Tragic Muse*', in *The Air of Reality, New Essays on Henry James*, ed. John Goode (London: Methuen, 1972) pp. 81–167.
54. *The Tragic Muse* (1889–90), chap. 37 (Harmondsworth: Penguin Books, 1978) p. 383.
55. Ibid., chap. 11, p. 138.

Chapter 4

1. 'The Middle Years' (1893), reprinted in *The Figure in the Carpet, and Other Stories* (Harmondsworth: Penguin Books, 1986) p. 235.
2. Ibid., pp. 237–8.
3. Ibid., p. 258.
4. *Henry James. Letters*, vol. III, p. 240.
5. Ibid., p. 209.
6. Ibid., p. 326.
7. *The Complete Notebooks of Henry James*, pp. 52–3.
8. *Henry James. Letters*, vol. III, p. 320.
9. See Leon Edel, *The Life of Henry James* (1953–72), vol. 2 (Harmondsworth: Penguin Books, 1977) pp. 137–66; and Leon Edel, 'Henry James: the Dramatic Years', Preface to Henry James, *Guy Domville* (Philadelphia: Lippincott, 1960) pp. 13–121.
10. *Guy Domville*, ed. cit., p. 200.
11. Henry James. Letters, vol. III, pp. 507–9.
12. Ibid., p. 510 and p. 513; Henry James. Letters, vol. IV, ed. Leon Edel (Cambridge: Harvard University Press, 1984) p. 18.
13. 'The Pupil' (1891), repr. *Complete Tales of Henry James*, vol. 7, ed. Leon Edel (London: Hart-Davis, 1963) p. 410; pp. 413–14.
14. Ibid., p. 417.
15. Ibid., p. 452.
16. 'Owen Wingrave' (1893), repr. *Complete Tales of Henry James*, vol. 9 (1964), p. 51.
17. Preface to 'The Altar of the Dead', in *The Art of the Novel*, p. 241.
18. 'The Altar of the Dead' (1895) chap. 2, repr. *Complete Tales of Henry James*, vol. 9 (1964), p. 237.
19. Ibid., chap. 3, p. 242.
20. *Henry James. Letters*, vol. III, p. 482.
21. 'The Autumn of the Body' (1898), in W. B. Yeats, *Essays and Introductions* (London: Macmillan, 1961) pp. 189–94.
22. *Henry James. Letters*, vol. III, p. 377.
23. *Complete Notebooks of Henry James*, p. 126.
24. To William James, quoted in Leon Edel, *The Life of Henry James*, vol.

2, p. 93; to Edmund Gosse, in *Henry James. Letters,* vol. III, p. 495 and p. 502.

25. *Complete Notebooks of Henry James,* p. 109.
26. Ibid., pp. 115–16.
27. Notes for *The Ivory Tower,* in *Complete Notebooks of Henry James,* p. 469.
28. *The Spoils of Poynton* (1896), chap. 1 (Harmondsworth: Penguin Books, 1963) p. 8.
29. Ibid., chap. 12, p. 98.
30. *What Maisie Knew* (1897), chap. 15 (Harmondsworth: Penguin Books, 1966), pp. 107–8.
31. Ibid., chap. 30, p. 228.
32. *The Awkward Age* (1898–9), chap. 28 (Harmondsworth: Penguin Books, 1987) pp. 234–5.
33. *The Sacred Fount* (1901), chap. 8 (London: Hart-Davis, 1959) pp. 99–100.
34. Ibid., chap. 8, p. 101.
35. *The Spoils of Poynton,* chap. 9, p. 79.
36. Ibid., chap. 16, pp. 134–5.
37. *What Maisie Knew,* chap. 31, p. 238.
38. 'The Autumn of the Body', pp. 190–4. See above, pp. 119–21.
39. *The Awkward Age,* chap. 21, p. 169.
40. 'John Gabriel Borkman', in *Henry James: the Scenic Art* (1948), ed. Allan Wade (New York: Hill and Wang, 1957) p. 293.
41. *Henry James. Letters,* vol. IV, pp. 19–21.
42. Letter to Francis Boott, quoted in Leon Edel, *The Life of Henry James,* vol. 2, p. 277.

Chapter 5

1. *Henry James. Letters,* vol. IV, pp. 705–6.
2. For a particularly vivid and detailed account of these years, see Miranda Seymour, *Henry James and his Literary Circle, 1895–1915* (London: Hodder & Stoughton, 1988).
3. *Henry James. Letters,* vol. IV, p. 41.
4. Ibid., p. 248.
5. Ibid., p. 508.
6. Ibid., pp. 494–5.
7. Quoted in *The Legend of the Master,* ed. Simon Nowell-Smith (London: Constable, 1947) pp. 11–12 – a book that is still an indispensable compendium of impressions and wonderful (if unreliable) anecdotes of James in his later life. One of the best of these is Edith Wharton's account of James, as a passenger in her car, helping to obtain directions to King's Road, Windsor, late at night:

    While I was hesitating and peering out into the darkness James spied an ancient doddering man who had stopped in the rain to gaze at us. 'Wait a moment, my dear – I'll ask him where we are'; and leaning out he signalled to the spectator.

'My good man, if you'll be good enough to come here, please; a little nearer – so,' and as the old man came up: 'My friend, to put it to you in two words, this lady and I have just arrived here from *Slough*; that is to say, to be more strictly accurate, we have recently *passed through* Slough on our way here, having actually motored to Windsor from Rye, which was our point of departure; and the darkness having overtaken us, we should be much obliged if you would tell us where we now are in relation, say, to the High Street, which, as you of course know, leads to the Castle, after leaving on the left hand the turn down to the railway station.'

I was not surprised to have this extraordinary appeal met by silence and a dazed expression on the old wrinkled face at the window; nor to have James go on: 'In short' (his invariable prelude to a fresh series of explanatory ramifications), 'in short, my good man, what I want to put to you in a word is this: supposing we have already (as I have reason to think we have) driven past the turn down to the railway station (which in that case, by the way, would probably not have been on our left hand, but on our right), where are we now in relation to ...'

'Oh, please,' I interrupted, feeling myself utterly unable to sit through another parenthesis, 'do ask him where the King's Road is.'

'Ah – ? The King's Road? Just so! Quite right! Can you, as a matter of fact, my good man, tell us where, in relation to our present position, the King's Road exactly *is*?'

'Ye're in it,' said the aged face at the window. (op. cit., pp. 46–7)

8. Ibid., pp. 131–2.
9. Quoted in Nowell-Smith, *The Legend of the Master*, pp. 133–4.
10. *The Ambassadors* (1903), bk 2, chap. 2 (Harmondsworth: Penguin Books, 1986) pp. 118–9.
11. *The Wings of the Dove* (1902), bk 4, chap. 1 (Harmondsworth: Penguin Books, 1986) p. 157.
12. *The Golden Bowl* (1904), bk 4, chap. 10 (Harmondsworth: Penguin Books, 1985) pp. 462–3.
13. Letter to Edward Garnett, 5 June 1914, *Letters of D. H. Lawrence*, vol. 2, ed. G. J. Zytaruk and J. T. Boulton (Cambridge: Cambridge University Press, 1981) p. 183.
14. 'The New Novel' (1914), in *Henry James. Literary Criticism*, vol. 1 (New York: Library of America, 1984) p. 127.
15. *The Ambassadors*, bk 12, chap. 1, pp. 476–7.
16. *The Golden Bowl*, bk 5, chap. 2, pp. 488–9.
17. *The Wings of the Dove*, bk 4, chap. 2, p. 169.
18. William James, *The Principles of Psychology* (1890), vol. 1 (New York: Dover Publications, 1950) p. 239.
19. *Henry James. Letters*, vol. IV, p. 466.
20. Ibid., pp. 382–3.
21. *Henry James, Literary Criticism*, vol. 1 (New York: Library of America, 1984) pp. 52–3.

22. William James, *Pragmatism: A New Name for Some Old Ways of Thinking* (1907), (New York: Longman, 1911) p. 128.
23. William James, *A Pluralistic Universe* (New York: Longman, 1909) p. 326.
24. *Henry James. Letters*, vol. iv, p. 313.
25. *The American Scene* (1907), (London: Hart-Davis, 1968) pp. xxv–xxvi.
26. Op. cit., pp. 116–17.
27. See, however, Michael Anesko's fascinating account of how James in the end totally compromised whatever grand scheme he may have had in mind for the arrangement of the New York Edition under the pressure of publishers, agent, and market place (*'Friction with the Market': Henry James and the Profession of Authorship* (New York: Oxford University Press, 1986) pp. 143–62.
28. *Daisy Miller* (1878), (Harmondsworth: Penguin Books, 1986) p. 65; ibid., New York Edition, vol. 18 (New York: Augustus M. Kelley, 1971) p. 27.
29. Penguin Books, p. 111; New York Edition, p. 86.
30. *The Art of the Novel*, ed. R. P. Blackmur (New York: Scribner's, 1934) p. 147.
31. Ibid., p. 16.
32. Ibid., p. 278.
33. *Henry James. Literary Criticism*, vol. 1, p. 98.
34. *The Complete Notebooks of Henry James*, pp. 209–10.
35. Ibid., pp. 260–1.
36. Quoted in Leon Edel, *The Life of Henry James*, vol. 2, p. 643.
37. Quoted in *The Legend of the Master*, p. 7.
38. *Henry James. Letters*, vol. 4, p. 551.
39. Ibid., p. 556.
40. 'The Lesson of Balzac' (1905), *Henry James. Literary Criticism*, vol. 2, p. 132.
41. *A Small Boy and Others* (1913), in *Henry James. Autobiography*, p. 18.
42. Ibid., pp. 3–4.
43. *Henry James. Letters*, vol. 4, pp. 713–14.
44. 'Gabriele D'Annunzio' (1904), *Henry James. Literary Criticism*, vol. 2, p. 934.

Suggestions for
Further Reading

The following list is selective only, being a cross-section of older and more recent writing, and is intended to supplement relevantly those primary works of fiction and non-fiction by James himself, and those main sources for his biography (such as the letters), details of which are given in the immediately preceding Notes. Bibliographies of James's own writings, as well as of criticism, can be found conveniently in the items listed below by Graham Clarke, vol. 1, pp. 9–30; Tony Tanner, pp. 133–42; and Judith Woolf, pp. 156–63.

Anderson, Charles R., *Person, Place and Thing in the Fiction of Henry James* (Durham, N.C.: Duke University Press, 1977).

Anderson, Quentin, *The American Henry James* (New Brunswick: Rutgers University Press, 1957).

Anesko, Michael, *'Friction with the Market': Henry James and the Profession of Authorship* (New York: Oxford University Press, 1986).

Auchard, John, *Silence in Henry James: the Heritage of Symbolism and Decadence* (University Park: Pennsylvania State University Press, 1986).

Bell, Millicent, *Meaning in Henry James* (Cambridge, Mass.: Harvard University Press, 1991).

Bewley, Marius, *The Complex Fate: Hawthorne, Henry James and Some Other American Writers* (London: Chatto, 1952).

Blackmur, R. P., *Studies in Henry James*, ed. V. A. Makowsky (New York: New Directions, 1983).

Bradbury, Nicola, *Henry James: the Later Novels* (Oxford: Oxford University Press, 1979).

Brooks, Peter, *The Melodramatic Imagination: Balzac, Henry James, Melodrama, and the Mode of Excess* (New Haven: Yale University Press, 1976).

Buitenhuis, Peter, *The Grasping Imagination: the American Writings of Henry James* (Toronto: University of Toronto Press, 1970).

Cargill, Oscar, *The Novels of Henry James* (New York: Macmillan, 1961).

Chatman, Seymour, *The Later Style of Henry James* (New York: Barnes & Noble, 1972).

Clark, Grahame (ed.), *Henry James. Critical Assessments*, 4 vols (Mountfield: Helm Information, 1991).

Crews, Frederick C., *The Tragedy of Manners: Moral Drama in the Later Novels of Henry James* (New Haven: Yale University Press, 1957).

Dupee, Frederick W., *Henry James* (New York: Sloane, 1951).

Dupee, Frederick W. (ed.), *The Question of Henry James: a Collection of Critical Essays* (London: Wingate, 1947).

Edel, Leon and Gordon N. Ray (eds), *Henry James and H. G. Wells: a Record of their Friendship, their Debate on the Art of Fiction, and their Quarrel* (London: Hart-Davis, 1958).

Fogel, Daniel Mark, *Henry James and the Structure of the Romantic Imagination* (Baton Rouge: Louisiana State University Press, 1981).

Freedman, Jonathan, *Professions of Taste: Henry James, British Aestheticism, and Commodity Culture* (Stanford: Stanford University Press, 1990).

Fussell, Edwin Sill. The French Side of Henry James (New York: Columbia University Press, 1990).

Gale, Robert L., *The Caught Image: Figurative Language in the Fiction of Henry James* (Chapel Hill: University of N. Carolina Press, 1964).

Gale, Robert L., *A Henry James Encyclopaedia* (New York: Greenwood Press, 1989).

Gard, Roger, *Henry James: the Critical Heritage* (London: Routledge, 1968).

Goode, John (ed.), *The Air of Reality: New Essays on Henry James* (London: Methuen, 1972).

Graham, Kenneth, *Henry James: the Drama of Fulfilment* (Oxford: Clarendon, 1975).

Graham, Kenneth, *Indirections of the Novel: James, Conrad, and Forster* (Cambridge: Cambridge University Press, 1988).

Habegger, Alfred, *Henry James and the 'Woman Business'* (Cambridge: Cambridge University Press, 1989).

The Henry James Review, ed. D. M. Fogel (Baltimore: Johns Hopkins University Press, from 1979).

Hocks, Richard A., *Henry James and Pragmatistic Thought: a Study in the Relationship between the Philosophy of William James and the Literary Art of Henry James* (Chapel Hill: University of N. Carolina Press, 1974).

Hocks, Richard A., *Henry James: a Study of the Short Fiction* (Twayne's Studies. Boston: G.K. Hall, 1990).

Holland, Laurence B., *The Expense of Vision: Essays on the Craft of Henry James* (Princeton: Princeton University Press, 1964).

Horne, Philip, *Henry James and Revision: the New York Edition* (Oxford: Oxford University Press, 1990).

Jacobson, Marcia, *Henry James and the Mass Market* (University: University of Alabama Press, 1983).

James, Alice, *The Diary of Alice James* (Harmondsworth: Penguin, 1982).

Kaplan, Fred, *Henry James: the Imagination of Genius. A Biography* (London: Hodder & Stoughton, 1992).

Kappeler, Susanne, *Writing and Reading in Henry James* (London: Macmillan, 1980).

Kaston, Carren, *Imagination and Desire in the Novels of Henry James* (New Brunswick: Rutgers University Press, 1984).

Krook, Dorothea, *The Ordeal of Consciousness in Henry James* (Cambridge: Cambridge University Press, 1967).

Lewis, R. W. B., *The Jameses: a Family Narrative* (London: Deutsch, 1991).

Long, Robert E., *The Great Succession: Henry James and the Legacy of Hawthorne* (Pittsburgh: University of Pittsburgh Press, 1979).

McWhirter, David, *Desire and Love in Henry James* (Cambridge: Cambridge University Press, 1989).

Matthiessen, F. O., *Henry James: the Major Phase* (New York: Oxford University Press, 1963).

Matthiessen, F. O., *The James Family: Including Selections from the Writings of Henry James, Senior, William, Henry, and Alice James* (New York: Knopf, 1947).

Maves, Carl, *Sensuous Pessimism: Italy in the Work of Henry James* (Bloomington: Indiana University Press, 1973).

Nettels, Elsa, *James and Conrad* (Athens: University of Georgia Press, 1977).

Norrman, Ralf, *The Insecure World of Henry James's Fiction: Intensity and Ambiguity* (London: Macmillan, 1982).

Poirier, Richard, *The Comic Sense of Henry James: a Study of the Early Novels* (New York: Oxford University Press, 1960).

Powers, Lyall H. (ed.), *Henry James and Edith Wharton. Letters 1900–1915* (London: Weidenfeld, 1990).

Powers, Lyall H., *Henry James and the Naturalist Movement* (E. Lansing: Michigan State University Press, 1971).

Rimmon, Shlomith, *The Concept of Ambiguity: the Example of James* (Chicago: University of Chicago Press, 1977).

Rowe, John Carlos, *The Theoretical Dimensions of Henry James* (London: Methuen, 1985).

Segal, Ora, *The Lucid Reflector: the Observer in Henry James's Fiction* (New Haven: Yale University Press, 1969).

Seltzer, Mark, *Henry James and the Art of Power* (Ithaca: Cornell University Press, 1984).

Seymour, Miranda, *Henry James and his Literary Circle, 1895–1915* (London: Hodder & Stoughton, 1988).

Sicker, Philip, *Love and the Quest for Identity in the Fiction of Henry James* (Princeton: Princeton University Press, 1980).

Smith, Janet Adam (ed.), *Henry James and Robert Louis Stevenson: a Record of Friendship and Criticism* (London: Hart-Davis, 1948).

Stowe, W. W., *Balzac, James, and the Realistic Novel* (Princeton: Princeton University Press, 1983).

Stowell, Peter, *Literary Impressionism: James and Chekhov* (Athens: University of Georgia Press, 1980).

Tanner, Tony, *Henry James: the Writer and his Work* (Amherst: University of Massachusetts Press, 1985).

Veeder, William, *Henry James: the Lessons of the Master. Popular Fiction and Personal Style in the Nineteenth Century* (Chicago: University of Chicago Press, 1975).

Ward, J. A., *The Imagination of Disaster: Evil in the Fiction of Henry James* (Lincoln: University of Nebraska Press, 1961).

Wiesenfarth, Joseph, *Henry James and the Dramatic Analogy: a Study of the Major Novels of the Middle Period* (New York: Fordham University Press, 1963).

Williams, Merle A., *Henry James and the Philosophical Novel: Being and Seeing* (Cambridge: Cambridge University Press, 1993).

Winner, Viola Hopkins, *Henry James and the Visual Arts* (Charlottesville: University of Virginia Press, 1970).

Woolf, Judith, *Henry James: the Major Novels* (Cambridge: Cambridge University Press, 1991).

Yeazell, Ruth Bernard, *Language and Knowledge in the Late Novels of Henry James* (Chicago: University of Chicago Press, 1976).

Index

Academy, The, 85
Adams, Henry, 140–1, 162, 165, 172, 182, 183
Alcott, Bronson, 6
Alexander, George, 108, 110, 111
Andersen, Hendrik, 139, 146, 182
Anderson, Mary, 93, 95
Anesko, Michael, 195 n. 27
Arabian Nights, The, 31
Archer, William, 94, 109, 110
Aristophanes, 36
Arnold, Matthew, 50, 74, 93
    Culture and Anarchy, 60
    'The French Play in London', 93
Asquith, Lady, 146
Asquith, Lord, 146, 187
Astor, Lord and Lady, 146
Athenaeum, The, 84
Atlantic Monthly, The, 19, 22, 24, 26, 45, 49, 54, 55, 62, 65, 70, 89, 94, 105, 112, 125, 180
Austen, Jane, 36, 45, 158

Bakunin, Mikhail, 71
Balestier, Wolcott, 121
Balzac, Honoré de, 12, 15, 20, 24, 45, 49, 51, 76, 77, 85, 140, 151, 174, 180, 184
Barrie, J.M., 182
Bartet, Julia, 105
Barthelme, Donald, 174
Barthes, Roland, 174
Bartlett, Alice, 27
Baudelaire, Charles, 119, 121
Beardsley, Aubrey, 118, 120, 121, 134
Beckett, Samuel, 142, 164
Beerbohm, Max, 144
Bell, Vanessa, 146
Bellini, Giovanni, 23
Bennett, Arnold, 110, 176
    A Man from the North, 110
    The Old Wives' Tale, 110
    Clayhanger, 110

Benson, A.C., 146, 148
Bergson, Henri, 166
Besant, Annie, 75
Besant, Walter, 79–80
Blake, William, 32, 120
Booth, Charles, 75
Booth, William, 75
Boott, Francis, 88, 193, n. 42
Boott, Lizzie, 27, 88
Bosanquet, Theodora, 139, 149–50, 176, 181, 182, 184, 185, 187
Bridges, Robert, 120
British Quarterly Review, The, 84, 85
Brontë, Charlotte, 158
Brooke, Rupert, 1, 147, 186
Browning, Robert, 50, 185
Burne-Jones, Edward, 23, 111
Byron, Lord, 31
    Manfred, 31

Caine, Hall, 52, 86
Campbell, Mrs Patrick, 108
Cannan, Gilbert, 160
Carlyle, Thomas, 32, 68, 72, 187
Century Magazine, The, 65, 70, 94
Cervantes, Miguel de, 12, 36
Channing, Ellery, 6
Chap Book, The, 125
Child, Theodore, 121
Churchill, Winston, 146
Cockerell, Sydney, 147
Coleridge, Samuel Taylor, 32, 40, 180, 188
    'Dejection: an Ode', 40
Compton, Edward, 105, 106, 107
Congreve, William, 128
Conrad, Joseph, 140, 145, 151, 165, 176
    The Secret Agent, 74
    Nostromo, 159
    Under Western Eyes, 163
    Heart of Darkness, 164
Contemporary Review, The, 86

Continental Monthly, The, 18
Coquelin, Benoît-Constant, 94
Corelli, Marie, 86
Cornford, Francis, 147
Cornhill Magazine, The, 50, 84
Crane, Stephen, 145
Cross, John, 53
Curzon, Lord, 146

D'Annunzio, Gabriele, 188
Dante Alighieri, 12, 20, 36
Darwin, Charles, 23, 66
Daudet, Alphonse, 46, 76, 78
Defoe, Daniel, 84
Derrida, Jacques, 174
De Vere, Aubrey, 22
Dickens, Charles, 2, 12, 20, 22, 24,
  36, 40, 46, 63, 72, 83, 113, 127,
  176, 187
  Martin Chuzzlewit, 3
  David Copperfield, 12
  Dombey and Son, 33, 40
  Bleak House, 33
  Little Dorrit, 33, 72
  Great Expectations, 33
  Our Mutual Friend, 33, 72
Diderot, Denis, 42, 43, 45, 95
  'Paradoxe sur le Comédien', 42,
  94
Dumas, Alexandre *fils*, 20
Du Maurier, George, 111

Edel, Leon, 22, 108, 109, 122, 166,
  171
Einstein, Albert, 159, 160, 166
Eliot, George, 12, 20, 23, 33, 40, 45,
  47, 52–5, 57, 65, 72, 83, 89,
  176, 183
  Silas Marner, 33, 40
  Felix Holt, 53, 190 n. 4
  Romola, 54
  Middlemarch, 54–5, 58, 61, 190 n. 4
  Daniel Deronda, 55, 58, 98,
    190 n. 4
  The Mill on the Floss, 58, 60
  Adam Bede, 59
Eliot, T.S., 12, 25, 119, 165
  'The Waste Land', 163
  'The Hollow Men', 164

Emerson, Ralph Waldo, 6, 7–8, 32,
  36–9, 44, 45, 64, 151, 168
  'Nature', 7, 37
  'The American Scholar', 37
  'The Divinity School Address',
  37

Faulkner, William, 162
  The Sound and the Fury, 164
Fields, James T., 22
Flaubert, Gustave, 20, 46, 49, 76,
  140
Forbes-Robertson, Johnston, 182
Ford, Ford Madox, 140, 142, 145
  The Good Soldier, 165
Forster, E.M., 146, 151, 187
  Where Angels Fear to Tread, 159
  A Room with a View, 159
Fortnightly Review, The, 23, 86
Fourier, Charles, 9
Freud, Sigmund, 160, 166
Fuller, Margaret, 6
Fullerton, Morton, 143, 147

Galaxy, The, 19, 26, 45, 46, 54
Galsworthy, John, 176
Garnett, Edward, 194, n. 13
Garnett, Olivia, 146
Gaskell , Elizabeth, 2, 58
Gautier, Théophile, 15, 20
George, Henry, 75
Gissing, George, 52, 145
  Workers in the Dawn, 52
Gladstone, W.E., 50
Goethe, Johann Wolfgang von, 20,
  168
Goncourt, Edmond de, 46, 76, 78
Gosse, Edmund, 65, 111, 122, 145,
  183
Granville-Barker, Harley, 182
Graphic, The, 115
Gregory, Lady, 146, 182

Haggard, Rider, 28, 82
  King Solomon's Mines, 52, 86
  Allan Quatermain, 86
Hardy, Thomas, 20, 84
  The Return of the Native, 52
  The Woodlanders, 102

Harper's Weekly, 138

Harrison, Frederic, 23

Hawthorne, Nathaniel, 7, 8, 9, 20, 40, 44–5, 48, 50–1, 59, 64, 86, 115, 158
   The Blithedale Romance, 9
   'Ethan Brand', 40
   The Scarlet Letter, 44, 51, 59, 60

Haydon, Benjamin, 11

Henley, W.E., 84, 85, 138

Henty, G.A., 86

Holland, Josiah, 27

Holmes, Oliver Wendell Jr., 19, 21, 145

Holmes, Oliver Wendell Sr., 24

Hope, Anthony, 86
   The Prisoner of Zenda, 138
   Rupert of Hentzau, 138

Houghton, Lord, 50

Howells, William Dean, 19–21, 24, 27, 49, 62, 76, 82, 85, 86, 102, 112, 153, 183

Hugo, Victor, 20

Hunt, William Morris, 14

Hutchinson, Anne, 36

Huysmans, J.K., *À Rebours*, 121

Hyndman, H.M., 75

Ibsen, Henrik, 105, 109, 128, 135–6, 158
   The Master Builder, 109
   Little Eyolf, 109, 135
   John Gabriel Borkman, 135

Impressionists, The, 49

Irving, Henry, 95

James, Alice (sister), 25, 27, 64, 87, 107, 121

James, Alice (sister-in-law), 183, 187

James, Billy (nephew), 146

James, Henry Sr. (father), 3–5, 7, 8, 9, 36, 46, 64, 168, 187

JAMES, HENRY
   Life
   Boston and Cambridge, 17–22, 23–4, 25, 26, 46, 64–70, 71–2, 183, 187
   Civil War, 1–2, 14, 16, 66, 67, 186

consciousness as theme, 5, 42, 44, 49, 57, 125, 136, 141–4, 151, 155–6, 161, 162, 165–9, 171–2, 177–8, 180, 185, 188

conversation, 148–9

as critic and theorist, 15, 20, 21, 28, 36, 46–9, 50–1, 54–5, 57–8, 63, 76, 79–82, 91, 94, 96–8, 123–4, 135–6, 140, 160, 165, 168–9, 172, 174–5, 176–80, 181, 184, 185, 186, 188

dictation, 139, 142–3, 149–50, 170

family, 2–6, 10–13, 24, 25, 40, 64, 121, 170, 183

Fin-de-siècle and Decadence, 97–8, 105, 116–21, 134–5, 136–7, 158

First World War, 1, 141, 186–7

Lamb House, Rye, 126, 137–9, 141–3, 145–7, 150, 170, 171, 181, 184, 187

late style, 99–101, 104–5, 112–18, 119–21, 124–37, 139, 143–5, 148–9, 151, 152–4, 155, 158–63, 171–3, 174, 175–6, 179, 180, 183, 188

letters, 16, 19, 21, 23, 25, 26, 50, 53, 62, 70, 71, 76, 79, 81, 101, 102, 107, 111, 112, 118, 121, 122, 137, 138, 141, 142–5, 167, 171, 181, 182, 183, 186

London, 22–3, 49–50, 51, 52–3, 61, 62, 65, 70–3, 78–9, 87, 88, 92, 105, 107–8, 137, 138, 141, 147–8, 187

Modernism, 105, 137, 139, 142, 148, 151, 154, 158–69, 174, 177

money and novel sales, 3, 22, 27, 45–6, 50, 62, 87, 102, 106, 108, 137, 138, 146, 170, 171, 182

Newport 13–17

New York, 6, 11–12, 24, 27, 45–6, 64–5, 66–7, 69, 77–8, 172–3, 174, 183–4

Notebooks, 21–2, 64, 65, 94, 106, 122–3, 124, 180–1

Paris, 4, 12–13, 46, 49–50, 75–6, 78, 87, 90, 105, 153

Realism, Naturalism, and Romance, 28, 52, 55, 57–8, 76–86, 89, 97–8, 138

Romanticism and Transcendentalism, 6–10, 28–45, 49, 68–9, 95, 105, 117

society and manners, 2, 3, 9–10, 13–14, 18–19, 24, 26, 28, 31, 42–3, 45, 51, 55, 61–2, 65–7, 69, 70–5, 92, 118, 146–7, 151, 154–5, 164–5, 171, 181, 186

theatre and the dramatic, 11, 93–6, 103–4, 105–12, 122–5, 128, 135–6, 182, 192 n. 53

travels in America, 25–6, 63–5, 140, 170–3, 183

travels in, and preference for, Europe, 3, 6, 12–13, 18, 21–3, 24, 25, 27, 45–6, 50–1, 62–3, 87–9, 122, 181

Works

'The Altar of the Dead', 104, 112, 116–18, 119, 136

The Ambassadors, 3, 8, 19, 43, 140, 148, 150, 151–4, 156, 160, 161–2, 165–6, 169, 170, 175

The American, 8, 9, 25, 28–31, 34–5, 37–8, 45, 49–50, 66, 129, 151

The American (play) 105, 106, 107–8, 109, 113, 116

The American Scene, 140, 170, 171–3, 179, 180, 184

'The Art of Fiction', 76, 79–82, 91, 168–9

'The Aspern Papers', 63, 88–9, 104, 156

'The Author of Beltraffio', 104

The Awkward Age, 24, 104, 124, 125, 126, 127, 129–30, 134–5, 136, 137, 138

'The Beast in the Jungle', 140, 164

'The Bench of Desolation', 180

The Bostonians, 2, 8, 9, 19, 52, 65–70, 71–2, 73, 74, 75, 76, 77–8, 87, 88, 97, 102, 119, 124, 129, 156, 158

Confidence, 50

'The Coxon Fund', 118

'Daisy Miller', 15, 25, 28, 30–1, 33–5, 39, 40, 43–5, 49–50, 65, 73, 85, 105, 158, 175–6, 178–9

'Daniel Deronda: a Conversation', 55

'The Death of the Lion', 97, 118

'Emerson', 36

The Europeans, 19, 25, 28, 30–1, 35, 38–40, 43, 45, 49–50, 53–4, 73, 124, 129

'The Figure in the Carpet', 104, 118

French Poets and Novelists, 50

'The Friends of the Friends', 136

'Gabriele D'Annunzio', 188

'George Eliot's *Middlemarch*', 54–5

'Georgina's Reasons', 104

The Golden Bowl, 3, 8, 140, 148, 150, 151, 156–8, 159, 161, 163–4, 165–6, 172, 189 n. 1

'The Great Good Place', 137

Guy Domville, 103, 104, 107–12, 116, 122, 123, 137

Hawthorne, 50–1

The High Bid, 182

'Honoré de Balzac', 46

'An International Episode', 5, 50

'Ivan Turgénieff', 46–9

The Ivory Tower, 180, 186

'The Jolly Corner', 4, 140, 180

'The Lesson of Balzac', 171, 175, 180, 184

'The Lesson of the Master', 89, 97, 118

'The Life of George Eliot', 54

'A London Life', 89

'Louisa Pallant', 89

The Macmillan Edition, 65

The Middle Years, 23, 53–4, 183

'The Middle Years', 99–101, 102, 103, 104, 108, 118, 136

'The New Novel', 160, 176, 185

The New York Edition, 140, 170, 171, 174–6, 182

'The Next Time', 118

Notes of a Son and Brother, 4–5, 17, 183, 185

JAMES, H., Works *cont.*
'The Novel in *The Ring and the Book*', 185
'The Novels of George Eliot', 54
The Outcry, 182, 183
'Owen Wingrave', 104, 112, 115–16, 136, 182
'A Passionate Pilgrim', 24
A Passionate Pilgrim, 45–6
'The Pension Beaurepas', 50
The Portrait of a Lady, 3, 5, 8, 15, 25, 39, 48, 52, 54, 55–63, 65, 67, 97, 115, 119, 124, 129
Portraits of Places, 26
Prefaces to the *New York Edition*, 28, 34, 57–8, 60–1, 63, 74, 85, 90, 97, 98, 128, 140, 171, 176–9, 180
The Princess Casamassima, 9, 32, 52, 65, 66, 68, 69–70, 70–6, 78–9, 81, 87, 88, 97, 102, 119, 129, 156
'The Pupil', 112–15, 116
The Reverberator, 89
Roderick Hudson, 3, 8, 11, 15, 19, 25, 27, 28–33, 35–6, 38–40, 45–6, 48–50, 66, 73, 89, 151, 159, 174, 178
The Sacred Fount, 104, 124, 125–6, 127, 129, 131–2, 135, 137, 189 n. 1
The Saloon, 182
'The Science of Criticism', 179
The Sense of the Past, 180, 186
'Sir Edmund Orme', 136
A Small Boy and Others, 4, 5, 10, 11, 12–13, 183–5
The Spoils of Poynton, 8, 48, 104, 112, 123, 124–8, 132–3, 135, 136, 137, 162, 164
'The Story of a Year', 1, 19
Terminations, 116
'A Tragedy of Error', 1, 18
The Tragic Muse, 8, 15, 32, 52, 89–98, 101, 102, 103, 105, 119, 129, 156, 158
Transatlantic Sketches, 45–6
'The Turn of the Screw', 115, 136, 137, 150
Washington Square, 3, 12

Watch and Ward, 23–4, 104
What Maisie Knew, 24, 104, 112, 124–6, 128–9, 133–4, 136, 163, 177–8
William Wetmore Story and his Friends, 170
The Wings of the Dove, 8, 15, 19, 39, 63, 140, 143, 148, 150, 151, 154–6, 159, 160, 164–6, 170, 172, 189 n. 1
James, Mary (mother), 27, 64
James, Peggy (niece), 146
James, Robertson (brother) , 14, 183
James, Wilky (brother), 14, 64
James, William (brother), 5, 10, 14, 16, 25, 27, 34, 50, 103, 111, 122, 166–70, 171, 183, 187
Varieties of Religious Experience, 167, 170
Pragmatism, 167, 169
The Meaning of Truth, 167, 180
A Pluralistic Universe, 169, 180
James, William (grandfather), 2–3
Jones, Henry Arthur, *The Dancing Girl*, 108
Joyce, James, 151, 160
Dubliners, 159
Stephen Hero, 159
A Portrait of the Artist as a Young Man, 163
Finnegans Wake, 165

Kafka, Franz, 142
The Trial, 164
Keats, John, 31–5, 38, 42
'La Belle Dame Sans Merci', 31
Odes, 34
Letters, 34, 42
Kemble, Fanny, 94, 105, 121
Keynes, Geoffrey, 147
Keynes, John Maynard, 147

Lafarge, John, 14, 16
Lang, Andrew, 86
Lawrence, D.H., 160, 165, 176
Sons and Lovers, 160
Women in Love, 162
Leighton, Lord, 111

Lewes, G.H., 53–4
Lewis, R.W.B., 166, 189 n. 2
Longman's Magazine, 79, 80
Loring, Katharine, 87
Lovelace, Lady, 146
Lowell, James Russell, 18, 19, 121

MacAlpine, William, 139, 149
MacCarthy, Desmond, 147
Mackenzie, Compton, 105, 160
Macmillan's Magazine, 52, 62
Maeterlinck, Maurice, 120, 134, 158
Mahler, Gustav, 118
Mallarmé, Stéphane, 119, 120, 121, 134
Mann, Thomas, 101
    Death in Venice, 101, 118
    The Magic Mountain, 162
Marx, Karl, 2
Matisse, Henri, 159
Matthiessen, F.O., 166
Maugham, Somerset, 183
Maupassant, Guy de, 46, 49, 76, 87
Melville, Herman, 7, 8, 9
Meredith, George, 50, 84
    The Egoist, 52
    Diana of the Crossways, 84
Mérimée, Prosper, 15, 24
Mill, John Stuart
    Autobiography, 40
    'On Liberty' and 'The Subjection of Women', 60
Millet, Jean François, 14
Moore, George, 52, 85–6
    A Modern Lover, 52, 85
    A Mummer's Wife, 85
    A Drama in Muslin, 85
Morrell, Lady Ottoline, 146
Morris, Jane, 22–3
Morris, William, 22–3, 75
Most, Johann, 71
Motley, John, 49

Napoleon Bonaparte, 68, 115, 187
Nation, The, 19, 26, 45, 93
New Review, The, 94, 125
New York Tribune, The, 46, 49
Nietzsche, Friedrich Wilhelm, 32, 68, 166

North American Review, The, 18, 19, 46, 170
Norton, Charles Eliot, 18, 19–20, 22, 25, 70
Norton, Grace, 19, 21
Nowell-Smith, Simon, 193 n. 7

Once a Week, 84
Osgood, James R., 65, 87

Pall Mall Gazette, The, 85, 94, 110
Pater, Walter, 50, 96, 97, 119
Perry, Thomas Sergeant, 19, 68, 79, 84
Persse, Jocelyn, 139, 146, 147, 182
Picasso, Pablo, 159
Pinero, Arthur Wing, 108
Poe, Edgar Allan, 7, 8, 118
    'Ligeia', 117
Pound, Ezra, 57, 146, 187
    Cantos, 159
    'Hugh Selwyn Mauberley', 164
Proust, Marcel, 19, 160, 162, 183
    À la recherche du temps perdu, 159
Pynchon, Thomas, 174

Quarterly Review, The, 85

Rachel (Élisa Felix), 94
Racine, Jean, 128
Rhymers Club, 118
Richardson, Dorothy, *Pointed Roofs*, 162
Richardson, Samuel, 84
Rimbaud, Arthur, 119
Robins, Elizabeth, 105, 109
Roosevelt, Theodore, 171
Rossetti, Dante Gabriel, 120
Rousseau, Jean-Jacques, 31, 36, 40
Ruskin, John, 22, 23, 83

St. Helier, Lady, 147
Saintsbury, George, 85, 86
Sand, George, 12, 20, 24, 45, 46, 140
Sarawak, Ranee of, 146
Sargent, John Singer, 65, 111, 185
Saturday Review, The, 110

Schoenberg, Arnold, 160
Scots Observer, The, 86
Scott, Sir Walter, 12, 46
Scribner's Monthly, 27, 50, 94
Scudder, Horace, 112
Senior, Nassau, *Essays on Fiction,* 18
Seymour, Miranda, 193 n. 2
Shakespeare, William, 12
Shaw, George Bernard, 75, 110, 146, 151, 182
   Man and Superman, 110
Shelley, Percy Bysshe, 32
Siddons, Mrs Sarah, 105
Spectator, The, 191 n. 37
Stein, Gertrude, 159
   Three Lives, 159
Stendhal (Henri Beyle), 12, 20, 42–3, 44, 45
   La Chartreuse de Parme, 42
Stephen, Leslie, 22, 50, 84
Sterne, Laurence, *Tristram Shandy,* 154
Stevenson, Robert Louis, 28, 79–82, 84, 87, 91, 101, 102, 122
   Treasure Island, 52, 86
   'A Humble Remonstrance', 80–1, 85
   Prince Otto, 86
   Kidnapped, 86
Story, William Wetmore, 170
Stowe, W.W., 77
Sturges, Jonathan, 147
Sturgis, Howard, 147
Swedenborg, Emanuel, 4, 7, 9
Swinburne, Algernon Charles, 23
Symons, Arthur, *The Symbolist Movement in Literature,* 119

Temple, Minny, 15–17, 19, 22, 30, 151
Temple Bar, 85
Tennyson, Alfred, Lord, 31, 50, 183
Terry, Ellen, 112, 182
Thackeray, William Makepeace, 12, 20, 45, 187
Thoreau, Henry David, 6, 7, 8, 39

Tintoretto, Jacopo, 11, 23
Titian (Tiziano Vecellio), 23
Trilling, Lionel, 68, 71, 73, 74
Trollope, Anthony, 12, 20, 83, 174, 176, 190 n. 8
   Dr. Wortle's School, 52
   Autobiography, 83
Turgenev, Ivan, 12, 45, 46–9, 51, 54, 57, 64, 76, 103, 140, 151
   On the Eve, 48
   A Nest of Gentlefolk, 48
Turner, J.M.W., 23

Verlaine, Paul, 119
Veronese, Paolo, 11, 23
Villiers de l'Isle-Adam, Philippe-Auguste, 120

Wagner, Richard, 118, 120, 121
   Tristan und Isolde, 118
Walpole, Hugh, 140, 146, 147, 182
Walsh, Catherine (Aunt Kate), 27, 121
Ward, Mrs Humphry, 65, 93–4, 111, 146, 147
   Miss Bretherton, 93
Waterlow, Sydney, 146
Watts, G.F., 111
Webb, Sidney, 75
Weld, Mary, 139, 149, 150, 170
Wells, H.G., 110, 145, 151, 176, 186
   The Time Machine, 110
   The Invisible Man, 110
   Kipps, 110
   The History of Mr. Polly, 110
   Boon, 186
Westminster Review, The, 84
Wharton, Edith, 140, 142, 143, 145, 147, 181, 183
   The House of Mirth, 145
Whistler, J.A.M., 120, 121, 134, 153
Whitman, Walt, 7, 8, 20, 42, 44, 176, 186
Wilde, Oscar, 97, 110, 117, 118, 121, 138, 158
   An Ideal Husband, 110

The Importance of Being Earnest, 110
The Picture of Dorian Gray, 119
Wister, Sarah, 27
Woman, 110
Woolf, Virginia, 22, 146, 151, 159, 160, 162, 165
  The Waves, 142
  To the Lighthouse, 163
Woolson, Constance Fenimore, 88, 121–2
Wordsworth, William, 32–4, 38, 40, 188
  Prelude, 32–3, 49

Yeats, William Butler, 119–20, 121, 134, 137
  'The Autumn of the Body', 119–20, 134, 137
  'Symbolism in Painting', 120
  'The Second Coming', 164
Yellow Book, The, 97, 118

Zola, Émile, 46, 49, 76, 77, 78, 82, 85, 86, 140
  Le Roman expérimental, 85
  Pot-Bouille, 85